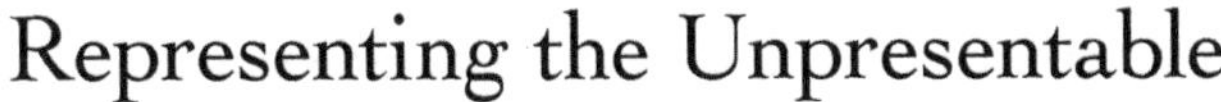

Gender, Culture, and Politics in the Middle East

miriam cooke, Suad Joseph, and Simona Sharoni, *Series Editors*

Other titles in Gender, Culture, and Politics in the Middle East

Arab Women's Lives Retold: Exploring Identity Through Writing
Nawar Al-Hassan Golley, ed.

Faith and Freedom: Women's Human Rights in the Muslim World
Mahnaz Afkhami, ed.

Gendering the Middle East: Emerging Perspectives
Deniz Kandiyoti, ed.

Intimate Selving in Arab Families: Gender, Self, and Identity
Suad Joseph, ed.

Missing Persians: Discovering Voices in Iranian Cultural History
Nasrin Rahimieh

Muslim Women and the Politics of Participation: Implementing the Beijing Platform
Mahnaz Afkhami & Erika Friedl, eds.

No Shame for the Sun: Lives of Professional Pakistani Women
Shahla Haeri

Rituals of Memory in Contemporary Arab Women's Writing
Brinda Mehta

War's Other Voices: Women Writers on the Lebanese Civil War
miriam cooke

Women of Jordan: Islam, Labor, and the Law
Amira El-Azhary Sonbol

Representing the Unpresentable

HISTORICAL IMAGES OF NATIONAL REFORM FROM THE QAJARS TO THE ISLAMIC REPUBLIC OF IRAN

Negar Mottahedeh

SYRACUSE UNIVERSITY PRESS

First Edition 2008
08 09 10 11 12 6 5 4 3 2 1

Permission to reprint chapter 1 from the following source is kindly acknowledged: "The Mutilated Body of the Modern Nation," *Comparative Studies of South Asia, Africa, and the Middle East* 18, no. 2: 38–50. Copyright © 1998 by Comparative Studies of South Asia, Africa, and the Middle East. All rights reserved. Used by permission of the publisher.

Permission to use material in chapters 2 and 4 from the following source is kindly acknowledged: "Resurrection, Return, Reform: Ta'ziyeh as Model for Early Babi Historiography," *Iranian Studies* 32, no. 3: 387–99. Used by permission of the publisher.

For a listing of books published and distributed by Syracuse University Press, visit https://press.syr.edu.

ISBN: 978-0-8156-3179-8 (hardcover) 978-0-8156-5666-1 (e-book)

Library of Congress Cataloging-in-Publication Data

Mottahedeh, Negar.
Representing the unpresentable : historical images of national reform from the Qajars to the Islamic Republic of Iran / Negar Mottahedeh.
p. cm. — (Gender, culture, and politics in the Middle East)
Includes bibliographical references and index.
ISBN 978-0-8156-3179-8 (hardcover : alk. paper)
1. Iran—History—20th century. 2. Iran—History—19th century. 3. Iran—Civilization—19th century. 4. Iran—Civilization—20th century. I. Title.
DS316.6.M68 2007
955.05—dc22
2007040774

The authorized representative in the EU for product safety and compliance is Mare Nostrum Group B.V.
Mauritskade 21D, 1091 GC Amsterdam, The Netherlands
gpsr@mare-nostrum.co.uk

◆ ◆ ◆

To Kasra and my parents,

Faezeh Seddigh and Hooshmand Mottahedeh

Negar Mottahedeh is assistant professor in the Program in Literature at Duke University. She is currently completing a book on contemporary Iranian cinema.

Contents

Illustrations

Acknowledgments

Representing the Unpresentable started off as a doctoral thesis, and although it has gone through several metamorphoses in the intervening years, the title has always seemed right for the project. John Mowitt, who was the director for my thesis, suggested it when I was attempting to knit the various threads of the argument together. "Representing the Unpresentable" fit in ways that reflected my attempt to theorize a national theory of history in Qajar culture and to cull the nation's self-representations in the last century and a half for the repressed figure of "the Babi" within. But John's role in relation to my work has never been that limited. His theoretical insights and methodological approaches never fail to inspire, whether my argument is about disciplinarity or about cinema. The introduction of two key terms to my vocabulary through his interventions, namely, antidisciplinarity and enunciation, situate my argument in this book, linking nineteenth-century Babi practice to the self-reflexive fold of enunciation inscribing the national representation of post-revolutionary Iran in cinema and marking this representation with an ambivalence that confronts the limits of both the field and the state.

My deepest thanks and appreciation also go to other members of my dissertation committee, John Archer, Donald Preziosi, Hamid Naficy and Nasrin Rahimieh. Besides her warm and constant encouragement of my work throughout the years, Nasrin helped me think through and develop my concerns around the future of the field and the disciplinary methods that have been used in the study of Babism. Nasrin and Hamid have both worked to introduce me to major texts and scholars in two key fields, Iranian studies and Cinema studies, and I owe a great deal to both of them. Bruce Lincoln and Nader Saiedi were involved at different moments in this writing, and my discussions with both of them have in later years structured certain insights in the argument in *Representing the*

Unpresentable. Members of the Internet lists Irfan1, 1997 and the H-Net list for Shaykhi, Babi and Baha'i Studies gave careful feedback on parts of *Representing the Unpresentable.* I am particularly grateful to the participants of Irfan1@umich.edu 1997, for their insights and clarificatory remarks on the Qurrat al-'Ayn in Karbala, Iraq, in 1845. My colleagues Kathryn Babayan, Juan Cole, Terry Culhane, William Garlington, Todd Lawson, Anthony Lee, Denis MacEoin, Susan Maneck, Ahang Rabbani, Peter Smith, Mohamad Tavkoli-Targhi, and Peter Terry were always encouraging and generous in their comments on H-Bahai. Mohamad's work inspired chapter 5. And Juan has found ways to involve me in projects that have informed my contributions to the field, for which I am grateful. Our acquaintance started on the Internet, over a paper he had written referring to the Karbala passions. We have had the occasion to meet, chat, and work on many projects since. But the occasion on which he introduced me to Jackson Armstrong-Ingram is the one moment that I will always keep dear. Jackson later joined me at conference presentations, kept me on toes, showed me what I had missed in images and texts, and engaged in rather animated arguments in the Q&As and after panels. He never failed to direct me to the newest piece by Afsaneh Najmabadi. I miss Jackson. The three of us, Afsaneh, Jackson, and I, always seemed to find the same things exciting at around the same time. Afsaneh continues to push me further in my research and to inspire, too. Her support of the project in *Representing the Unpresentable* has helped me keep faith in the importance of "the Babi" to the constitution of the modern Iranian self. Keya Ganguly, whose passion for Walter Benjamin I also share, played a similar role in inspiring the discussion of history as image in *Representing the Unpresentable.* I do also miss Hamila Seddigh, who would read from the books I would bring home from my nonstop sprees in Tehran. She would eagerly read passages with me, listen to traditional musical scores, watch new and old films, and discuss aspects of Iranian cultural and religious life. Those visits to her sickbed in Tehran between January 2001 and February 2005 were formative.

My mother, Faezeh Seddigh, seems always to have been there for these adventures in Tehran and, to my surprise, all over the world, and my dad and my brother, Hooshmand and Kasra Mottahedeh, have been constant, supportive, and eager to listen from afar. Michael Hardt read an early draft of *Representing the Unpresentable* and provided important suggestions. I am also grateful to my colleagues Farzaneh Milani, Andrew Janiak, Anna Krylova, Claudia Koonz, Jan Radway, Ken Surin, Toril Moi, Alice Kaplan, Wahneema Lubiano, Jane Gaines, Antonio Viego, Frank Lentricchia, Walter Mignolo, Tim Lenoir, Alberto Moreiras, Valentin Mudimbe, James Rolleston, Barbara Herrnstein Smith, Tomiko Yoda, Robyn Wiegman, Philip Stewart and Jean-Jacques Thomas for their support and encouragement. D. J. Whyte, Payman Nadimi, Lynne Yancy, Martha Schweitz, Selin Ever and Lisa Klarr worked so hard on various aspects of the manuscript's final draft, and I am forever grateful for Lisa's detailed work on the index. My editor Mary Selden Evans is remarkable. She has been my rock throughout. My friends—Antonio Arce, Anja Lee, Ranji Khanna and Srinivas Aravamudan, Fred Jameson and Susan Willis, Ariel Dorfman, Sherlock and Anyema Graham-Haynes, Paul Sobin, Shilyh Warren, Ifeona Fulani, Nancy Kimberly, Mazyar Lotfalian, miriam cooke and Bruce Lawrence, Gerry Mischke, Michael Murphy, Mana Rabiee, Ali Reza Tavakoli, Michelle Lach, Stephanie Merkel, Amit Rai, Rebecca Stein, Diane Nelson and Mark Driscoll, Emily Adams, and that adorable girl I've known forever, Amy Sexton—made my life so much fun in New York, in Tehran, in Oslo, in Minneapolis, in Delaware, and in Durham, too. Antonio played the part of an unassuming muse and was that trusty cheering voice in the last years of writing, while Griffin sat on my drafts and books when I needed them most and put himself on my fingers when he knew I was too tired to move them about on the keyboard anyway. These friends will never appreciate how well they kept me. I do.

Representing the Unpresentable

Introduction

A Traveller's Narrative, the chronicle of Babi history published in English in 1891 by the British orientalist Edward G. Browne, gives an account of an Iranian disciplining photograph. This account traces the peregrinations of a young Persian man from the borders of Europe and the Ottoman Empire to the court of Nasir al-Din Shah Qajar (b. 1831, r. 1848–96) in Iran. This young Babi, whom the chronicle calls Mirza Badi, bears a letter written by a Persian nobleman exiled in Adrianople.[1] Mirza Badi takes the letter to the shah, who is stationed at the time outside of Tehran. The young man waits on a rock outside the Royal Pavilion until he is summoned. Three days pass in the state of fasting. "On the fourth day," the chronicler records, "the Royal Personage was examining all quarters and directions with a telescope when suddenly his glance fell on this man who was seated in the utmost respectful attitude on a rock. It was inferred from the indications [perceived] that he must certainly have thanks [to offer], or some complaint or demand for redress and justice [to prefer]. [The King] commanded one of those in attendance at the court to inquire into the circumstances of this youth" (Browne 1891, 58).

1. Although the author of *A Traveller's Narrative* was initially anonymous, Abdu'l-Baha, the son of Mirza Husayn 'Ali Baha'u'llah (1817–1892), was later known to Browne as the author of the text. The nobleman in question in this passage is Baha'u'llah himself, the founder of the Baha'i faith, which was established as an independent world religion around that time. Baha'is were what the majority of the surviving Babis became by the mid- to late 1860s. Mirza Badi, like Baha'u'llah himself, was an early follower of Sayyid 'Ali Muhammad, the Bab (1819–1850). Although the image informing recollection often takes a different path than that traveled in the writing or the righting of history, Mirza Badi is retrospectively considered a Baha'i in contemporary historiography, in that he traveled to the court of the Shah in Iran on behalf Baha'u'llah. The processes by which the image of "the Babi" is rooted in recollection are discussed in chapter 1 of *Representing the Unpresentable.*

A Traveller's Narrative captures with these words a precious moment of encounter between the mediated gaze of the Qajar dynast, Nasir al-Din Shah, and the "emaciated body and enfeebled spirit" of the nation's other. Aware of the ultimate sacrifice, the young Babi receives permission to approach the royal pavilion with the letter. His dispatch delivered with "dignity, composure and respectfulness surpassing description," Mirza Badi addresses the shah: "O King, I have come unto thee from Sheba with a weighty message!" (Browne 1891, 59). The shah, according to *A Traveller's Narrative,* "commanded to take the letter and arrest the bearer" (59). The *Narrative* claims that the shah's intention was to "deliberate on the matters raised in the letter" (59). Shocked at this gesture of almost uncritical acceptance, others in the shah's company are said to have reacted with reprehension. As a result, the *Narrative* reports, the young Babi was ordered by the shah's ministers to suffer punishment and torture for his presumptuous approach to the royal court. The spectacle of his mutilated body was made a disciplinary measure, like many others under Nasir al-Din Shah's rule, for the edification of the masses. "[W]hen the torture gave no result," the *Narrative* continues, "they [first] photographed him (the executioners on his left and on his right, and he sitting bound in fetters and chains beneath the sword with perfect meekness and composure), and then slew and destroyed him" (59).

The author of *A Traveller's Narrative* then records that he sent for the photograph and found it "worthy of contemplation, for he [Mirza Badi]

1. Mirza Badi photographed before his execution.

was seated with wonderful humility and strange submissiveness, in utmost resignation" (Browne 1891, 59). This photographic image of the young Babi became a fixed image in time. It was one of many that appeared in Iran under Qajar rule (1785–1925), which, according to Bahram Beiza'i, "brought the nation face-to-face with its own image" for the first time. The coming of the photograph represented the presence of the present to itself, rendering the previously unpresentable present (Beiza'i 1996, 373). "Photography," as Walter Benjamin famously observed, "with its time lapses, enlargements, etc. makes such knowledge possible. Through these methods one first learns of this optical unconscious, just as one learns of the drives through psychoanalysis" (1999b, 47). It is this, the link between the detail captured by the momentary "click" of the camera and the psychoanalytic recovery of the unconscious in quotidian life that signals the birth of modernity in Iranian historiography.

The tradition of photography in Iran, with its roots in the early personal photographs taken and collected by Nasir al-Din Shah and in the commercial photographs taken by foreigners, is marked by the presence of the unpresentable, the *haram,* in ordinary national life.[2] Photography was

2. "Iranian hermeneutics is based on the primacy of hiding core values (that is, of veiling) and of distrusting manifest meaning (that is, vision)," Hamid Naficy observes (1994, 136–37). This traditional distrust of vision and of public visibility has had a significant impact on pictorial representation in Iran. Notions of veiling have thus gained centrality in the national construction of social and cultural life and articulate themselves in a variety of ways. Visual culture is not the only discourse affected by this dynamic. Hamid Naficy notes: "The practice of veiling motivates people to search for hidden, inner meanings in all they see, hear, receive in daily interaction with others; to interpret constantly all products of social interaction, while trying to conceal their own intentions at the same time" (136–37). As such what veiling represents is caught in a web of diverse media and materials.

The division of space and the construction of architecture in Iran are symptomatic of cultural perceptions of veiling and visuality. Traditional homes have two distinct arenas within which action takes place: the space known in Persian as the *biruni* or "exterior," where guests are received, and the *andaruni* or "interior," where the family (and, in particular, the women) may carry on their lives without outside interference. "Outside the home, this need for privacy is continued by means of the veiling of women. The word for 'veil' in Persian, *chador,* actually means a tent, as though the home itself were somehow transported into the public sphere. This covering of the self is not restricted to women. . . . In traditional

used to capture the everyday, but in doing so, photography also dissolved the stringent boundaries between the public space of visibility, the *biruni,* and the private and sacred space of interiority, the *andaruni* or *harem.* Photographs of everyday life brought interior *(baten)* pure and holy spaces to the exterior realm of visibility *(zaher).* Nasir al-Din Shah's prolific photographs of his harem and concubines adorned in their private outfits, as well as the exoticized photographs taken by foreigners of the Qajar women lifting their facial veils, immersed early Qajar photography in the realm of the *haram,* the unpresentable, marking the technology's future subjects and its practitioners with a stigma of prohibition and the apprehension of immodesty. Absorbed in the realm of the forbidden and unpresentable, the photo image unveiled an interiority in Iranian modernity beyond the purified limits of Shi'ite Islam—this was a realm subject to the convergence of cultures.

If we return briefly to the passage on Mirza Badi in *A Traveller's Narrative,* we will note the degree to which the photograph and the commentary on it are configured by the tensions of a history of cultural confluence in representation and the uncanny measure by which they together represent that history in an abbreviated form. In his commentary, the narrator of *A Traveller's Narrative* suggests that in the photograph that he acquired after the execution of the young man, Mirza Badi is seated in the center with the executioners seated on his right and left. Similar photographs of criminals emerged and were circulated in Iran as a means to warn, discipline, and instill fear in the shah's subjects under the reign of the Qajars. Yet the commentary around this photographic encounter emphasizes the

---

painting, the faces of the Prophet and other sacred figures are regularly depicted with a long white veil" (Easterman 1992, 217). Notions of female privacy are both semantically and conceptually connected to the Islamic legal category of forbiddenness, expressed through the Arabic root h-r-m. This is a complex root from which a range of words may be derived; words which indicate how spatial divisions bear upon built forms as directly as they do conceptual distinctions and rational practices. "Three things seem to join forces . . . to develop the sense of what is *haram:* holiness; impurity (as with pork or wine); and sexual activity (or, by extension, women, in whom [heterosexual] sex is invested). All exist within conceptual spaces that mark them off from ordinary life. All define boundaries that may not be crossed, spatial, social and moral circles of inviolability" (Easterman 1992, 218).

inefficacy of this disciplinary gesture. The narrator's eyes rest on the photograph to contemplate the heroism and integrity of the sword's victim. Rather than embracing the discourse of the law, the commentary issues a challenge to those who attempt to pose the subject of the photograph in terms that are destructive of the common good. The commentary similarly challenges the claims to documentation and hence "truth," which underwrite both the disciplining measures adopted by the shah through photography and the tradition of distance and objectivity in foreign travelers' textual and visual accounts of nineteenth-century Iranian culture, a tradition on which the *Narrative*'s own labor admittedly rests. As such, the commentary configures a critique that derives its force from the specificity of reading a photograph as an *antidisciplinary* object.

Although the commentary challenges the disciplinary measures ascribed to the photograph by the royal court and undercuts the tradition of scientific truth attributed to photography, especially in the contemporary Western disciplinary discourse, the photograph itself embraces another irony on the level of its content: with fetters around his neck and feet, the young man rests his left hand on the chain. Not unlike the first photographs of Nasir al-Din Shah taken by his own camera, the sword's victim stares directly at the lens. Yet it is not the direct look, but the hand that is remarkable. Mirza Badi's hand placement in this photograph is reminiscent of a time in early Western traditions of photography when it was necessary to give the models support, so that they would remain steady for the duration of the exposure in photo-ateliers. In these early Western photographs, columns appeared next to drapes and awkwardly standing on rugs. Models stood with their fingers braced in their jacket-buttons to hold still (Benjamin 1999b). Mirza Badi's hand gesture, a traditional sign of humility in Iranian culture, like the polite raising of a hat on nineteenth-century Manhattan promenades, awkwardly replicates Western traditions of photography. One has to wonder if this gesture, like Nasir al-Din's top hat and imported chairs in his own court photographs, was not inherited from the early Western styles of photographic portraiture—a gesture shaped in the context of modern Western technological development and remembered and mimicked even to last moment of one's life. In an uncanny current of antagonistic articulation, and thus linked to the veiled condition of interiority, the *baten,* Mirza Badi's photograph externalizes a gesture with its connotations of (interior) integrity to the visual and exterior world of the *zaher.* It does so in its exposure of the abject Iranian subject to technological advances in photography.

The young Babi's hand gesture is a photographic index buried for decades and directing the vision of its reader looking back. It instructs the reader in an *antidisciplinary practice.* It is through the specificity of this reading practice that the chronicler articulates a critique of state. The term "antidisciplinarity" names an engagement with the specificity of the object of knowledge in ways that disrupt the disciplinary structures that make it. As such, this engagement has global significance. Because of the multiple ways in which antidisciplinarity informs Babi practice, it offers itself as a model for my reading of Babi texts and conditions my attempt to trace the discursive role of the "the Babi image" in the constitution of the modern Iranian nation.

Although shackled to a stigma of abjection, the Babis were in truth not altogether different from other Iranian Shi'ites that formed the majority of the Iran's population in the nineteenth century. While the Babis eventually differentiated themselves from Shi'ites by undermining the foundations of Shi'ite orthodoxy, like all Shi'ites the Babis believed that the Prophet Muhammad assigned political and spiritual authority only to the ancestral line of the Imams. When the Twelfth Imam went into occultation in 939, the exercise of authority was handed to the *ulama* (the learned in Islam) and to good Muslim rulers. Thus, in Shi'ite thought, political and religious authority would only be legitimate in the absence of the Twelfth Imam. In the mid-1840s, Sayyid 'Ali Muhammad declared himself the Bab, "the Gate" to the Twelfth Imam, later modifying this claim by asserting the return of the venerated figure of the Imam as *Mahdi,* or *Qa'im,* in his own person.[3] With the Imam in the world—a claim largely accepted by the Bab's followers and understood by all Iranian Shi'ites, all religious and political institutions were subject to his sufferance. Thus, as Denis MacEoin suggests, "From the point of view of both local and national government,

3. The Bab's claims actually progressed from being "the Gate" to the imam, to being the Imam Mahdi/Qa'im himself, to being a divine revelator as was Muhammad.

the Babis were manifestly insurrectionaries bent on subverting existing religious and social order" (1982, 121). "The authorities recognized the revolutionary implications of the claims of the Bab and acted accordingly" (Walbridge 1996, 347). Yet, "[i]t is vital to bear in mind," MacEoin warns concerning the period after the Bab's assumption of Mahdihood, that although laws and practices changed for the Babis themselves, "the Bab's particular role was far from clear to his followers." In fact, "Babism in this period was far from being a doctrinally homogenous movement" (1982, 115). The authority to speak on behalf of the Qa'im often fell to Babi leaders such as Qurrat al-'Ayn Tahirih, Mulla Husayn Bushru'i, Mulla Muhammad Ali Quddus, and Hujjat Zanjani, who "were accorded considerable respect and veneration and were regarded by many as incarnations of the Imams or other sacred figures of Shi'i hagiography." Chroniclers of the period refer to one of the early Babi leaders, Mulla Muhammad Ali Quddus, for example, as "the Qa'im of Jilan" attributing to him the station of the Twelfth Imam, Mahdi, himself (MacEoin 1982, 115).

Suggestions of Babi incarnation, coupled with the movement's claim that the Qa'im had returned in the figure of the Bab, produced the now-time of Iran's modernity as Judgment Day, a day of religious revolution and social reform, a day coincident with the messianic cessation of time. The Babi incarnation into popularized conceptions of the Last Days could have provided the means for the popular acceptance of the Babis as the image of Iran on the cusp of a new era in history. Instead, the Babis emerged in popular consciousness as the cause of the shocks perpetuated by Iran's confrontation with the vicissitudes of modernity. "The Babi" was captured in recollection as Iran's modern scapegoat and as the very measure of modernity's abjection.

The reputed public unveiling of Qurrat al-'Ayn Tahirih (born Fatimih Zarin Taj Barghani) at the Babi conference in Badasht, a gathering that would establish Babism's complete break from Shi'ite traditions, provided modernity with a dialectical image for the abject figure of "the Babi." The public perception of such a public gesture by a woman of great reputation and heritage, combined with the radical claims made by the Babis as the representatives of the returned Twelfth Imam on the Day of Judgment, made it increasingly difficult for the Shi'ite nation to deal with the Babi movement as a passing occurrence and as insignificant to the formulation of modernity in Iran. Cryptic references to Qurrat al-'Ayn Tahirih's unveiling represented the act as a sign of Iran's degeneracy in the hands of foreign and European powers and conversely as a trope capable of instilling awe in the movement's revolutionary claims, its brave following, and its mighty achievements in the course of its short history. In the decades that followed, the image of Qurrat al-'Ayn Tahirih's unveiling oscillated in the literatures, the chronicles, the travelogues, and the memoirs to become the abject bearer of the ambivalences of Iran's own modern identity.

In *Representing the Unpresentable,* I will argue that it was in fact against "the Babi," an image of the self as the embodiment of the nation's "abject other," that modern Iran could emerge as homogenous and whole. The development of this image and its afterimages stands as the core problematic of the book.

The historical photograph that captured the young Persian Babi, Mirza Badi, before his death, stands for the dialectical image of the modern Iranian self as Other in this text. Lodged in the confluence of cultures, this technologically produced image and other photographic images like it mark the birth of modern representational forms in Iran and function, like the pictures that flitted by the viewer in those photo booklets of old "under pressure of the thumb," as the predecessors of contemporary Iranian cinema under the rule of the Islamic Republic.[4] Every one of these photographic imprints marks the cinema's technologies from its inception with the polluting presence of the abject and the seal of the foreign Other in Iran. Inscribing the multiplicity of cultural influences informing the birth of the camera in Iran, the photographic image marks its inventors and its subjects as the representatives of the *haram*—the unpresentable.

That I foreground this history of cultural confluence as it configures the photographic index ultimately to reflect on the historical image of "the Babi" and thus to articulate the presence of an unpresentable presence in the constitution of the modern state is not to contrast historical representations of the modern Iranian subject with the contemporary self-representation of Iran in its cinema under the Islamic Republic. My

4. Cf. Benjamin 2003c, 280n. 39.

effort is rather to recover the cinematic precondition for the contemporary state's self-representation to the world. As Garrett Stewart remarks, "The confident differentiation of film *from* mere photography cannot . . . be secured without the reciprocal implication of those differences *between* successive photograms upon which all film is fashioned" (1999, 39). It is the successive presence of the abject body as the very figure embodying Iran's own cultural confluence in the historical and the technologically mediated image marking the birth of the nation's modernity that poses a constant threat to Iran's meticulous and highly successful representation of itself in its cinema after the Iranian Revolution of 1978–79.

"Representing the Unpresentable" the organizing theme of this book, which brings "the image" to the concept of history, has its provenance in the work of the German literary and cultural critic Walter Benjamin. In his last known work, "On the Concept of History," Benjamin argues that history becomes knowable in image form. Thus, for Benjamin, it is from within the image that historical writing takes shape, not as a testimony to progress, but in the recognition of its relevance for a present that is illuminated by its momentary relation to the past. "Articulating the past historically means recognizing those elements of the past which come together in the constellation of a single moment. . . . In drawing itself together in the moment—in the dialectical image—the past becomes part of humanity's involuntary memory" (2003b, 403). A sudden and flitting amalgamation takes shape. The conjunction of the present and the past constitutes a "now-time" that for Benjamin is at once the mark of a messianic redemption of the all-time of history and a revolutionary break from the continuance of historical and progressive time. The past gains its urgency in articulation with the present as *Jetztzeit*—"now-time" in image form. "The dialectical image," which captures the historical moment in abbreviated form, is defined by Benjamin "as the involuntary memory of a redeemed humanity" (2003b, 403). This vision of the historical embraces for Benjamin, "a conception of the present as now-time shot through with splinters of messianic time" (2003a, 397).

The problematics involved in the temporal confluence of the historical as dialectical image are apparent in the title, *Representing the Unpresentable,* as well. The past cannot become a present without ambivalence. The past is an un-present and remains unpresent-able without the intervention of a gesture of "witnessing." It is the condition of the present of witnessing that brings a sense of urgency to the past.

The connection between the act of witnessing and the act of writing about the past is held together by the etymological roots of the concept "theory." The word stems from the Greek verb *theorein* which means "to contemplate, to look at, to survey." In his "Tiger on the Paper Mat," Wlad Godzich writes about the genealogy of the concept in ancient Greece. "The Greeks designated certain individuals . . . to act as legates on certain formal occasions. These individuals bore the title *theoros,* and collectively constituted a *theoria.* They were summoned on special occasions to attest the occurrence of some event, to witness its happenstance, and to then verbally certify its having taken place" (1994, 165). Godzich notes further that the functional structure of *theoria* is such that between the event and its entry into public discourse, there is mediation. The *theoria* is the authority that puts the seen into socially acceptable and reliable language, and it is this discourse that is then brought to the polity. Historical representation, a theory, a witnessing of past events, is caught in the web of visuality and language, a mesh created out of the seen and the said. Although the *theoria* witnesses an event, it is the meaning that the *theoria* brings to that event from within the preoccupation of the present that formulates the significance of the witnessing to posterity. Theory creates a representation of an event through discourse. Discourse comes to stand in for vision or experience. Theory in this sense represents experience and materializes itself as the replacement for that experience.

Nineteenth-century Iran understood this conception of history and its representation well. It brought history to life on the stage, creating a medium through which the past could make itself present to vision. More important, it did so in a space that doubled as the original space of happening. The space of the stage was the double of the historical one, but as double or copy it transformed the past for the present. Significantly, ancient religious history, deprived of its real presence in the now, was made present through a replacement. That historical past, which in the nineteenth century was the antiquity of Islam, was both witnessed and represented through the Shi'ite passion play, the *ta'ziyeh.*

The *ta'ziyeh* drama recalled in the nineteenth century, as it does today, the fundamental break between Shi'ism and Sunnism. The drama reenacts the story of the battle at Karbala in which the differences between the followers of the Imams (i.e., the familial successors of the Prophet Muhammad) and the rest of the Muslim world were finally determined. In 680, because of his refusal to acknowledge Caliph Yazid as a just and rightful ruler, Imam Husayn, the grandson of the Prophet Muhammad, was killed in battle at Karbala, and his head was delivered to the governor of Kufa. Unwilling to submit, the remainder of his family was slaughtered or taken along with the women and children in chains to the court of Caliph Yazid in Damascus. The *ta'ziyeh,* an Iranian passion play performed by men and young children throughout the first month of the Muslim year, represents these moments of historical brutality in graphic terms.

In the nineteenth century, a century that marked the high tide of the *ta'ziyeh*'s popularity, Iran's history as a Shi'ite nation was recalled through the medium of the *ta'ziyeh.* In *Representing the Unpresentable* I argue that this drama represented the antiquity of Islam through its reenactment as theory or discourse on the present. In the *ta'ziyeh* the actors were seen as role-carriers who incarnated the forebears of Shi'ite Islam for the drama. These highly venerated figures have been addressed, since the beginning of the Shi'ite tradition, as the "Fourteen Pure Souls" or "Fourteen Infallibles." They include the Prophet Muhammad himself, the Twelve Imams, starting with Imam Ali, and Muhammad's daughter Fatimih, the mother of the important Shi'ite Imams—Hasan and Husayn. The past incarnated itself *figuratively* in the quotidian present in the reenactment of these figures by role-carrier on the *ta'ziyeh* stage. The *ta'ziyeh* theater became that copied space in which the past made itself known within the present. Enacting a present that is mimetic of the past, the *ta'ziyeh* produced a theory of the modern nation for its audience. On this stage, two particulars were unpresentable, namely, women and the Shi'ite Infallibles. Veiled young men played the role of women on the *ta'ziyeh* stage, and the Shi'ite Imams were played with veiled faces to maintain their venerated status. So, while the modern present demanded their historical representation for the nation's constitution, women and the Fourteen Infallibles remained unpresentable to vision—that is, unfit to be seen and the eyes as unfit to see them.

This contradictory logic of representation and unpresentability permeates a culture concerned with its own status as a modern nation in the nineteenth century. For while the image of "woman," as we shall see, is one determinant in the construction of the identity of the modern nation, her body remains unpresentable and must remain veiled in public space according Islamic law. And while the Imams were fundamental to the historical conception of the nation as a nation of Shi'ites, the mortal eye remains unfit to see them. As Matthew Arnold noted: "The Ta'ziyeh is an innovation which they [the Muslim clergy] disapprove and think dangerous; it is addressed to the eye; it departs from the limits of what is revealed and appointed to be taught as truth, and brings novelties and heresies;—for these dramas keep growing under the pressure of the actor's imagination and emotion of the public and receive new developments everyday" (1871, 677). To represent on this stage was then meant "to stand in for," that is, "to make the opportunity available for," the incarnation of the Imams in the present. It also meant "to make present," that is, to bring the past into the here and now of discourse. What the theologians identified as a problem, therefore, was not only history's address to the eye, but the transformation that the *ta'ziyeh* perpetuated in religious history by virtue of a copy that transformed its "truth" into discourse. The *ta'ziyeh* took history and transformed it into a discourse that then stood in for history's truth. As such, this act of representation was an unauthorized, but in fact a collective *theoria,* an act of witnessing the past in the present for both the actors and the audience, who all became representatives of those who had gone before. The *ta'ziyeh* stage became the copied stage through which historical events were represented anew, but now as the foundation of a collective national discourse—a theory of the present.

Emile Benveniste has suggested that discourse, unlike the category of history, carries within it the linguistic markers (deixis) that situate the speaker in the text. History, he argues, speaks from the position of a disembodied, disinterested subject (1971). Unlike history, discourse refers to the place and time of its speaker. It does so through its deixis. "Deixis," Godzich writes, "is the linguistic mechanism that permits the articulation of all . . . distinctions between the here and the there, the now and the then, the we and the you. It establishes the existence of an 'out there' that is not an 'over here,' and thus is fundamental to the theoretical enterprise" (Godzich 1994, 166). In the transition from history to discourse produced by the *ta'ziyeh,* religious history could take on new truths. For "the here" of the actor and of the audience also became "the there" of the historical characters he (and sometimes she) would represent. The *ta'ziyeh* thus took liberties with "the there" of history, making it "the here" of the dramatic stage. History's transformation took shape by its transition through the deictic markers of the *ta'ziyeh* discourse. By doing so, the drama created the possibility of a multitude of other such transformations.

It was, in fact, the very structure of the *takiyeh* in which the *ta'ziyeh* was performed for the first time in the nineteenth century that was among the first cultural sites to be influenced by these deictic transformations. *Ta'ziyeh*-style religious iconography first appeared in the *takiyeh.* The *takiyeh* walls translated *ta'ziyeh*'s historical representation of the past onto a new medium as a new historical truth—a truth about the past that was essentially and deictically transformed in the process of its staging. Muhammad and the Imams began to appear with long veils on tile paintings on the theater walls. Thus in the nineteenth century, the image surrounding the stage of the *ta'ziyeh* became the modern medium for the representation of an unpresentable history, clinging tenaciously to its deictic roots in the *ta'ziyeh.* Linked in this way, the image remained unrecognized for its capacity to represent the nation to itself in forms that were commensurate with its coming modernity: forms such as the photographic and then, later, the cinematic image.

As the first chapter of *Representing the Unpresentable* will suggest, my concerns in this text are primarily with modern national discourses. My attempt is to uncover the discourses that have constituted the image of "the Babi" within Iran's national history, focusing on the ways in which this image came to represent the prototypical image of the modern Iranian nation in the figure of its abject Other. That this identification has been by and large obscured, I argue, has much to do with the way that Babism has been constituted as an object of disciplinary study since Edward G. Browne's early historical and doctrinal investigations of the movement. Thus, though much work remains to be done on the specificities of Babi doctrine and the doctrine's relation to historical happening, my concerns diverge fundamentally from the academic investigation of the doctrinal and theological. I devote chapter 3 to discussing the problems associated with such disciplinary approaches to the materials Browne collected in his search for the history and doctrinal coherence of the Babi movement. The texts unearthed and translated by Browne, I argue, suggest, in fact, an urgency of a different kind. The texts configure a theory of a present without equal. Sirenlike, they signal a "now" that is the Day of Judgment itself. The theory of the present embedded in these texts creates a vantage point from which the abject image of "the Babi" as the Iranian self gains clarity. The image that these texts configure suggests a belonging to the nation from which the Babis were forcibly othered.

As I discuss in chapter 4, *A Traveller's Narrative* (1891), Browne's first translation of a chronicle on the Babi movement, articulates a protomodern discourse in the guise of a narrative history of the Babis, staging the cruelty meted out to the Babis by the clergy and the envoys of the nineteenth-century Qajar dynasty as the condition for modern Iran's impossible continued imperial dominion in the world. By appealing to the history of the Babis, the narratives call the nation to take radical measures for reform. *Tarikh-i-Jadid or New History of Mirza Ali Muhammad—the Bab* (Browne 1893) modeled after Mirza Fath 'Ali Akhundzadih's fictive travelogue *Kamal al-Dawla,* and told from the perspective of an objective foreign observer, situates the Babi movement within a discourse of modernization, based in mythified descriptions of the European nations, a discourse typical of Persian travelers to Europe in the eighteenth and nineteenth centuries. *Nuqtat al-Kaf* (Browne 1910) presumably containing the earliest description of the movement by an eyewitness, and Browne's last major publication on the Babi movement, situates the movement within the tradition and history of the ancient Arab Muslims and casts the Babi figures as the return and resurrection of the Fourteen Infallibles. Important to this representation is the chronicle's casting of the Babis in accordance with the tropes of the Karbala drama, the *ta'ziyeh.* The temporal and spatial deictics of the *ta'ziyeh* are used to situate the Babis as integral to Iran's history and through its tropes to call on the nation to participate in its own reform.

Although modern Iranian history has been witness to many different approaches to the Karbala story, my reading of "the Browne chronicles" suggests that the preferred perspective on that story in these texts was one of martyrdom on the narrative level and one of national regeneration on the enunciative one. In chapters 3 and 4, I argue that this perspective was closely tied to the tropes of the *ta'ziyeh*'s performance of the tragic carnage of Imam Husayn and his family in Karbala. On the narrative level, the *ta'ziyeh* emphasizes the role of the meek Imam who, prepared for his ultimate sacrifice, again and again takes his ancestral place as the leader of the Muslim community and faces his final defeat on the stage of martyrdom on the plains of Karbala. On the enunciative level, however, the appropriation of the *ta'ziyeh,* as a representational tool is understood as a call for national regeneration.

The enunciative, as Benveniste (1971) argues, is the reflexive marker of the pronoun in utterances. In utterance, deixis marks the speaker's time and space, signaling the status of the utterance as discourse or enunciation. Yet, deictic markers become slightly more complicated to place when historical texts become embodied—when the actors speak of themselves as the incarnations of past figures, of their present as the past, and of their space as that of another. The whole issue of the reliability of *theoria* rests on its ability to make its visuality take the place of its witnessing—in effect, to make its language, its speech, refer to the here and now of the act that was witnessed (Godzich 1994, 166–67). But on the *ta'ziyeh* stage, the here and now, the deictic markers of time and place take on an ambivalence in which the past, represented in the figure of Imam Husayn, becomes the present of the modern Shi'ite nation. Because the *ta'ziyeh* was used to celebrate the constitutive differences of Shi'ite Iran from all other neighbors, whoever inserted him/herself into its narrative as a role-carrier enacting the story of Karbala, as my reading of the Babi chronicles suggests they did, also inserted himself/herself in a narrative that was formed in this period by the *ta'ziyeh*'s nationalist discourse. He/she inserted him/herself in a discourse that aligned him/her with the defense of national interests. On the *ta'ziyeh*'s patriotic character in the 1860s Comte de Gobineau writes the following:

> [Husayn] is not only the son of Ali, he is the husband of a princess of the blood of the Persian kings; he, his father Ali, the whole body of the

> Imams taken together represent the nation, represent Persia, indeed, ill treated, despoiled, stripped of its inhabitants, by Arabians. The right which is insulted and violated in [Husayn] is identified with the right of Persia. The Arabians, the Turks, the Afghans—Persia's implacable and hereditary enemies—recognize Yazid as legitimate caliph; Persia finds therein an excuse for hating them the more, and identifies itself with the usurper's victims. It is patriotism therefore, which has taken the form here, of drama to express itself. (quoted in Arnold 1871, 683–84)

What seems to be at stake in identifying the Karbala story as the story of choice for the early chronicles of Babi history, such as the ones collated by Browne, is first to identify one's story with a story about the plight of the nation and of work toward its regeneration. Second, the Karbala story enables identification with the acts of the Third Imam, Imam Husayn, who despite his knowledge of his ultimate martyrdom, went through with his mission, and who, because of this heroic sacrifice, would be remembered forever in popular national memory.

While at the end of the day the position taken by the Babis as the incarnated figures of the Karbala tragedy may seem irreconcilable with the later messianic claims of its membership that the Bab was the messianic return of the Twelfth Imam, the Qa'im after his major occultation, the narrative, and the spatial and temporal structures of the *ta'ziyeh* drama enabled such overtures quite readily. Abbas Amanat argues that despite the discrepancies in Shi'ite messianic traditions, "one can discern a distinction between the Day of Return and the Day of Resurrection" (1989, 194). For the Babis themselves the Day of Return was the period when the Babis, as the symbolic reincarnations of the past holy figures, fulfill certain tasks before the Day of Resurrection, hastening its advent. After the return of the Qa'im, the Prophet Muhammad, the Imams, and all the faithful companions are resurrected to face the forces of evil and witness the Qa'im as he takes historical vengeance for all that was postponed by the Imams to the proper future (195–96). Theologians have disagreed about the proper sequence of events during the Last Days, but at least in the popular belief of Qajar Iran, Imam Husayn plays the most important role on the Day of Resurrection (Arabic: *al-yaum,* literally "the day"). He chooses Karbala as the site of his resurrection. According to the popular traditions, those who remember Imam Husayn, mourn him, and reenact his tragic death enter Paradise with him on Judgment Day, *al-yaum.*

On the enunciative level and through the ambivalences of the deictic markers, then, the *ta'ziyeh* stage sets up a situation in which the time and space of the past and the present coincide in a kind of *Jetztzeit,* (now-time, or *al-yaum*) so that the "audience" became both the troops supporting Imam Husayn in Karbala *and* his mourners, mourning his death in the present. Both actions are recognized as important means for the believers to enter Paradise on Judgment Day. The Babi messianic expectations and the chronicler's vision of them reenacting the events of Karbala fit right into this construction on the popular stage. Lasting a little short of two decades, the day of the Babi present *(al-yaum)* was in fact Judgment Day. In response to the shocks of this recognition, a recognition the nation violently denied, the image of "the Babi" emerged as the nation's figure of the unpresentable self as other. I pursue this argument in detail in chapter 1, in scraps of memoirs, travelogues, and everyday gestures that were recorded in the years that followed the execution of the Bab, the persecution of his followers, and the exile of some key Babis from Iran.

The dramatic tropes of the *ta'ziyeh* and the historical vision of the present as a *Jetztzeit,* continued to play a significant role in the production of the nation's historical and revolutionary consciousness after the *ta'ziyeh*'s rise to popularity in the nineteenth century. The *ta'ziyeh* rearticulated itself as the most important discourse in overthrowing the Pahlavi regime, which was perceived as the dominant impetus behind the country's enforced move toward the modernization and the consequent Europeanization of Iran in the 1970s. More important, the dramatic artform, significant to the formation of a national consciousness and a uniform national language in the nineteenth century, became a tool for political and national critique. The Pahlavi regime had feared the *ta'ziyeh*'s power and popularity to the extent that it was unwilling to lift the ban on its performance in the late 1970s.

What survived from this national tradition in culture was its historical formulation of the present—a representation of the present imbued with and in revolutionary constellation with a history of a national past.

When the popularity of the cinema displaced the traditional forms of entertainment such as the storytelling session in coffeehouses and participation in the *ta'ziyeh,* it inherited the temporal and spatial tropes of the *ta'ziyeh* along with its enunciative processes. There was a dual inheritance in the cinema, of course, and, as we shall see in chapter 5, the other inheritance was one that was embedded in the inscriptive technologies of vision and sound that were to become constitutive of the representation of the nation's new revolutionary identity.

As a government opposed to the growing influence of Western imperialism on Iranian culture, the Islamic Republic attempted to reclaim the cinema as a national art after the revolution in 1978–79. The government attempted to purify the film industry and the cinematic screen from foreign intervention and directed the industry, rather, toward the promotion of revolutionary and Islamic values. In part, this reclamation meant the reconstruction of the Iranian film industry in light of theologically dictated rules of modesty and women's veiling. Such dictates pitted the moral superiority of contemporary Islamic Iran against the technological superiority of the West and aimed, through a constellation of isolationist moves, to create a national cinema that was distinct from both East and West. It was clear that media technologies would be used to create and represent the nation's identity to itself and to the world at large. At issue for the film industry was how a national cinema was to be configured, however. How was the nation to be represented in film? How would film technologies mediate the national? What role did the representational technologies of film play in the production of national images and national sounds? Did the mediating technologies affect this representation or did they not? How did their histories, attached as they were to a Western and an imperial heritage, affect the representation of a national culture that was produced within a purified national film industry under the Islamic Republic?

In close readings of the dialectics that inform the genealogy of representation in Iranian modern culture, and the genealogy of Iranian cultural modernity in representational form, *Representing the Unpresentable* focuses on the terms of two unpresentables: women and national history.

The first chapter introduces the image of "the Babi" as a trope for the unpresentable nation. It discusses the problematics associated with the fetishized image of the unveiling of the great nineteenth-century Babi poet Qurrat al-'Ayn Tahirih, and the consequences of this fetishism in the formulation of the nation's identity as whole. The second chapter traces the "chunneling" of ideas of patriotism, blood, and nation in the work of the "Father of Racism," Joseph Arthur Comte de Gobineau (1816–1882) who, in engaging both the history of the Babis and the popularity of the *ta'ziyeh* in the nineteenth century, brought further evidence to his vision of a degenerated Europe and, indeed, world civilization. The chapter pursues an in-depth discussion of the *ta'ziyeh.* I use this chapter as a foundation for my discussion of the image of "the Babi" in modern Iranian chronicles. The chapter also offers opportunity to foreground some of the *ta'ziyeh* tropes that come to configure the revolutionary and resistant strategies of postrevolutionary Iranian cinema as discussed in the concluding chapter. Chapter 3 follows the orientalist gaze of Edward Granville Browne and his efforts to pursue the history of the Babis in Iran and around the globe. It situates the roots of the historical studies of the Babi movement in the blind spot of the orientalist's vision, arguing that another anaphoric position, such as the study of culture, would indeed uncover other, possibly more nationally rooted concepts for the representation of the movement and for understanding the grounds for its unpresentability in modern Iranian culture. Evoking the notion of "antidisciplinarity" to define the strategy used by the Babis in the analysis of Iran's modernity I submit, in this chapter, that Babi antidisciplinarity, the object of Babi studies, is the very tool that will functionally transform approaches to Iranian modernity, shifting in this way the very representation of Iran's contemporary identity. Chapter 4 is a study of the translations and the major publications of Babi historical chronicles by Browne. "The Browne chronicles," I argue, return the orientalist gaze and envision the history of the Babi movement, as a return or resurrection of the protohistorical figures of Shi'ite Islam using *ta'ziyeh* tropes. Conversely they stand as the embodiments of modernist vision that represent the best of European culture as models for Iranian modernity. In this chapter I discuss why the moment of Qurrat al-'Ayn Tahirih's unveiling is left unrepresented. I argue that this is because "the Browne chronicles," in contrast to other narratives, such as *Nabil's Narrative,* fail to recognize the medium that is commensurate with the modernity they attempt to depict in image form. In my argument, the medium capable of this representation is the photo image that, though unemancipated from its place within a chronological history of progress, is capable of grasping the accelerated shocks associated with the nation's encounter with modernity and of developing these, as some narrators attempt to do, from negative clichés to positive photo images.

In the final chapter, the problematics informing the representation of the nation in the cinema of the Islamic Republic are articulated in allegorical conjunction with the flickering image of "the Babi" as the emblem of European modernity and of Shi'ite antiquity. In a close reading of director Ali Hatami's *Delshodegan* in this chapter, I maintain that although engaged in the project of national purification and regeneration, Iranian cinema speaks of the modern nation as it once did when reflecting on the abject image of "the Babi," as both self and other—an image of a nation shaped by the force cultural confluence articulating its revolutionary character with tropes drawn from the *ta'ziyeh.* In tracing the relay of the occidental and the oriental gazes and the inscription of sound on the gramophone in the process of national representation, I argue that Iran's postrevolutionary cinema, considered one of the leading examples of a "national cinema" in the 1980s and 1990s, and as a representative of an isolationist nation in the world, is significantly marked by an international articulation. This, I suggests, is an unpresentable hybridity that was derived simultaneous with the nation's very first contact with modern representational technologies and in the nation's encounter with its own internal Otherness, that is, with the "shocked" images of its scapegoat, the abject figure of "the Babi." Against the attempt to purify the nation from this Otherness, contemporary Iranian cinema speaks reflexively of its own productive technologies and of its own coming into being, in national representations that are inscribed, not by Shi'ite purity, but by traversals in space and time. These traversals situate the nation's will to reform, resist, and revolt while revealing the nation's deep attachment to the enunciative tropes derived from the *ta'ziyeh* drama. These tropes repeatedly configure the present of the Islamic Republic as the Babis once did: "Today is Judgment Day. A day scheduled to redeem all pasts in one messianic abridgment." In the process of representation and in moments of reflexivity, the cinema's technologies externalize, reinscribe, and internalize the modern nation itself in an unpresentable image that is wedged, like the dialectical image of "the Babi," in the contradiction of cultures.

1

The Mutilated Body of the Modern Nation

The Babi movement, established in 1844 in Shiraz, Persia (Iran), by Sayyid 'Ali Muhammad, known as the Bab (the Gate), is considered in contemporary Western historiography a messianic movement aimed at the transformation of a society conditioned by Twelver Shi'ism. Persisting a mere decade as a coherent entity, Babism was in nature a social and religious revolution. In spite of an extensive and comprehensive persecution of its membership by the Shi'ite clergy and the Qajar despot's representatives, the Babi movement nevertheless affected varied sectors of Iranian society. A perusal of contemporary academic writing published in Europe and in the United States, however, suggests that the Babi movement's chief achievement was its egalitarianism and particularly its impact on the status of women in Iran during the nineteenth century. This perception may be related to the public visibility of one of the Babi movement's female leaders, the poet Qurrat al-'Ayn Tahirih, and her conspicuous unveiling at a Babi gathering popularly referred to as the Badasht Conference.

The vast majority of the Bab's early followers, including Qurrat al-'Ayn Tahirih, were learned scholars in Shi'ite jurisprudence and the traditions of Islam. They came out of what is now referred to as the Shaykhi school. The school was situated in Karbala (Iraq), a city that was a major center for Shi'ite religious training. The Shaykhi school, associated with Shaykh Ahmad Ahsa'i, was known for its progressive teachings and reformist attitudes. A significant number of the early adherents of the Bab had received six to nine years of formal religious training with the school's leaders. Indeed, much of the students's messianic leanings and their thinking about the day of Resurrection, the advent of the Imam Mahdi, and the theory of prophetic cycles came from their contact with the instructor and later leader of the school, Sayyid Kazim.[1] After the death of Sayyid Kazim, many of them found the fulfillment of their teacher's promises of the return of the Imam Mahdi (as the victorious promulgator of Islam) in the teachings and the personage of the Bab. Typically the Shaykhi-Babis opposed the corruption of Shi'ite doctrine within Shi'ite orthodoxy and had a strong awareness of the way in which it accommodated the needs of the Qajar rule.

The Bab's followers, in their own particular ways, accepted his social and religious teachings and acknowledged his ultimate claim to be the return of the Twelfth Imam (the Mahdi or Qa'im). After the Bab's cruel public execution in Tabriz in 1850, most of the notable Babis who survived the ensuing fierce attacks by the clergy and the government acknowledged the claims of the prophet-founder of the Baha'i faith, Baha'u'llah, and recognized his leadership and successful establishment of an independent religion.

Writing in 1863–64, Mirza Fath 'Ali Akhundzadih, one of the early spokesmen for Iranian reform, promoted his book *Kamal al-Dawla* as an anti-Babi polemic intended to further the cause of Islam in Iran.[2] In *Kamal al-Dawla,* Akhundzadih celebrates the greatness of pre-Islamic Iran, through the fictive persona of a foreign traveling prince, and aspires to re-create Iran's glory by drawing on the technology and the sciences of the West. He argues that "these objectives can never be achieved without destroying the foundations of religious beliefs, which obstruct people's vision and impede their progress in secular affairs."[3] Although the Babis were perhaps the main source of resistance to the doctors of Islam (the *ulama*), who were Akhundzadih's main target of criticism, he calls the

1. *Kitab-i Nuqtat al-Kaf* reviews these aspects of Shaykhi thought in great detail. Refer to E. G. Browne's version of *Nuqtat al-Kaf* (Browne 1910). Also see Juan Cole's three papers on Ahsa'i (1993b, 1994, 1997). Cole also pursues these themes in some detail in the work of Baha'u'llah in his article "'I Am All the Prophets'" (1993a). Also consult: Abbas Amanat (1989); Denis MacEoin (1979); Vahid Rafati (1979); and Idris Hamid (1998).

2. Of course Akhundzadih was not promoting the work to save Islam from Babism, but to save the civil state from "the Babi threat." He represented the Babis as just more Islam-type fanaticism.

3. Letter to Shaykh Muhsin Khan dated Feb. 1879 (quoted in Sanjabi 1995, 50).

Babis "the deceivers of the people" whose "absurd words" renewed "sedition and revolts." For Akhundzadih "the Babi threat," as perceived by most Persians in his time, could be used to distract the attention of the priestly class away from his own antagonistic modernist rhetoric and his suggested reforms for the nation (Sanjabi 1995, 50). "The Babi" was for Akhundzadih a scapegoat and hence a readily available, indeed a stereotypic, popular target that could identify the symptoms of social ills from which Iran's modernity suffered.

The call for reform from this period until the Iranian Constitutional Revolution of 1906–11 often focused on the representation of the Iranian woman.[4] Her image, which was also defined by her interactions with men, was fundamental to shaping the image of the modern nation. Some Iranian observers looked to the "moon-faced," "ruby-lipped," "cypress-countenanced" unveiled Western woman as the quintessential image of European progress and set the Western woman as a model of modern Iranian femininity. But increased European hegemony in world politics, as Mohamad Tavakoli-Targhi points out, and the "constant threat of colonization and subversion of religion and cultural orthodoxy led to the scapegoating of European women in the political struggle against Iranian modernism" (Tavakoli-Targhi 1990a, 80). While many nineteenth-century observers of the West were "fascinated by Europeans," others portrayed the same unveiled fairy-faced women as demonic and saw the threat of European influence on Iran as directly connected to the "sexual debauchery of European women" (Tavakoli-Targhi 2001, 66). Their increased influence was measured by the secularization of Iranian Shi'ite society. European women were threatening because they were not veiled, revealing thereby their sexual appetite. In his *Shab Nameh,* devoted to the characteristics of European women, Mirza Fattah Garmrudi reports from his diplomatic mission that, "In this land of diverse persuasions, women and girls are generally pantsless and without a veil and have a constant desire for able pummelers. . . . They have escaped the trap of chastity into freedom and have masterly leapt from the snare of purity" (quoted in Tavakoli-Targhi 2001, 66).

4. For more on the Constitutional Revolution of 1906–11 see Janet Afary (1996).

The unveiled bodies of European women were directly linked through this rhetoric to untamed appetites and unwholesome mores. Their bodies as models of Iranian womanhood became figures of abjection in the more extreme anti-moderninist tracts, bearing the threat of Europe's imperialism in Iran.

Julia Kristeva's definition of abjection may bear some relevance in this discussion, for the abject is experienced "at the peak of its strength" as that impossible thing within the subject that simultaneously produces the subject's very being (1982, 5). While it seems that in Garmrudi's rhetoric the figure of the unveiled woman is in some ways associated with her lack of purity and chastity without that essential sartorial shield, her abjection in the nineteenth-century Iranian context, as we shall see in the figure of "the Babi," must be read, more incisively, as that which "disrupts identity, system, order. What does not respect borders, positions, rules" (Kristeva 1982, 4).

The manner in which the term "Babi" gained currency as a way to denote negative notions of modernity in common parlance in late-nineteenth- to early-twentieth-century Iran is worthy of note. For as derogatory as its resonances were, they seem to be imbedded, more often than not, within a context of sartorial innovation and Europeanization. The term "Babi," as we shall see, was a stereotypic attachment to any gesture of resistance to traditional Islamic values. It was a simplification, of course, and like most stereotypes, an arrested and fixed type of representation that masqueraded behind an untold carnival of images of foreignness, of modernism, of nihilism, and of irreligion. As such, this stereotype was a fixed memory in miniature—an image—constructed on the basis of events that took place at a specific time in Iranian history while simultaneously detached, reformulated, and recovered to illuminate other times and places. One may speculate along with Huchang Chehabi on the role played by the Babi poet Qurrat al-'Ayn Tahirih's public unveiling in the association between sartorial innovation and heresy (1993, 210). For while a "Babi" could be a man or a woman, only the Babi woman could be directly linked to images of public unveiling associated with European values. In the nineteenth century, the image of "the Babi" became connected to a sartoriality that connoted difference, indeed foreignness.

In this chapter I discuss the enforced participation of the Iranian people in the extermination of the Babis. While recognizing the difficulties of reconciling psychoanalytic concepts with a historical endeavor, I consider Sigmund Freud's discussion of the usefulness of an "intruder" for the constitution of a "communal love." I outline, through a series of historical images, the way in which the stereotypic term "Babi" entered into a complex and ambivalent play of fetishism in modern Iranian history. This "play of fetishism," a concept whose various formulations inform the analysis of race relations and national imagining in the work of writers such as Homi Bhabha and Frantz Fanon, organizes around itself the ambivalences of the modern nation's self-relation and the traumatic experiences of self-annihilation in Iran between 1848 and 1852. I argue here that the concepts of fetishism and abjection in psychoanalytic and postcolonial theory may be useful in understanding how a stereotypic image such as "the Babi" can inform a historical study of Persian modern subject formation and the subject's relation to the problems of formulating a modern nation's sense of its own identity. I therefore establish the ground for a reconsideration of historical thinking about the Babi movement and the constitutive role of the movement's historical image in the coming of modernity in Iran. In this chapter, too, I set up the dynamics that inform my discussion of postrevolutionary Iranian cinema as a "catharsis par excellence." Although less concerned with cinematic representation than with the problems informing representations of national belonging and difference, I aim to set the foundation for a discussion of postrevolutionary Iranian cinema as the nation's representative artform. In a longer discussion of cinema as the representative of the Islamic Republic in the world, I will argue in the final chapter that cinematic representations of the nation, while rooted in the abject figure of modernity discussed here, attempt to purify themselves from it in order to produce the Islamic Republic's religious and national difference in the world.

Veiled Threat

The famous orientalist Edward Granville Browne's reflections on the clothes he had acquired for his travels from Yazd to Kirman in his travelogue dated

1887–88 may illuminate the stereotypical link between a piece of cloth and a threat. The following anecdote relates a scene in which an abridged memory connected to the Babis is recalled, shedding light on the present moment of Browne's vogue:

> I had arrayed myself in a new suit of clothes made by a Yezdi tailor, of white shawl-stuff, on the pattern of an English suit. These were cool, comfortable, and neat; and though they would probably have been regarded as somewhat eccentric in England, I reflected that no one at Yezd or Kirmán would doubt that they were the ordinary summer attire of an English gentleman. Haji Safar [Browne's young Persian assistant], indeed, laughingly remarked that people would say I had turned Bábí (I suppose because early Bábís were wont to wear white raiment), but otherwise expressed the fullest approval. (Browne 1926, 452)

The term "Babi" in this anecdote designates not only the general eccentricity of the foreign other, but the wearing of an extraordinary configuration of clothing, the color of which may connote an act of dissent. The anecdote represents not only what Browne as a British orientalist associates with his suit, but fortuitously reveals an assumption about the Yazdi and Kirmani mind. Although Browne was extremely interested in and driven to understand the Persians and moreover the Babis, he failed to grasp the historical connection (made by his travel companion) between what he was wearing and the perceived role of the Babi in innovating fashions in Iranian culture.

In Browne's recollection, it is the native informant who is cast as the one who resorts to stereotypes (and it is this conundrum in colonial relations that, according to Frantz Fanon, is important in understanding the colonial psyche). The native informant, Haji Safar, identifies the "foreign" or threatening element. The mob associates this element with "the Babi" in Browne's clothing. "The Babi," as the scapegoat for the ills of Iranian society, is here recognized by the white color of the foreign scholar's suit. So, while Browne may have been correct in assuming that no one in Yazd or Kirman would assume the suit to be any different from an English gentleman's suit, what he could not predict was the extent to which the suit's color would recall "the internal foreigner." In effect the color of Browne's suit neither represented him as a proper gentleman, nor an eccentric one, but as "the Babi"—the nation's self as other.

The unveiled Qajar princess Taj al Saltanih's memoirs (1884–1914) also situate the stereotypical link between a veil and a threat through the connotative values of the term "Babi." The stereotypic image "Babi" is used in this anecdote to convey the negative vicissitudes of modern education, naturalism, and irreligion, all terms associated with the "Babi" unveiling. Speaking of the effects of her education on the development of her mature identity she writes:

> Right up to my eighteenth year, I had held beliefs taught to me by my nanny that the heavens were pulled by a chain in an angel's hand, or that when God's wrath was incurred, the sound of thunder came. . . . As I progressed in my studies day by day, my irreligiosity grew until I was a complete naturalist myself. Since these ideas were new to me, I was eager to impart them to my mother, my relatives, and my children. As I would begin to talk, however, my mother would curse at me, "You have turned Babi!" My relatives would invoke God's forgiveness and keep their distance, refusing to listen. (Amanat 1993, 309)

Taj's memoir as a whole constructs clear connections between her modern education, her unveiling, women's liberation, and her desire and respect for European ideals as encountered by her in various French literatures and philosophies. Yet in this brief anecdote set in the chamber of familiarity, the image "Babi," and not *farangi* (European, stranger) arises to effect the connection between her modern subjectivities and her alleged naturalism and irreligion. It would be relevant to recall an observation made by Kristeva, that abjection is characterized in some sense by a failure to recognize kinship—the kinship between selfhood and otherness, in this case (1982, 5).

Another literary reference to the derogatory term "Babi" is found in a short story by Rasul Parvizi that humorously relates the effects of the panoptic enforcement of modern clothing policies under the Reza Shah (1925–41) in the young man's hometown of Shiraz. As is well known, Reza

Shah's dynastic legacy in Iranian history falls within the realm of modernization as evidenced in his enforcement of European clothing on men, and the forced injunction to unveil Iranian women in the late 1930s and early 1940s. Houchang Chehabi sketches this "progressive move" from the institution of the Pahlavi hat (similar to the French *kepi*) as the official hat for all Iranian men in 1927 to the decree in 1935 that established the chapeau in an effort to construe an Iranian Westernization (1993, 212–15). While becoming a nation meant insisting on Iran's uniqueness, a nation "distinct from all others," implicit in the project, as Charles Kurzman has also emphasized, was the "global multiplication of nationalisms: each nation is unique, just like all others" (2005, 137). Chehabi notes the violent reproach by the general populace toward the new policies enforced by Reza Shah on a nation that reluctantly transformed from a complex diversity of cultural practices in clothing to the mobilization of a national front through the forced uniformity of dress. This done, the institution of new policies in the 1930s, and especially the injunction to unveil, introduced "the people" into a foreign system of clothing and etiquette that would distinguish Iran from its bordering countries on the basis, oddly enough, "of a cross-national similarity" (Kurzman 2005, 156).

The panoptic enforcement of the rules of clothing through the active engagement of the police force, the school system, the traffic comptrollers, and even undercover agents in bathhouses to monitor compliance, especially with respect to the rule to appear unveiled in public places, seems almost surreal. The general reaction toward this totalized foreign mimicry enforced by the disciplinary institutions resonates in the young Shirazi's chant, in Rasoul Parvizi's story, as he walks around town knocking off people's Pahlavi hats and ripping them to pieces:

> We don't want a blue hanky,
> We don't want a Babi guv'nor,
> We don't want a foreign hat. (Chehabi 1993, 230)

The survival of the stereotype "Babi" in this piece of prose, three-quarters of a century after the virtual collapse of the nineteenth-century Babi movement, is remarkably linked not only to the enforced introduction of foreign values and internationalism, but also to a variety of associations with a change of clothing. Abjection as linked to the figure of "the Babi" signals here what Kristeva would call "a kind of *narcissistic crisis*"—a narcissism associated with an emerging desire for a defined nation—and more to the heart of the matter: a clear definition of the nation's uniqueness (1982, 14). For it should not go without notice, as Afsaneh Najmabadi points out, that "[t]he modern Iranian man's effort to look like a European man from the start made him look like the *amrad*," the cultural equivalent of the paradisical young beardless man or *ghilman*, and the very signifier of homosexual desire. Although this identity was acceptable for young men who could be objects of inspiration and desire for their older counterparts, such appearance in and practice between older men was considered quite dishonorable. For some conservatives, the Europeanization of Iranian modernity could be received not only "as effeminizing but," as Najmabadi emphasizes, "perhaps more threateningly as amradizing" (2005, 303n. 6). Representative of the foreigner within, the modern subject as an effeminate and Europeanized male was inscribed alongside the unveiled and Europeanized woman as a polluting force that was ushered in by the shocks of modernity (303n. 6). For Iranian women to appear unveiled in the public sphere and for Iranian men, young and old, to circulate in Western-style clothing, cast the darkest shadow of taboo over Iranian men's sexual practices and their sense of honor, elevating the compulsion for a heteronormalization of desire in late Qajar Iran (150–51). Of the many notable cultural achievements of Iranian modernity and women's bodily presence in the public sphere, then, was the necessary erasure of the effeminate European-looking man, of male-male gazing, and of homosexual practices (2005, 150–51).

History's Fetish

The stereotypical image "Babi," as a memory in miniature in the anecdotes discussed above, ambivalently joins the two poles of outside appearance and personal identity—the traditional realms of the *zaher* and the *baten* in Persian. Remarkably, it conflicts with the official attempts to dissociate the two realms during the reign of Reza Shah, whose counterimposition of the veil on prostitutes was meant to prevent "the association of unveiling with unwholesome mores" (Chehabi 1993, 219).[5]

The contradiction associated with the use of veiling—that is, the contradiction residing in the fact that the veil at once hides "the perverse" as it preserves the modesty of the Muslim believer in modernity, speaks to the verdant space created for the ambivalence of the fetish in the national context. This ambivalence, which I will elaborate on momentarily, is that spatial relation that connects the fetish at once to the desirable but scrambled[6] female body in the act of protecting the fetishist and to an object that is both in the perceptual sphere of and beyond the control of the fetishist.

Historically organized around the problems of spatiality and visuality invested in the constitution of gender relations, the concepts of external appearance and personal identity have a fundamental relation to Persian models of subject formation.[7] By embracing a fluctuating negative stereotype such as "the Babi" in the act of formulating a modern national identity, these relations of externality, comparable to traditional models of identity formation, play themselves out on the uncanny scene of fetishism. As such they are caught in the problematics of an abject and "scrambled" identity, associated with the pleasure and horror to which the fetishized image of "the Babi" gives rise. I use the term fetishism (or the stereotype as fetish) here to discuss the subject's desire for a pure origin that is threatened by a realization of an impossible difference. This understanding of fetishism is informed by the work of the postcolonial theorist Homi K. Bhabha, who in rereading the work of Edward Said on "orientalism"

5. Chehabi remarks that despite the efforts to elucidate the intentions of the policy, "traditional Iranians saw it as an attempt to turn a virtue into a vice" (1993, 219).

6. The term "scrambled" refers to the way in which the body is perpetually reconfigured by the dynamics of fetishism, according to Freudian psychoanalysis.

7. For further elaboration on this notion (i.e., the dynamics of *zaher* and *baten*), see Beeman (1986), especially chapter 4, "The Marking of Parameters." Roxanne Varzi's thoughtful ethnography of post-revolution youth culture in Iran in *Warring Souls* (2006) probes the dynamics of this play between individual reality and appearance in the construction of national identity on the societal and individual level. Her discussions of identity in the introductory chapter, of city life in chapter 4, and of the collapse of Islamic identity in the post-Khatami era in chapter 8 pay specific attention to this problematic in contemporary Iran.

and Frantz Fanon on the problematics of representation in the colonial context redefines the stereotype or fetish. Bhabha defines the fetish as a concept that gives "access to an 'identity', which is predicated as much on mastery and pleasure as it is on anxiety and defense." The fetish or stereotype, in Bhabha's reading, is a form of "multiple and contradictory beliefs in its recognition of difference and its disavowal of it" (1994, 75). This rereading of fetishism by Bhabha and its role in the subject's reckoning with difference is imbricated in the Foucauldian apparatus of knowledge and power.[8] Drawing on that discussion, I argue below that the fetishized image of "the Babi," attached as it is to the perception of Qurrat al-'Ayn Tahirih's unmentionable unveiling and to aspects of Iranian modernity, complicates the modern subject's relation to him/herself and to the constitution of the modern nation as pure, homogenous, and whole.

It is clear from the historical records of the Babis, reproduced in both Shi'ite polemics and in court chronicles, that the fetishized image does not simply refer to the gesture of unveiling, but that it carves out an ambivalent relation between different spaces that then define each other through the ambivalence of the fetishized image of "the Babi."[9] The ambivalence of the fetish, as John Mowitt points out, is "the spacing that complicates the fetish by connecting it simultaneously to a desirable body (a body scrambled in the act of protective self-representation) and to an object which is both in the possession and beyond the control of the fetishist" (Mowitt 1992a, 173). The discussion of some historical accounts of the Babi movement will elaborate and delineate the ambivalence of the fetish further while illustrating its spatial proximity to and remove from the poet's unpresentable unveiled presence. But, as the issue of fetishism bears on the problematics of sexuality and spatiality, let me pause to reflect on the ways in which sexuality and territoriality conflate in Islamic discourse.

We have come to learn that sexuality, in the context of Islam, is territorial (Mernissi 1975, 81). Sexuality is mapped, as it were, unto the specific

8. For a review of the latter's position see Foucault's chapter on "Panopticism" in *Discipline and Punish* (1979) and on "The Confession of the Flesh" in *Power/Knowledge* (1980).

9. Bhabha's "Signs Taken For Wonders" and "Of Mimicry and Man" in *The Location of Culture* (1994) bear out well this claim on the ambivalence and the spatial status of the fetish.

topology of the public and the private. The female is "it," Shahla Haeri remarks, "the embodiment of sex itself" (1989, 222). From this perspective, the veiling of women is a way to ensure the purity of the public sphere, generally a sphere designated as male. Veiling thus functions as a shield within public space, a gesture of dissimulation that also produces the female space beneath the veil as a private space: "So long as women use the 'prophylactic' veil, both sexes are presumably protected, the dangerous gender is isolated beneath her veil, and the endangered species is safe and saved, at least momentarily! But once the wall of the veil is removed, men have no choice but to gravitate to these bundles of sexuality" (Haeri 1989, 222).

Configured in this way, sexuality in Muslim discourse permits a definition of female identity as an identity split. On the one hand, in the context of the perception of her natural constitution, the female is seen as a distraction that interrupts or otherwise complicates the male's formulation of his identity as pious or divine. Her presence as a sexual being in the public sphere, in other words, interferes with the Muslim man's relation to Allah. On the other hand, in the context of her cultural status and as the embodiment of the community's identity, the female is seen as in need of protection. The veil thus covers over her constitutional split, creating a unified or whole subject that is both dangerous by nature and incapable of defending herself or the community's identity within the public domain. Without the veil this dual and dangerous quality is thought to come to the fore, unveiling a "scrambled" identity, dangerous and mutilated.

The unveiled woman in the Muslim public realm is perceived as naked.[10] Her unveiling, especially in the Irano-Islamic context, is a sure sign of her sexual promiscuity, her unleashed sexuality and transgression.[11] In seeing this naked body, men participate in the transgression. Such is the force of female sexuality, at least in modern Muslim rhetoric on which the heteronormalization of desire has cast a defining light. Its purchase in the nineteenth-century culture is also evident, especially in the

10. For an excellent discussion of these issues, consult Fatima Mernissi's discussion of unveiling in *Beyond the Veil* (1975, 85).

11. Farzaneh Milani (1992, 7–9) discusses the perception of recent unveilings by female poets in these terms.

public claims made against the Babis during the Zanjan upheavals in the late 1840s and early 1850s in which the *ulama* and government officials claimed that the Babis fought for the love of "a regiment of Babi virgins."

John Walbridge's history of the Babi uprising in Zanjan, an account derived largely from *Tarikh-i Vaqayi-i Zanjan* and written by Mirza Husayn Zanjani (1880) illustrates my point by linking the stereotypical image of "the Babi" with the excesses of love. In one of the chronicle's passages we come across a rendition of the activity of the women during a Babi siege against the government in Zanjan. Zanjani reports what follows: "The government officials and the ulama together wrote to the Shah in this wise [giving a list of excuses for their failure to defeat the Babis]:'Fourth, there is a regiment of Babi virgin girls. The Babis fight for love of them.' They wrote a great deal in this vein and sent it to the king" (Walbridge 1996, 355).

Although this letter claims that the Babis fought because of their infatuation with the Babi maidens, Zanjani argues that the truth of the matter is essentially different. He portrays the Babi women as strong and active participants of (not distractions to) the Babi defense. Zanjani's narrative goes on to describe the activities of one such woman within the Babi faction.[12] Yet in the official letter to the shah, the mere presence of the Babi women is seen as generating desire for their unveiled bodies. These bodies are represented in the official report as the object-cause of male transgression against the nation from within its very borders. The sight of the presumably unveiled, active bodies of the Babi women is articulated as the cause of the uprising against the government. Their abject presence in the public domain, caught in the participating look of Babi men, poses a threat to the body of the nation itself.

It is on the basis of such perceptions that I would propose a conjunction between the moment of Qurrat al-'Ayn Tahirih's unveiling in a garden in Badasht, systematically, and however erroneously, signaled as the first act of public unveiling in Iranian history, and the psychoanalytic account of fetishism. For the sake of clarity, let me restage the scene of fetishism before making the historical connection.

12. See also Walbridge (1998).

Freud's fable describes the scene of fetishism in very specific terms (Freud 1971b). It is set on the stage of maternal undressing where the boy discovers the absence of the penis. Recognizing the threat of castration (his own) in the form of the castrated mother, he creates a substitute. The terrifying sight of the castrated maternal figure forces the child to disavow what he has seen by masking it. In the act of disavowal, the boy transfers the importance of the penis onto another object—the substitute object or fetish. This conflict between the "weight of the perception" and the force of the "counter-wish" situates in the substitute-object the former pleasure in the penis as well as the horror of castration. Affective value is thus transferred onto the fetish. The mixture of horror and pleasure in the fetish renders it therefore ambivalent. Produced on the basis of recognition and disavowal, the object retains within itself the affective pleasure of continued belief (that the mother actually has one), the unshakable horror of recognition (that she doesn't), and the anxiety of castration (that the father did it and may strike again!). The ambivalent fetish object serves to maintain the male child's sense of wholeness (Freud 1971d, 154). Bhabha's rereading of Freud's account, which I use here, draws out the ambivalence of the fetish as a spatial relation. It suggests that the contradictory affects, which the perception of difference (or otherness) situates in the fetish, configure the limits of the viewer's own identity in relation to the fetish.[13]

Unveiling the Threat

A glance at the various historical accounts of Qurrat al-'Ayn Tahirih's unveiling presents us with a dynamic of historiographic recognition and disavowal similar to the processes of fetishization. The historian Abbas Amanat's disparate discussions of various historiographic and autobiographical sources betrays an uncanny ambivalence in the affirmation of Qurrat al-'Ayn Tahirih's unveiling—so much so that an "act of nudity"

13. Joan Copjec's discussion of Clérambault in chapter 4 of *Read My Desire* (1995) supplies a sustained reading of some of the issues that I raise here with respect to the fetishism of the veil.

becomes concomitant with an absolute and unremitting disavowal. According to Amanat's assertions, many sources claim that Qurrat al-'Ayn Tahirih did indeed unveil in public at some point. Most say, however, that she only did so in the gathering of "believers" (i.e., other Babis). And though most sources agree that she never unveiled publicly before the Badasht Conference in 1848, others even doubt that she did so on that occasion (Amanat 1989, 295–316). A double disavowal takes place in the reconfiguration of these various narratives, wherein, first, none but the "believers" are incriminated by this public violation and second, no one is at all. It seems, then, that while Qurrat al-'Ayn Tahirih was seen unveiled in the chronicle of history, no one is willing to admit to having seen her that way.

The ambivalence of affirmation and disavowal that gives shape to the myth of Qurrat al-'Ayn Tahirih's unveiling in history constitutes a popularized stereotype-fetish representing Babi acts of deviance. For as Rene Girard (1986) remarks on the historical image of the scapegoat, there is a real subject behind the threat.

The Bab's teachings, as championed by Qurrat al-'Ayn, called for the abrogation of national and religious laws: in his innovative writings, the Bab declared the confidentiality of mercantile correspondence inviolate. He called the specification of coinage necessary and argued the need for a stable monetary system. He made the discharge of debts obligatory, the organization of the postal service and communication in the West commendable and asserted the need for both to be organized in Iran. A new calendar was introduced, replacing the Islamic lunar calendar with the solar year of nineteen months of nineteen days. The year began not on the Islamic month of Muharram, but on the pre-Islamic Iranian New Year. In addition to the reinvention of time, the Bab substituted the old Islamo-Arabic understanding of space with a new Persianness. The old centers of pilgrimage in the Arab world were replaced by new ones in Iran (Bayat 1982, 108). The Bab's residence became the *qibla* (the direction faced for prayer) toward which his followers turned in prayer at all times. This spiritual and territorial substitution reoriented the pious body and situated it within new geographic boundaries.

It is clear from even a rudimentary overview of the Bab's innovations that "the Babis," in the figure of the unveiled poet, represented a messianic movement firmly rooted in the nation, but without the former national belonging. The Babis claimed a new Iran as their home and embraced as their most holy book a book written, not in Arabic, but in the Persian language, the *Persian Bayan*. Rather than countenance the loss of the nation, the Iranian Shi'ites produced "the Babi" as a fetish. As such, the fetish represents the unpresentable surrogate for the absent nation: as both a fierce threat to the identity of the national subject and as a pleasurable assurance of the subject's continued wholeness. "The Babi" thus emerged as the fetish, representing otherness—a term, as we have seen, that could cover any gesture of deviance associated with the forceful coming of modernity. Qurrat al-'Ayn Tahirih's reputed unveiling came to stand as the abject sign, an image of this modernity.

Historiography remains suspect, however, and any search for the true origin of the narratives around Tahirih's innovations is doomed to failure. For although Qurrat al-'Ayn Tahirih, as a renowned niece of a Qajar cleric, was watched and condemned, the terms of the witnessing and of the historiographic depiction of her conflict and contradict one another. That is perhaps why Friedrich Nietzsche, in his critical discussions of the historiographic project, pointed out that "a monkey stands at the entrance" (Nietzsche 1974, 49). But in the wildly hallucinatory account of the "moonfaced" Qurrat al-'Ayn in the work of the Qajar court chronicler Sipihr (known as "The Tongue of the Kingdom"), we can only imagine the extent to which her acts entered into popular imagination as moments of primal fantasy. From this chronicler's shamelessly sensual account of Qurrat al-'Ayn, we can perhaps gather up the traces of her gestures (whether rhetorical or physical), which activated the processes of recognition and disavowal in the minds of those who believed her to be the reincarnation of Fatimih, the Muslim Prophet's daughter—"a representation which guaranteed her sanctitude by lineage, marriage and motherly love."[14] Traces such as the ones we will find in the court chronicler's account cast a revealing light on the abject figure that "the Babi" represents

14. In Islamic history, Fatimih is known as the daughter of the Prophet Muhammad, the wife of Ali and, perhaps most important for Shi'ite Islam, as the mother of Imam Hasan and Imam Husayn.

in historiography. For two parts of that essential distance necessary for the subject's protection against the "cataclysmic power" of the abject body, Kristeva reminds us, have to do with the body's status as the archaic figure of the mother and the general taboo against incest as the substructure of social life itself (1982, 77).

Sipihr, the Qajar court chronicler, mustering the full force of his sobriety, reports that Qurrat al-'Ayn not only believed in the unveiling of women but endorsed the marriage of one wife to nine husbands. For her public addresses, he says:

> She would decorate her assembly room like a bridal chamber and her body like a peacock of Paradise. Then she summoned the followers of the Bab and appeared unveiled in front of them. First she ascended a throne and like a pious preacher reminded them of Heaven and Hell and quoted amply from the Qur'an and the Traditions. She would tell them: "Whoever touches me, the intensity of Hell's fire would not affect him." The audience would then rise and come to her throne and kiss those lips of hers which put to shame the ruby of Ramman, and rub their faces against her breasts, which chagrined the pomegranates of the garden. (Amanat 1989, 321; Sipihr 1353 A.H. [1958], 3:220)

The dynamics of pleasure, fear, recognition, and disavowal in the juxtaposition between this scene of fantasy, probably derived from the renowned conference at Badasht, and the scene of utter horror described in the eyewitness records of that same conference in *Nabil's Narrative* (when, at the sight of Tahirih's unveiling, an Isfahani zealot is said to have cut his own throat in an act of self- mutilation)[15] is an uncanny reactivation of the

15. For further reference see Amanat's discussion of the Badasht conference in *Resurrection and Renewal* (1989, 325–26). We will, in chapter 4, learn more about the scene of horror recollected with unambiguous clarity by *Nabil*'s informant, Shaykh Abu Turab. But the shocks of the scene reverberate in this passage recorded in *Nabil's Narrative:* "After the historic gathering of Badasht, a number of those who attended were so amazed at the fearlessness and outspoken language of that heroine, that they felt it their duty to acquaint the Báb with the character of her startling and unprecedented behaviour. They strove to tarnish the purity of her name. To their accusations the Báb replied: 'What am I to say regarding her

moment of terrifying recognition and phantasmagoric substitution in the psychoanalytic scene of fetishism.

The conjunction between the act of unveiling and the psychoanalytic scene of fetishism gains more clarity as we go on to observe the ways in which the precursors and the consequences of this event are constituted in a variety of historiographic texts. What seems to drive this fundamental conjunction, moreover, is the way in which the dynamics of public law inform the economy of recognition and rejection of the subject's private relationship to the Nation-Thing.

According to Slavoj Zizek, the bond linking members of a community implies a relationship with "the Thing," which in his terms can be defined as enjoyment incarnated or, in Jacques Lacan's terms, the "objet a"—the object-cause of desire. This relationship, Zizek explains, is structured by means of fantasies, and it is this relationship that is at stake when we say that the other is a "menace to our way of life." National identification, according to Zizek, is "by definition sustained by a relationship toward the Nation qua Thing" (1993, 210). The Nation-Thing is structured by a series of contradictory properties that the other cannot grasp by virtue of its only being accessible to us. But if one asks any given person what that Thing is to which they claim a belonging, the answer that one receives is an elusive entity that represents "our way of life"—indeed a way of life, which upon further investigation only leads to a notion of belief embedded in that person's belief in the communal credence to "the Thing" (202). In this regard, the historical terms that depict "the Babi" as "a menace to our way of life" and that represent Qurrat al-'Ayn Tahirih's chamber of enjoyment in Sipihr are very illustrative.

The scene of Qurrat al-'Ayn's unveiling is preceded in this chronicler's measured beat by a register of land exchange, and by the rise and fall of leaders in public life. For, as Walter Benjamin notes in his review of Nikolai Leskov in the 1936 essay known as "The Storyteller," the chronicler,

whom the Tongue of Power and Glory has named Tahirih [the Pure One]?' These words proved sufficient to silence those who had endeavoured to undermine her position. From that time onwards she was designated by the believers as Tahirih" (Zarandi 1996, 83).

unconcerned with "an accurate concatenation of definite events," shows in his work the manner in which these events are "embedded in the great inscrutable course of the world" (2002, 153). In that year, Sipihr notes, regional land was exchanged between two princes. A man of state traveled to Baghdad to sign a treaty with the three leaders of Rome, Russia, and England regarding the boundaries of states. "Mirza Jafar Khan, Persia's envoy left from Tabriz," Sipihr remarks, "and his trip to Baghdad took four years." It is in the midst of these records that Qurrat al-'Ayn's hair, her polyandry, and her unveiling are considered, immediately followed by the vivid description of her chamber of indulgence. Death inevitably follows the episode, "as the Reaper does in the processions that pass around the cathedral clock at noon" (Benjamin 2002, 152). For, although it is not the place of the chronicler to say, in her disregard for father and husband, she brought death to her household, indeed to one of the great Shi'ite scholars of Iran, her uncle Mulla Muhammad Taqi.

Even the chronicler who, in Benjamin's interpretation, has from the very start "lifted the burden of demonstrable explanation from [his] own shoulders," presents "the Babi" as an encroachment upon the fantasy of the nation (Benjamin 2002, 152–53). Regions are conquered by the daring and able princes. National boundaries are agreed upon in Baghdad. The scene of Qurrat al-'Ayn's unveiling follows with death at its heel. It is as if the nation is being devoured by the excesses of the Qurrat al-'Ayn's pleasure chamber. Yet it is impossible to pin down what this encroachment is to be about. Is the Babi too beautiful to be learned? Too intelligent to fall in the trap of the Bab? Is it that the Babi is a foreigner to the nation? Is it that she is immoral? Irreligious? Antitheocratic?

The early chronicles and memoirs withhold their explanations. But in the attachment of the image of "the Babi" to various local subjectivities as the educated princess or the modernizing governor, in popular discourse it would seem to appear that "the Babi" is in fact associated with a singularly national subject. The historical anecdotes that introduce this chapter clearly point up the fact that "the Babi" is indistinguishable from the modern subject in that he or she is precisely that which simultaneously constitutes the nation, and which, because of his or her curious activities, threatens the nation's dissolution. Regardless of its close association with the nation per se, "the Babi" as fetish is recovered over the course of the decades as a threat, both to the very constitution of the Iranian nation and to its subjects as well.

According to Zizek, what we impute to the nation's other is an excessive enjoyment: he or she is thought to steal our enjoyment and have access to a secret store of perverse enjoyment of its own. As a constitutive element of the psyche in psychoanalysis, this thief is also known as the superego. The superego in Freud's theoretical construction is that entity and mechanism by which the law is enforced upon the id. Hence, the superego, that which makes the law an object of respect for us, is always in violation of it. The superego hoards and takes enjoyment away from the id in the name of the law. And yet, as it continues the enforcement of the law, it gains in its own enjoyment. As Zizek notes, "The superego is, so to speak, the agency of the law exempted from its authority: it does itself what it prohibits us from doing . . . the more we follow the superego's order and renounce enjoyment, the more guilty we feel, for the more we obey the superego, the greater is the enjoyment accumulated in it and, thus, the greater the pressure it exerts on us" (1991, 160).

The chronicler, Sipihr, speaking on behalf of the court, which prohibits the association of its subjects with the Babi, takes pleasure in an exaggerated description of the poet's unveiling before the audience of men. Indeed she unveils in his statement to become the object-cause of national desire, a desire that then is prohibited and condemned by the force of the law in such a way that the national subject is hailed to destroy it. We will see soon that the-other-as-the-law, which gains in its enjoyment by the pressure it exerts on the subject, must necessarily be also associated, in popular imagination, with "the Babi." This is because of the movement's own dramatic association with the early figures of Shi'ite Islam, who are said to be resurrected in the present in the figures of the Babi heroes and heroines. As such, the Babi movement fixes the present as the Day of Judgment, a day on which every subject is to be called before the Divine Law. But for the purposes of the immediate argument, the historical records of the communal efforts in the destruction of the Bab's followers will be sufficient to address the horror and enjoyment that produced "the Babi" as the abject body and the fetishized image against which and through which the modern nation identified itself.

The Failed Fetish: The Babi Massacres, 1848–1852

Historical sources agree that the Badasht Conference took place in 1848, the summer of one of the main Babi uprisings in Iran. By 1852 the Babi claim that a communal effort toward the reform of the nation was no longer imminent, but rather long overdue, became too much to take for the majority of Iranians. The Babi statement of the urgency of the present was articulated with the apocalyptic proclamation that the coming of the Bab represented Judgment Day. As a result of theocratic disagreements on this and other accounts, a number of violent confrontations between the Babis, the Shaykhis, and the orthodox Shi'ites combined with episodes of stupefying and humiliating public torture. Together they drove many Babis to their wits' end. The French agent Joseph Phillip Ferrier records the butchery of the Babis in Mazandaran (Momen 1981, 95). The Russian minister Dologorukov relates an episode in which he witnessed executioners dragging still-writhing bodies of strangled Babis through the streets outside Tehran (101). Mirza Mahmud, the British agent, reports on the display of the heads of slain Babis in Nayriz. With drums beating, the soldiers suspended the heads of the Babis on the Isfahan gate (110). By the end of 1848, "the Babi" emerged as the name of Iran's modern and feared scapegoat.

Qurrat al-'Ayn Tahirih's uncle, one of the leading Shi'ite scholars in the town of Qazvin, is said to have been humiliated by the rumors of his niece's alleged immoralities—and her public unveiling may have been one of these (Amanat 1989, 322) These whispered defamations, thought to bring ill repute to his house, added to his pronounced hatred for the Babis, thus aggravating the situation between the Babis and the Shi'ite Muslims all the more. One morning, while praying at his mosque, it is claimed, the well-known religious leader was murdered by a Babi sympathizer (Amanat 1989, 322). The most notable Babis of Qazvin, all suspected accomplices, were rounded up, charged with the murder of the Mulla Muhammad Taqi, and summarily executed. Typical of later anti-Babi killings, the Qazvin executions were carried out by a mob. Most sources claim that they were incited by religious leaders who both promised rewards in the hereafter and encouraged the tortures as gestures in active defense of Shi'ite Islam (Amanat 1989, 324).

An undeniably potent space was set up in the leaders' religious rhetoric that calls up a conjunction between, if not a complete superimposition of, the scene of absolute terror and the phantasmic space of the hereafter. The fear of humiliation (castration, if you will) was virtually displaced in the activation of a scene of bliss and pleasure—the scene of paradise—and transferred into the active Shi'ite "body." The site/sight of the mutilated Babi was disavowed and simultaneously retained through the appropriation of this discursive and palimpsestic space by the popular imaginary, giving way to a fetishistic scene of fantasy and of the Qur'anic paradise such as the one figured in the court chronicler's narrative.

After these horrifying public executions, Qurrat al-'Ayn Tahirih was also accused of co-conspiracy in her uncle's assassination and was put under house arrest until after the suppression of the above-mentioned uprisings. Various recollections assert that she was then sent to Tehran, where she was brought to the court of Nasir al-Din Shah Qajar. Upon inspecting her the monarch reportedly exclaimed, "I like her looks: leave her, and let her be" (Browne 1891, 313). One can only wonder what the shah saw and heard, for he is said to have asked her for her hand should she stop expounding her beliefs. Her reply was a somewhat poetic but nonetheless defiant "No!":

> Kingdom, wealth and power to thee
> Beggary, exile and loss for me
> If the former be good, it's thine
> If the latter is hard, it's mine. (quoted in Milani 1992, 88)

One will search in vain for a record of this transaction in the court chronicler's recollections, "whose ears," according to Browne, "must hear what is pleasant rather than true and whose actions must be not only justified but extolled as models of wisdom and virtue" (1891, 187).

It was perhaps four years later, in August 1852 according to most documents, that an idea was hatched by a Babi, Shaykh Ali Mirza, known as Azim, to murder the young dynast, Nasir al-Din Shah. The monarch was only wounded by the birdshot, but this act set the scene for massive arrests and a general massacre of all Babis.[16] The "Babi threat" reached

16. For foreign accounts of this massacre, see Momen (1981, 128–46).

its full force. "The Qajar officials, alarmed by the potential threat of the 'nihilists' and 'anarchists' devised 'Machiavellian means' for their extermination" (Browne 1891, 328). Convinced of the existence of widespread disaffection toward his four-year reign, the shah agreed to instigate a widespread plan for the extermination of the Babis. Browne describes the plan in these words:

> It was suggested that if the responsibility for the doom of the captives rested solely on the Shah, the Prime Minister, or the ordinary administrators of the law, these would become thereafter targets for the vengeance of the Babis. If, on the other hand, a partition of the prisoners were made amongst the different classes; if a representative body of each of these classes were made responsible for the execution of one or more Babis; and if it were further signified to the persons thus forced to act the part of executioners, that the Shah would be able to estimate their loyalty to himself by the manner in which they disposed of their victims, then all classes, being equally exposed to the retaliation of the survivors, from whom they would therefore be effectually and permanently alienated, while at the same time the Shah himself would avoid incurring the odium of the massacre. (Browne 1891, 328)

Many Babis were killed during this massacre, including Qurrat al-'Ayn Tahirih herself. But in the involvement of representatives of every class in the massacre, the shah managed to transfer his actual "fear of castration" (decapitation, in another register) onto his subjects.[17] Masked in a rhetoric of nihilism and anarchism, this threat of ultimate mutilation was thus perpetuated by the agitation of representatives of every class throughout the national body, allowing for numerous permutations. The most important of these was the accusation of "Babi" difference.

17. As Judith Butler points out in an extended discussion of the historical relevance of the psychoanalytic fable of fetishism in *Bodies That Matter:* "The failure to submit to castration appears capable of producing only its opposite, the spectral figure of the castrator Holophernes's head in hand." (1993, 102). For further elaboration on the thematics of "the threat," see Butler's chapter "Phantasmatic Identification and the Assumption of Sex." See also Hélene Cixous (1981).

Western accounts of the Nayriz upheaval in the summer of 1850 supply us with perhaps the first of such accusations grounded in the "difference" of "the Babi." As Peter Smith suggests, the Bab's opponents had asserted early on that the Bab possessed a miraculous potion by which he could cause people to convert to the new religion. Regarding Nayriz, Mirza Mahmud, the British agent in Shiraz, reported that only one quarter *(mahallih)* was plundered and destroyed by the upheavals and that the government soldiers *(sirbaz)* had procured a good quantity of stolen property from their interactions with the Babis: "Syed Yahyah is reported to have had four or five vessels of Pomegranate Syrup, a single drop of which was sufficient to make a man become Babi and join him. One bottle was drunk by four Sirbaz, who instantly turned Babees, and fought against their own Commanders. They say this Syrup has been brought to the Prince" (quoted in Momen 1981, 111). Ferrier, a French soldier who had been brought to Persia to train Muhammad Shah's army, reported to the French Foreign ministry that a dish containing a curious confiture was found at Nayriz "and considered by the Babis as being a miraculous substance which it was not possible to taste even the smallest amount without becoming Babi" (quoted in Momen 1981, 112). Writing from Tehran, Ferrier goes on to say that the shah is now "awaiting this mysterious sherbet impatiently, with the intention of testing its properties on several state prisoners who are at this moment detained in Tihran" (quoted in Momen 1981, 112).

That the "miraculous substance" associated with the figure of "the Babi" is also the essence of the pomegranate should not go unnoticed. In ancient Persian traditions, the pomegranate symbolizes invincibility in battle. But as we have heard in the court chronicler's graphic description of the paradisiacal scene associated with Tahirh's "chamber of pleasure," the pomegranate is also that paradisiacal fruit that appears most often in nineteenth-century texts and in Qajar paintings to represent fecundity, sexuality, and desire. The pomegranate is almost exclusively coupled with the delights of maidens and with the pleasures of a woman's breast in these accounts of earthly life. Thus the pleasures embodied in this fruit are rooted firmly in the affects and in the delights of comely maidens in paradise, yet they also blossom in the exuberance of the much feared and desiring bodies of earthly women. Capable of "bleeding" the pomegranate embodies, in ancient mythologies, the force of life and death itself, and therefore appears often as a symbol of the mother's menstruating and fertile body. These associations clearly underwrite the rumors reproduced in official communiqués. The syrup that can beguile an army so to embrace the cause of the Bab stands for an ecstasy that can be imbibed from a fruit grown primarily on Iranian soil, a fruit that in the pleasures of tasting "even the smallest amount" leads to an immediate discharge of the self. For as Kristeva remarks on that otherness within the self, "The eroticization of abjection, and perhaps any abjection to the extent that it is already eroticized, is an attempt at stopping the hemorrhage: a threshold before death, a halt or a respite" (1982, 55). "The Babi essence" as an affective substance both desirable and disruptive in distilled syrup-form, is awaited with palpable anticipation by the court. Palpable anticipation—yes, for its continued circulation represents, the expulsion of the self, the ursurpation of power; actually, death itself.

In *The Scapegoat,* Girard claims that such stereotypes of accusation were made against the Jews and other scapegoats during the plague in Europe as well. One persecutor, Guillarme de Machaut, accuses the Jews of poisoning rivers and thus causing the plague. "The persecutors," writes Girard, "imagined such venomous concentrations of poison that even very small quantities would suffice to annihilate entire populations. Henceforth the clearly lightweight quality of magic as a cause is weighed down by materiality and therefore scientific logic. Chemistry takes over from purely demonic influence" (1986, 16).

Alchemy is precisely the accusations leveled at "the Babi" scapegoat. For if violence was the only charge against the Babis, then it would be obvious that the mobs were implicated in it. The accusation of lustful magic and of poisoning lay the responsibility for the destruction of peace in Iran, on a people "whose activities," to quote Girard, "have not been really proven criminal" (1986, 16). Thanks to the pomegranate syrup, "it is possible to be persuaded that a small group, or even a single individual, can harm the whole society without being discovered" (16). Hence "the Babi," associated with the fruit that embodies the pleasures and powers of seductive female desire, of a body unveiled, could be identified as that element that, unbeknownst to the populace, was tearing the whole fabric of society apart. "The Babi"'s powers lay dormant in the syrup of the fruit that was sown on national soil—a fruit whose paradisiacal pleasures would ultimately reveal the horror of a subject deprived of a self. No! More crucially, deprived of a nation. For "filth," as Kristeva argues, "is not a quality in itself, but it applies only to what relates to a boundary and, more particularly, represents the object jettisoned out of that boundary, its other side, a margin" (1982, 69). At risk in asserting the dangerous otherness of "the Babi," it would seem, is the ground on which the nation could delimit its frontiers and claim a uniqueness and purity in the process of nationalization. "The Babi" stood in essence for an abject being, "a pharmakos" who, "having been ejected," like Oedipus, allows the emerging nation to be freed from all defilement and emulation—a nation unique onto itself with clearly demarcated borders and boundaries within a greater world (Kristeva 1982, 84). As Kristeva brilliantly qualifies, "prohibition and ideal are joined in a single character in order to signify that the speaking being has no space of his own but stands on a fragile threshold as if stranded on account of an impossible demarcation" (Kristeva 1982, 83–84).

Careful attention to the anecdotal examples that enumerate the way in which the term "Babi" was used to connect various instances of innovation and modernization in the modern period in Iran will serve to remind us that the stereotypical image does not merely refer to the absent "originary" act of sartorial innovation. Its point of reference is not, to quote psychological discourse, "the source memory." In its various permutations the image of "the Babi" carries within it traces of desire and pleasure as well as fear and anxiety—the affects associated with the "Babi threat." I have argued that "the Babi" carries these traces because of its entanglement in the dynamics of fetishism.[18]

18. We should be reminded here that Freud links the fetish to objects of clothing, which come to stand in for the absent penis (1971d, 153). The boy in Freud's analysis does not merely replace the absent maternal penis with a new one. In some cases, Freud maintains, "the replacement of the object by a fetish is determined by a symbolic connection of thought." (155) What resides in the fetish nonetheless are the affects of fear and pleasure that situate the encounter with the maternal body.

Freud remarks that the fetish object is instituted at the moment of traumatic amnesia, the fixing of perception at the moment of shock (1971d, 155). This shock, in historical terms, occurs at the moment when perception stops in reaction to the threat of the subject's own endangerment in the apprehension of profound pleasure. In terms of the historical materials gathered here, this endangerment is the threat of decapitation that is transferred to the masses from the endangered body of the shah and the *ulama.* It occurs through the activation of the subject's own threatened identity in the accusations of nihilism and anarchism, both terms associated with the "Babi threat." The subject, in turn, is encouraged to mutilate the Babis on behalf of the shah/*ulama* and in doing so, be given the promise of his or her own preservation in the rhetoric of a deferred but imaginable paradisiacal hereafter.

Neurologists argue that three things can occur to memories at moments of psychological stress or moments of fear, horror, or endangerment: (1) the memory of the moment is repressed and lost; (2) it is repressed and retrieved in parts; (3) it is recovered with errors in the memory trace. Memories can also be implanted, constructed on site or in retrospect. From within the dynamics of Freud's account of fetishism, I have argued that at the sight/site of the mutilated body of a Babi, a memory in miniature is created in defense against the claims of the external reality (the threat of the father/shah/mulla). This substitute image, whether "implanted" or constructed, is grasped by the subject as the relation that mutually defines the two spaces of externality—the mutilated and the sovereign body of the nation. As a fetishized image, "the Babi" is used as a means to ensure the subject's continued wholeness.

This image of "the Babi" is then reactivated at other times and places when the threat of the subject's disintegration occurs: in the introduction of foreign values and ideas, in the threat of change and innovation, and in the loss of a secure identity in the absence of religion's stabilizing reassurance. Thus the "novel" statements of the unveiled princess Taj al-Saltanih, as evidence of a scrambled body, pose a threat to her immediate family and relatives. Their reaction is to recall the fetishized image of "the Babi" and invoke "God's forgiveness," securing thereby the preservation and wholeness of their own identity. Freud's references to this process, in his discussions of belatedness or Nachträglichkeit in hysteria, are best summarized by John Forrester as a "transferential function, whereby the past dissolves in the present, so that the future becomes (once again) an open question" (Forrester 1990, 206). Past traumas thus "operate in a deferred fashion as though they were fresh experiences; but they do so unconsciously" (Freud 1962, 167n). What is activated in this process is an image ("picture"), which is grasped at a distance, not only as a fresh event, but as a new trauma (Freud 1971c, 109).

This image of "the Babi" is thus fetishized as "the relation" that makes different spaces and times "interactively and precariously define one another" (Mowitt 1992a, 175). The bliss of paradise, the evil of nihilism, and the parade of naturalism erupt at the site/sight of the sybaritic carnival that is "the Babi." This memory, therefore is not only an ambivalent and charged image, it is also multiple and layered—a palimpsest. Its various spaces cancel out time and inform one another through their superimposition. Any act of innovation or foreignness, thus, instinctively recalls a history of unveiling, of perceived promiscuity, of heresy, and of mass slaughter in a massive abridgment.

Any representation of Qurrat al-'Ayn Tahirih's reputed unveiling can be said to be an instance of affectivity in Iranian modern history, which in light of its unpresentable nature in the context of historiography is doomed to repression.[19] Its recollection in the work of the court chronicler (as a moment that characterized all her behavior), and the historical statements of Shaykh Abu Turab reproduced in *Nabil's Narrative,* must be said to give the retrieval a shock. Freud argues, in his classic discussion of the movement of unconscious material to the conscious, that this shock is necessary, in that the relocation of repressed material from the unconscious to the conscious can only occur through the operation of the negative particle "no."[20] What is retrieved from the repressed unconscious is therefore brought to consciousness in the negative.

19. In his discussion of the "uncanny," Freud notes that the prefix "un-" must be considered "the token of repression" (1971e, 245).

20. For reference, see Freud's 1925 paper on "Negation" (1971a).

This repressed history, crystallized into an image, "flashes up," in Walter Benjamin's words, "at an instant when it can be recognized" (2003a) but in guises other than itself: in the foreign English gentleman's clothing, in the curious confiture that is retrieved during battle, in the love of European literature, or in the general injunction to wear a chapeau.[21] Browne's white suit retroactively defines the "originary" sartorial gesture by signaling the innovation as a change from veil to white clothing while the fetishized notion of a heresy simultaneously defines the very constitution of Browne's "foreign" gesture.

The recovered fetishized image, as an abridgment of history, introduces a conjunction between at least two different spaces and times each defining the other with uncanny reverberations, making the familiar unfamiliar and the unfamiliar the very structure of familiarity. An instance such as this is perhaps best summed up in Sadeq Hedayat's haunting mirroring "that Khomeini," the prototype of modern Shi'ite Islam and Iranian politics, "was more than a little a Babi in his rhetoric and his slogans" (Fischer and Abedi 1990, 245). It is this dialectical image of "the Babi," which simultaneously represents Iran's modernity and its internal otherness, that haunts the Islamic Republic's efforts to represent the nation in terms of a manufactured and synthetic purity—a manufactured purity especially in the cinema, which has remained the Islamic Republic's main representative in the world. But this aspect of the nation's historical will to purity and its relation to cinematic representation under the rule of the Islamic government is part of a discussion that will have to wait until the final chapter.

21. For further elaboration of "history as image," refer to Walter Benjamin (2003a).

2

Scheduled for Judgment Day

> The messianic world is the world of universal and integral actuality. Only in the messianic realm does a universal history exist. Not as written history, but as festively enacted history.
>
> —Walter Benjamin, "Paralipomena to 'On the Concept of History'"

Comte de Gobineau was in the prime of his youth when he moved to Paris in 1835 and still only thirty-four when, after a brief collaboration with Alexis de Tocqueville on the historical study of moral attitudes in 1848, he published in 1850 what is today recognized as one of the founding texts of racism, *Essays on the Inequality of the Human Race.* Gobineau's biographer, Michael Biddiss, in an introduction to Gobineau's political writings, remarks somewhat apologetically that there were extenuating circumstances for his entry into racist discourse: "In 1835 he went to Paris to seek his fortune and, after clerical work with a gas company and in the postal service became a journalist and entered fully into the social life of the legitimist salons. His experience of Parisian society convinced him that France, having rejected the Bourbons, was gripped by a profound mediocrity embodied in the growth of bourgeois power and the rise of revolutionary ideas of liberalism, democracy and socialism" (Biddiss 1970b, 16). This experience of the Parisian society, Biddiss claims, initiated Gobineau's search for the origins of the contemporary state of French degeneracy. He found at its root what became his crowning theory of the inequality of the races:

> Recognizing that both strong and weak races exist, I preferred to examine the former, to analyse their qualities and especially to follow them back to their origin. By this method I convinced myself at last that everything

> great, noble and fruitful in the works of man on this earth, in science, art and civilization, derives from a single starting point, is the development of a single germ and the result of a single thought; it belongs to one family alone, the different branches of which have reigned in all civilized countries of the universe. (Gobineau 1970, 42)

The image that captures for Gobineau what he soon "will not have around" anymore, that reflection of a decrepit Paris that had rejected the only family capable of raising France to its past grandeur, introduces the opening paragraph of his final chapter of the *Essays*. Here Gobineau portrays the vanishing image of world history as an intricate tableau:

> Human history is like an immense tapestry. The earth is the frame over which it is stretched. The successive centuries are the tireless weavers. As soon as they are born they immediately seize the shuttle and operate it on the frame, working at it until they die. The broad fabric thus goes on growing beneath their busy fingers. The two most inferior varieties of the human species, the black and yellow races, are crude foundation, the cotton and wool, which the secondary families of the white race make supple by adding their silk; while the Aryan group, circling its finer threads through the noble generations, designs on its surface a dazzling masterpiece of arabesque silver and gold. (Gobineau 1970, 163)

Gobineau thus presents an image of the purity of the races, which he sees as swiftly vanishing in his time. He saw the intermixture of cultures as the cause of the extinction of the human race. His concern was not, however, with the extinction alone. He writes at the very end of his *Essays:* "What is truly sad is not death itself but the certainty of meeting it as degraded beings" (Gobineau 1970, 176). He had in mind, as Biddiss reports, "the degradation of a humanity levelled into mediocrity by blood-mixture" (1970b, 32). He saw in this vanishing image, the superiority of the Aryan blood, "which alone supports the edifice of our society," a blood that in Gobineau's time was "already diluted so many times, . . . moves closer each day towards total absorption" (Gobineau 1970, 172). Based upon these predicaments, he predicts that the intermixture of bloods "will lead eventually to mediocrity in all fields: mediocrity of physical strength, mediocrity of beauty, mediocrity of intellectual capacities—we could almost say, to nothingness. Everyone will share this sad heritage in equal measure" (173).

When the later two volumes of Gobineau's *Essays* were published, Gobineau had already left for Tehran on diplomatic duties. This was his first visit outside Europe (of which he had only seen Germany, France, and Switzerland). Gobineau took the post of chargé d'affaires to Persia from October 15, 1856, to January 20, 1858. And in August 1861 he returned to take the position of French minister to Persia, a post he kept until October 1864.

Gobineau's *Les Religions et les Philosophies dans l'Asie Centrale,* published in 1865, graphically captures the processes of decay and innovation at work in modern Iran. Once again, this new world opened to him allowed him the opportunity to understand the process of degeneracy consuming his Europe. The process of degeneracy in Asia helped him understand a continent that was, in his view, well on its way to disintegration, indeed on the verge of democracy. It was, however, Wagner's Bayreuth Circle that, after the death of the author and of the composer, would be "responsible for Germanizing Gobineau's ideology and for converting its pessimistic acceptance of inexorable ethnic degeneration into a messianic creed of racial redemption" (Biddiss 1977, 117).

For Gobineau, whose search for a singular origin of any idea and morality would be the preoccupation of a lifetime, Persia was a place of true illumination. "Everything that we think and all the manners of which we think have their origin in Asia" (Gobineau 1900, 1). And for Gobineau, Iran represented all of Asia (Amanat 1989, 433). The reasons for Gobineau's belief were, certainly, grounded in a philological understanding of culture at the time and emerged out of a general acceptance that the root of all that was good in Europe was inherited from the Aryan races.[1] In the words of

1. Biddiss writes in *The Age of the Masses:* "Like most who wrote earlier in the century about 'Aryan' dignity, Gobineau gave some particular weight to linguistic evidence. Just when many philologists were, however, recanting previous expressions of simple equation between language and race, Aryan or otherwise, Darwinism came into vogue. Racists then tended to rearrange their priorities of evidence. By adopting and developing for their own

an American medical doctor working in Iran and one of Gobineau's fellow commentators on life under Qajar rule: "[Persia] is especially interesting to us as a place from which the white race sprang. Its name is known in the Persian language as Iran, pronounced E-ron, which is from Arya, hence the Aryan races" (Wishard 1908, 10).

Waiting close to the optician's shop for his eyeglasses, Maxime du Camp was inspired to write a book about his own Paris in 1862. Like his contemporary, Gobineau, his inspiration for this historical text arrived as an image and as a reflection of his own sadness over old age. "The slight deterioration of his eyesight which had been demonstrated on his visit to the optician *reminded him of the law of the inevitable infirmity of all human things.*" Du Camp, like Gobineau, recognized the ancestry of Paris in the dust of the dead Orient: "It suddenly occurred to the man who had travelled widely in the Orient, who was acquainted with the deserts whose sand is the dust of the dead, that this city, too, whose bustle was all around him, would have to die some day. . . . In a flash of inspiration, of the kind that occasionally brings one an extraordinary subject, he resolved to write the kind of book about Paris that the historians of antiquity failed to write about their cities" (Benjamin 1983, 86). Gobineau, like Du Camp, hurriedly portrayed in his book on Central Asia what would seem to be fleeting into oblivion. On the one hand, it seemed, his desire to depict life in Persia was a desire to capture the origin of the Aryan race and thus the antiquity of France. On the other hand, Iran was a country whose contemporary signs of degeneracy were reflected in his experiences of modern Paris. "There is no doubt," writes J. M. Hone, that Gobineau, "loved Persia and the Persians; he could excuse all their faults in the most charming and witty manner; and yet this people, as he well knew, was no longer Iranian or Aryan, but a hotch-potch of all the races" (1914, 29).

A man whose notoriety rested on the pillars of three volumes outlining the theory of the inequality of races, perhaps inexplicably turned to affirm—between the covers of *Les Religions et les Philosophies dans l' Asie*

---

purposes such phrases as 'struggle for existence' they could emerge with an aura no less scientific" (1977, 115).

Centrale—the force of the new religious movement, Babism, and the dramatic innovations of the Persian passion play (the *ta'ziyeh*). He was to be the first to record these dual forces as foundations for what would constitute Iran's modern identity. He positioned both developments within the discourses of modernism and democratization, trends that he witnessed and rejected with the force of his convictions on human inequality in France. He saw in these vivacious dynamics of renewal a germination of life that already signaled the death of world civilization. As Biddiss observes, Gobineau saw in the life of these populist movements a parallel destiny for Europe under the influence of socialism (1970a, 186–87):

> The Cause of the Bab is on the road to great achievements. We have now shown how there has taken place a religious movement which absorbs the deepest attention of Central Asia, that is to say, of Persia, several regions of India and a section of Asiatic Turkey; a religious movement, therefore, truly remarkable and worthy of being studied. Through it, we witness events, manifestations, catastrophes such that one could only imagine possible in remote ages when the great religions were born. I even confess that if I were to see appear in Europe a religion like unto Babism, with advantages such as Babism possesses, with complete faith, an undaunted enthusiasm, tried courage and proven devotion, winning the respect of the indifferent, frightening its adversaries and, moreover, a tireless proselytism constantly gaining adherents in every social class,—if I were to see such a phenomenon in Europe, I would not hesitate to predict that, within a given time, power and sovereignty would of necessity belong to a group so richly endowed. (Gobineau 1900, 328)

The Babi movement constituted a revolutionary movement for social change. This kind of revolutionary fervor signaled the degeneration of the planet for Gobineau: "Whence asked Gobineau, do our modern revolutions proceed? . . . From the adulteration of German blood; the adulteration of Iranian blood in ancient Persia had like effects. Whither do they lead? Today, to the complete destruction of humanity, since in the German was contained the last reserve of Aryan power and energy. 'The earth falls asunder being old'" (Hone 1914, 38).

Gobineau thus heard in the modernity of Central Asia the death knell of the planet. The corruption of the institutions, concern solely with material well-being, the processes of urbanization and its associated vices, social movements and ethnic disorders, Gobineau witnessed in Persia a land on the verge of breakdown: "This whole country [Persia] is full of the idea of God. Decrepitude, old age, extreme corruption, in short, death is present everywhere in institutions, customs and characters; but this constant absorbing preoccupation with what is holy singularly ennobles all this ruin" (Gobineau 1933, 88).

Gobineau had addressed his dialectical vision of the germination of life with the seed of death more explicitly in his *Essays,* weaving his melancholic and desperate vision of a degenerated Paris into the warp and woof of world history: "we are forced to affirm that every assemblage of men, however ingenious the network of social relations that protects it, acquires on the very day of its birth, hidden among the elements of its life, the seed of an inevitable death" (Gobineau 1970, 43).

Comte de Gobineau's *Les Religions et les Philosophies dans l' Asie Centrale* can be divided roughly into two parts. The first part of *Religions* captures a vivid and complex description of religious life in modern Iran and posits the rise of Babism in the context of Sufi Shi'ism. This primary section of the text, Gobineau's dramatic description of the life and death of the Bab that was influenced largely by Sipihr's chronicle of Qajar history, eventually caught the imagination of a multitude of poets and playwrights in France and elsewhere (Momen 1981, 18; Amanat 1989, 433). The second part of *Religions* comprises an enchanting description of the *ta'ziyeh,* the Persian passion play. Gobineau's detailed descriptions of the drama suggest that he witnessed it. He is said to have considered it equal in rank to the Greek drama. "Latin, English, French and German drama is, [Gobineau] says, in comparison a mere pasttime [*sic*] or amusement, more or less intellectual and elegant" (Arnold 1871, 673).

Gobineau, disillusioned with the Europeans, constantly complained to his friends and associates in letters written during his service abroad about the tepid reception given to the ideas he put forward in the *Essays* on race. In contrast, when *Les Religions et les Philosophies dans l' Asie Centrale* was first published in 1865, it won great acclaim and became so popular that a second edition was called for in less than a year. A third edition came out in 1900. It inspired numerous reviews and references from important figures of nineteenth-century Europe, among them Ernst Renan (Momen 1981, 22), and Matthew Arnold and historians such as E. G. Browne (1924, 153; 1926, 329) and A. L. M. Nicholas (Momen 1981, 26). Yet a hundred years later, his biographer contends that this book was the most "erratic" piece of scholarly work produced by Gobineau's pen (Biddiss 1970a, 182).

Matthew Arnold, in a 1871 lecture delivered at the Birmingham and Midland Institute based on Gobineau's now infamous book, casts a glance at the first part of the book on the Babis and adds an interesting comment, no doubt owing to the enthusiasm around Gobineau's addition of the novel word "Babi" to nineteenth-century European vocabulary: "most people in England have at least heard the name" (Arnold 1871, 669). He then goes on to enumerate, albeit briefly, some minor details about the movement's founding and principal figures. Matthew Arnold finally focuses on Gobineau's lengthy descriptions of the *ta'ziyeh*, the Persian passion play.

Resting on the dual forces that drive Gobineau's reflections on Iranian modernity, I set out in this chapter to describe the *ta'ziyeh*, its prologues, and the Karbala eulogies attached to it. The *ta'ziyeh*'s plots and participants, as well as its temporal and spatial tropes, will be discussed. In the course of this discussion of the *ta'ziyeh*, I intend to lay out a framework for the study of nineteenth-century Iranian historiography and to show the continuing importance of the reenactment of antiquity in and through these performances in grafting the limits of a modern national identity in Iran. I will insist on the mediating function of the *ta'ziyeh* form and its tropes as these emerge in forms that animate and shape the representation of modern Iranian identity and its history in late-nineteenth- and early-twentieth-century Persian historiography. In the following two chapters I will suggest the ways in which *ta'ziyeh* deictic tropes and *ta'ziyeh* narratives give shape to early Babi historiography, strengthening Babi revolutionary claims regarding the Babi present as the Day of Judgment. My discussion in chapter 5 of director Ali Hatami's cinematic representation of modern national history in *Delshodegan* will reflect on the ways in which the *ta'ziyeh*'s spatial and temporal tropes are engaged as a strategy of resistance to Hollywood's homogenization of culture and the standardization of cinematic technique by the cinema of the postrevolutionary period. The move to analyze the articulation of national identity in Iran's contemporary representative media will not only reiterate Gobineau's insight into the importance of the *ta'ziyeh* tradition to the constitution of Iranian modern identity but will also show the ways in which the utilization of the drama's narratives and tropes in Babi historiography come to articulate Babism's role in the production of Iranian modernity and its function as the unpresentable kernel of Iranian identity and difference in the globe.

What Is *Ta'ziyeh?*

The annual *ta'ziyeh* performance cycle commemorates the slaughter of the family of the Prophet Muhammad in Karbala. An indigenous Persian performance tradition, the *ta'ziyeh* draws on the "central narrative of Shi'ite Islam, the story of Karbala which is remembered and reenacted every year in the month of Muharram" (Afary and Anderson 2005, 40). "The slaughter at Karbala came to be considered by [Shi'ites] as the ultimate sacrifice, the pinnacle of human suffering. The month of Muharram became the month of mourning, when [Shi'ites] all over the world commemorate [Husayn's] sacrifice in stationary and ambulatory rituals of unequaled intensity. It was from these ritual observances that *ta'ziyeh,* which literally means 'to mourn' or 'to console,' arose as a dramatic form" (Chelkowski 2005, 16). Although the reenactment of the Karbala tragedy as a theatrical artform can be traced back to the sixteenth century, when Shi'ism was officially recognized as a state religion in Iran, the *ta'ziyeh* itself was born as a result of "the stationary and ambulatory aspects of the ritual merged in the mid-18th century, . . . a distinct type of music drama" (Chelkowski 2005, 16). It only became popular as a performance tradition in the nineteenth century. But the extent to which this tradition represented Islam's antiquity with any degree of accuracy, as we shall see, depended largely on that history's urgent relevance to nation's modern constitution.

Ta'ziyeh or *shabih* is traditionally known in Iran as the historical drama and passion play that recounts the life of the family of the Prophet Muhammad. Referred to in the Shi'ite tradition, as the "Fourteen Pure Souls" or "Fourteen Infallibles" the figures who appear in the Shi'ite drama include Muhammad himself, the Twelve Imams starting with Imam Ali, and Muhammad's daughter, the mother of Imams Hasan and Husayn, known as Fatimih. In the *ta'ziyeh,* the Fourteen Infallibles come alive on stage and take part in the dramatic enactment of Islam's antiquity—a resurrection in time, historically scheduled for Judgment Day.

The *ta'ziyeh* drama, enacted during the month of Muharram, which is the first month of the Muslim year and the Shi'ite month of mourning, revolves around the tragic death of the Third Imam, Imam Husayn, who to this day claims a significant position in Iranian history, religious interpretation, culture, and political outlook. The drama is enacted in recollection of the days in which Imam Husayn, his meager army, and members of his family were slaughtered on the plains of Karbala by the claimants to the Prophet's successorship and the military army of Yazid.

> [T]he ta'ziyeh performance, which is similar to Christian passion plays and was influenced by them ... is a theatrical representation of the Karbala events. Ta'ziyeh is one of the oldest forms of theatre in the region, and ordinary citizens eagerly anticipate the annual performances. This highly melodramatic performance, which is a fusion of ... [street processions and the recital of Karbala eulogies or *rauzeh-khani*] with European theatrical ... [performances] is staged by local groups throughout the country before large audiences. The performances single out the suffering of [Husayn's] entourage, especially that of the women and the children, on Ashura day. The narrator and the actors describe in great detail the thirst of the besieged community in the heat of the desert of Karbala and the deviousness of Yazid, who chose Friday at noon, the time of Muslim communal prayer, to slaughter his rivals. The audience weeps bitterly during the last scenes of the play and is reminded of the treachery and guilt of the Kufa community, which did not side with its savior [Husayn], thereby allowing the tyrant Yazid to commit his dastardly deed. (Afary and Anderson 2005, 44)

Muharram is a month of recollection. It is the month in which the pious Shi'ite remembers these stirring moments in Islam's antiquity, knitting together fragments of broken time. For theater, as Peter Brook remarks, "must always be a religious action and its action is very clear: it is that by which fragments are made whole" (1979, 50–51). *Ta'ziyeh* is a sacred theater and, like all ancient performance traditions, it relies on its audience to know the story and grasp its references and gestures as shorthand for much larger happenings.

In 1979, Brook describes his encounter with *ta'ziyeh* performances in a remote Iranian village as "the strongest things" he has seen in theater: "A group of four hundred villagers, the entire population of the place, sitting under a tree and passing from roars of laughter to outright sobbing—although they all knew perfectly well the end of the story—as they saw [Husayn] in danger of being killed and then fooling his enemies, and then being martyred. And when he was martyred, the theatre became a truth—there was no difference between past and present. An event that was told as remembered happening in history 1,300 years ago, actually became a reality in that moment" (1979, 51–52).

John G. Wishard, who opened the first American clinic in Tehran, wrote in 1908 about the rituals of the month of mourning and the *rauzeh-khani.*[2] During the month of Muharram, he says, "little black flags over many doorways serve as an invitation to the passerby that daily readings a sort of cottage prayer-meeting is being held for the public. At these meetings, the priest reads from the Koran [Qur'an], recites poems touching upon the life and character of their martyrs and follows these with an exhortation that generally meets with a response on the part of the audience, of tears and amens" (1908, 156). These "prayer" meetings or gatherings for the purpose of reading Karbala eulogies, called *rauzeh-khani,* are said to be one of the roots of the modern *ta'ziyeh.* The *rauzeh-khani*s are among the first popular cultural spaces in which Shi'ites recalled

2. *Rauzeh-khani*s are gatherings where eulogies on the tragedies of Karbala are recited in detail. These are ritual sermons that are inspired by Husayn Va'ez Kashefi's 1502 text *Rawzat al-shohada (The Garden of Martyrs),* a text that remains "one of the most often quoted sources in later narratives and histories retelling the story of the battle and its aftermath." (See Aghaie 2005a, 6). Other similar forms of ritual mourning such as *dastih-i azadari* (ritual funeral processions) and *sofrih hazrat-i abbas* (ritual gatherings to fulfill a vow) convene throughout the year. See also Thaiss (1972).

the sect's fundamental difference and independent character within the greater religion of Islam. This memory is preserved in the stories of the Karbala tragedy.

Although the break between the Sunni and Shi'ite sects occurred some thirty years earlier, the tragedy at Karbala represents the moment in which this schism within Islam is effectively justified and in which it takes root in Shi'ite discourse, national ideology and popular cultural practice (Momen 1985, 33). The *ta'ziyeh* spectacle recollects this momentous break and helps the Persians "to preserve their hatred and resentment against the Sunnis" (Tancoigne 1820, 197). In slight contrast to J. M. Tancoigne's assessment and, as always, acutely mindful of the descent of passions, Gobineau suggests, that the appeal of the Karbala tragedy, as enacted in the *ta'ziyeh,* arises from a feeling of patriotism. Persians, he claims, find similarities in their own experiences with Husayn (understood as a compound religious, political, and military figure) vis-à-vis the Arabs who surround them. "[Husayn] is not only the son of Ali, he is the husband of a princess of the blood of the Persian kings; he, his father Ali, the whole body of the Imams taken together represent the nation, represent Persia, indeed, ill treated, despoiled, stripped of its inhabitants, by Arabians. The right which is insulted and violated in [Husayn] is identified with the right of Persia" (Gobineau, quoted in Arnold 1871, 683).

The Karbala tragedy recollected in the month of Muharram encapsulates the fundamental differences inherent within the Shi'ite and Sunni sects of Islam in the late Qajar period. This difference came to animate the populist nationalist struggles in the years immediately following. Thus *ta'ziyeh,* seen through Gobineau's eyes, must be recognized as a space in which a phantasmatic national identity is forged. The annual commemorative events surrounding the *ta'ziyeh* not only offered a spiritual renewal for the Twelver Shi'ites but situated the cultural difference of the Qajar Persians vis-à-vis their neighbors. The performances themselves stamped Persian national identity with the mark of difference. This difference could be formulated as an identity associated with the meek but no less victorious Imam, who loved the Persians. This close association between the nation and the Third Imam validated an identity that could be neither robbed nor destroyed by the machinations of the nation's Sunni others.

The historical roots of this identity are evident in the traditions of the first Shi'ite imam, Imam Ali.

Shi'ite tradition claims that Imam Ali, who was the Prophet's son-in-law and cousin, was appointed by the Prophet Muhammad as his legitimate inheritor of power and spiritual successor. At the Prophet's death, historians claim, Imam Ali was passed over and the Caliph Abu-Bakr, the chief lieutenant of the Prophet in the government, was recognized as his successor. This left Imam Ali with only spiritual and religious power. After the Caliph Abu-Bakr's death and the death and murder of his two successors, Imam Ali finally and legitimately took the caliphate. However, to the dismay of Shi'ites, he was assassinated within a short period of time. The Twelver Shi'ites recognize only Imam Ali and his sons Imam Husayn and Imam Hasan as the legal successors to the Prophet Muhammad and reject the first caliphs as usurpers. The year 661 marks the official break between the Sunnis and the Shi'ites.

In 680, historians of Islam note, the two sons of the deceased Imam Ali resided in Medina close to their grandfather's grave. In the Euphratian city of Kufa, where their father, Imam Ali, had moved his headquarters after the Battle of the Camel in 656, a change of power was taking place once again.[3] The people of Kufa, who claimed to be unhappy with this change, sent for Imam Husayn (Imam Ali's second son) to support them in overthrowing the Caliph Yazid and his Syrian troops. If he could with their help defeat Caliph Yazid, they claimed, Imam Husayn could take on his legitimate role as caliph in Kufa.

The tragedy of Karbala takes place on the plains where Imam Husayn, having gathered his possessions and family and on his way to claim his rightful place in history, is killed. On the second day of the month of Muharram, having reached the plains, about thirty miles from his destination, it becomes clear that his communication with the inhabitants of Kufa has been intercepted and that his band is surrounded by

3. The revolt referred to as the Battle of the Camel was an uprising led by Muhammad's favorite wife, 'Aisha, and the daughter of the Caliph Abu Bakr against the rule of Ali. For a thorough historical rendition of 'Aisha's role in the early days of Islam and her future legacies, see Spellberg (1994). Fatima Mernissi also discusses the Battle of the Camel and suggests that the Muslim title given to it obscures 'Aisha's leadership in this uprising (1987, 5–7).

the enemy's, Caliph Yazid's, troops. They are cut off from Kufa and from accessing water. Hostilities ensue on the tenth of Muharram. This is the day Shi'ites call the Ashura. Refusing to acknowledge Caliph Yazid as a just and rightful ruler, Imam Husayn is killed in battle, and his head is delivered to the governor of Kufa. Unwilling to submit to the rule of the caliph, the family of the Prophet is brutally murdered on the battlefield. The survivors are taken, along with the women and children, as prisoners in chains to the Caliph Yazid in Damascus.

The *ta'ziyeh* spectacles performed by men and young children throughout the month of Muharram in middle to late Qajar Iran recollect and reenact these moments of brutality in graphic terms. Commemorating each day the heart-wrenching details of those bygone days of Muharram, the performances conjure the irrational fact that despite the defeat of the Third Imam and the brutal massacre of his family, he is remembered for his undaunted integrity despite impossible odds. *Ta'ziyeh* performances climax on the tenth day of Muharram, the Ashura. On this day the drama of Imam Husayn's slaughter is reenacted by the *ta'ziyeh* troupes. Mourning Imam Husayn's death on the day of Ashura is recognized as an advantage for the believer who begs for the intercession of the meek Imam on his or her behalf.

> The word ta'ziyeh literally means expressions of sympathy, mourning and consolation. As a dramatic form it has its origins in the Muharram processions commemorating [Husayn's] martyrdom and throughout its evolution the representation of the siege and carnage at Karbala has remained its centerpoint. Ta'ziyeh has never lost its religious implications. Because early Shi'ites view [Husayn's] death as a sacred redemptive act, the performance of the Muharram ceremonies was believed to be an aid to salvation; later they also believed that participation, both by actors and spectators, in the ta'ziyeh dramas would gain them [Husayn's] intercession on the day of the Last Judgement. (Chelkowski 1979, 2)

After the Ashura, writes Wishard, "the play takes on a lighter character and drifts into comedy" (1908, 157).

On the tenth of Muharram every year, the city awakes to commotion in the street. It is a public holiday, and the processions commemorating the massacres in Karbala start early. Wishard, whose general sympathy for Persia and all things Persian are evident throughout his recollections, shows restraint and a will to confine his participation in Persian cultural life on the anniversary of the day of Imam Husayn's martyrdom:

> The morning is given up to great processions moving through the streets, composed of men and boys dressed in white, carrying swords, with which they inflict deep gashes into their shaven heads. Others, with bare chests, strike themselves with pieces of chain or with their hands, calling in unison the names of the martyrs. Other bands made up of boys and some men are content to carry banners and cry the names of [Husayn] and [Hasan]. As a rule, Europeans find it pleasanter and safer to remain indoors on the day of this religious celebration. (1908, 158)

The Muharram procession of 1820 is described in a document by a French officer on official duty in Tehran, J. M. Tancoigne. He recognizes the street procession as the ritualized funeral procession that it customarily represented in early Qajar culture:

> Naked and bleeding men marched behind. . . . They were followed by a long train of camels mounted by men dressed in black, as were female mourners, and an infinity of persons of that sort, who threw ashes and chopped straw on their heads in token of mourning. A more pompous and imposeing [*sic*] spectacle suddenly came to variegate these hideous scenes. There appeared two great mosques of gilt wood, carried by more than three hundred men: both were inlaid with mirrors, and surmounted with little minarets: children placed in galleries sang hymns, the soft harmony of which agreeably recompensed the spectator for the frightful shouting they had heard just before. (1820, 196–201)

Modern dramatic forms of the *ta'ziyeh* are said to have emerged out of an amalgamation of these ceremonies associated with the mourning processions for Imam Husayn, as well as the *rauzeh-khani*s that were held in individual homes and in public mosques. By the middle of the nineteenth century the Shi'ites gathered for these ritual plays in the houses of the rich or in *takiyeh*s, which according to Gobineau in 1865, could be found in each neighborhood (1900, 339–41).[4] Private residences were opened to the public during the month of mourning as a way for the affluent to offer public and religious service (Chelkowski 1979, 4). Johan ter Haar notes that *ta'ziyeh* dramas were performed in over two hundred locations, each accommodating between three to four hundred spectators in Tehran (1993, 165). They were staged so that city dwellers could relive, recollect, and identify with the events of Karbala on the first ten days of the Muslim year. Each day a different *ta'ziyeh* was performed, culminating in the reenactment of the tragedy of Imam Husayn's murder on the anniversary of his slaughter. In the years of Gobineau's residence in Tehran, the *ta'ziyeh* performance was accompanied by a fictive procession to the court of Yazid in Damascus close behind the decapitated head of Imam Husayn mounted on a pole in effigy.[5]

The *ta'ziyeh* spectacles as culminations of the street processions were first staged at street intersections and squares but were later moved into courtyards of caravan serais, bazaars, and private homes. "An advantage of smaller sites such as a mosque or a private residence was the *houz* [pool] which, customarily a feature of the courtyard, could easily be converted into a stage by covering it with wooden planks" (Peterson 1979, 65). This stage, completely exposed, would be left barren, except for a few symbolic objects significant to the history of the Karbala tragedy: a basin of water representing the Euphrates River, from which Imam Husayn and his companions were cut off by the Caliph's troops (Chelkowski 1988, 16), and a branch of a tree representing a palm grove. The *ta'ziyeh*'s emphasis on stagecraft and place in a permanent theater did not culminate until the last five decades of the Qajar reign, according to ter Haar (1993, 164). And even then, little was done by way of elaborate costumes, stage props, and so forth. In the constitution of dramatic meaning, "the public," Arnold says, "meets the actor halfway" (1871, 676). This statement rings true, too, of the early conditions for the staging of the *ta'ziyeh*. In 1820 Tancoigne noted that only "the last five representations of the Karbala story were

4. A *takiyeh* is a converted private yard or theater with a stage used for the performance of the *ta'ziyeh*.

5. For a literary critique of one of these scenes in contemporaneous Persian writing see Cole (1993a).

performed on a theatre erected opposite the king's kiosk in the Gulestan Palace" (1820, 198). The remainder, we must assume, took place during the processionals themselves.

The *Takiyeh:* Fixing the Place of History

Fath 'Ali Shah (1797–1834), writes Said Amir Arjomand, "gave considerable impetus to the development of the passion plays of the martyrdom of Husayn and the tragedy of Karbala. The *ta'ziyeh* was first performed in the houses of notables as a part of the ceremonies of the month of Muharram alongside long recitations of the afflictions of the house of the Prophet, known as *rawzah khani*" (1984, 240). Under the long reign of Nasir al-Din Shah Qajar, the *ta'ziyeh* became a sovereign art form, however, and it was given a permanent residence and a royal following. Royal encouragement of individual commemorations of Husayn's martyrdom for the purpose of patriotic and religious zeal was already an established custom under the Safavid dynasty (1502–1736), whose reign is associated with the construction of Shi'ite Iran. Under the Safavids the pageantry of the Muharram festival achieved extraordinary forms and these Muharram celebrations became a unifying force for the country. Despite this earlier introduction of the *ta'ziyeh* to Iranian cultural life, Nasir al-Din Shah Qajar would become the monarch known for his frivolous love of the mourning ritual in the dramatic form of the *ta'ziyeh*.,

The Royal Takiyeh in Tehran was a theater built for the purpose of *ta'ziyeh* performances under the watchful eye and perseverance of Nasir al-Din Shah. This seat of the *ta'ziyeh* in Tehran held several thousand spectators. During the other months of the year, when the *ta'ziyeh* was not usually performed, the Royal Takiyeh was used for the royal menagerie. It became Nasir al-Din Shah's temporary burial ground when he was assassinated on May Day 1896 (Peterson 1979, 70).

It was Nasir al-Din Shah who insisted that this phenomenal brick construction be built in the image of the Royal Albert Hall in London. He visited London for the first time in 1873. Nasir al-Din Shah describes this visit to the Albert Hall in his travel diary as if entering paradise: "Passing through, we came to a place the very picture of paradise. All the corridors, apartments and manufacturies [around the hall] were lighted up in various wonderful manner by jets of gas. The very concert itself was in an exceedingly spacious enclosure with a roof in shape of a dome where seven tiers of seats all occupied by people, all filled with beauteous women magnificently apparelled. . . . Multitudes of gaslights were burning" (Qajar 1874, 165–66). The shah was mesmerized by the dome at Albert Hall and was annoyed shortly after his visit to find out that his staff was unable to create the same spectacular effect at home. It took the intervention of the foreign community to convince him "that the dome he envisioned was physically impossible with the materials available to the Persian builders" (Peterson 1979, 64). Instead, the builders devised an ingenious system by which canvas awnings, representing Imam Husayn's tent in Karbala, would be stretched across wooden arches that were reinforced by iron braces. Every

2. *Every photograph of a* ta'ziyeh *performance staged in this period features these marvelous white awnings suspended over a spectacular crowd. Photograph by Antoin Sevruguin, courtesy of the Freer Gallery of Art and Arthur M. Sackler Gallery Archives, Smithsonian Institution.*

photograph of a *ta'ziyeh* performance staged in this period features these marvelous white awnings suspended over a spectacular crowd.[6]

Under Qajar rule, the theater that dramatizes the antiquity of Islam found a permanent royal home. The Royal Takiyeh opened a space of recollection, redemption, and mourning for the Shi'ite *millat* (people). Yet Gobineau would argue that those who attended the spectacle participated without regard to the divergence of religious opinion (1900, 382). Observing their enthusiasm for the spectacle, Gobineau writes that the Persians recognize in this history of brutality the legitimation of their belief in the rightful claimants of the prophet Muhammad's throne and see their national identity revealed in the *ta'ziyeh.* Indeed, Gobineau's "observation of Iranians' love for their past, as demonstrated by their twin loyalty to Anushiravan and Ali, persuaded this Frenchman . . . to refer to Iran as a 'nation' as early as the 1850s" (Kashani-Sabet 1999, 44). "The Arabians, the Turks, the Afghans—Persia's implacable and hereditary enemies—recognize Yazid as legitimate Caliph; Persia finds therein an excuse for hating them the more and identifies itself with the usurper's victims. It is patriotism therefore, which has taken the form here, of drama to express itself" (Gobineau, quoted in Arnold 1871, 684).

As William Beeman points out, the "Ta'ziyeh performance offers the opportunity for the spectators ritually to renew their commitment to a religious and ideological order of which they are an integral part. This ideological order does not limit itself strictly to religious dimensions but includes a political and nationalistic dimension as well" (1979, 30). The *ta'ziyeh* decidedly gave shape to and was shaped by the rationalities that filtered through various modern Persian institutions. Its dialectical forces animated personal and collective initiatives in different eras in Persian history. Although at times the structural elements of the *ta'ziyeh* were used to reinforce religious distinctions by casting "the good" as the Imam and his family and "the evil" as the Caliph Yazid and his Sunni adherents, at other times the *ta'ziyeh* dramatic format was used to call the people

6. For an impressive collection of photographs of the *ta'ziyeh* in Isfahan, a city known for its superb productions of the *ta'ziyeh,* see Jennifer Scarce's review of the amateur photographer Ernst Hoeltzer's collection (1976).

to revolutionary action and to emphasize the role of the nation as Imam Husayn's representative in the world. Similarly, literatures, travel narratives, and invocations of various kinds, especially those belonging to the Qajar period, demonstrate the marked influence of the *ta'ziyeh* throughout the culture.[7]

Evidence of that influence can be seen in the exchanges between these dramatic representations and the *ta'ziyeh*-style depictions of the Karbala massacres appearing on tile panels in nineteenth-century *takiyeh*s throughout the country. Benjamin writes about this act of quotation in the dramatic sphere as *literarization* (1992, 7). Citing from the work of Bertolt Brecht on epic theater, Benjamin uses the term literarization to refer to the connections made between the epic stage and other institutions for intellectual activity (a gesture not unlike footnoting the play). Among these connections Benjamin mentions those between the media (he suggests books) and the epic stage: "Neher's background projections for such 'turns' are far more like posters than stage decorations. The poster is a constituent element of 'literarized' theatre. 'Literarizing' entails punctuating 'representation' with 'formulation'; gives the theatre the possibility of making contact with other institutions for intellectual activities" (1992, 7).

Using material that is already known to the audience, namely historical material, the epic theater, like the *ta'ziyeh,* instructs the actor to transform it, to give it a new twist.[8] "One must, however, expect the dramatist

7. Several historical texts, among them works published under the titles *Kitab-i-Nuqtatu'l-Kaf* and *The New History of Mirza Ali Muhammad the Bab,* and the narratives of the Babi upheavals in Nayriz by Mulla Muhammad-Shafi, discussed in later chapters, show a strong reliance on the *ta'ziyeh* historical model as a way to validate and justify the messianic and revolutionary acts of their protagonists in relation to what they perceived to be corrupt and oppressive political and religious systems.

8. Andrzej Wirth argues against equivalencies drawn between *ta'ziyeh* and Brechtian epic theater. He writes "The paradox of Ta'ziyeh is that being basically a non-epic and non-dramatic event, it produces an epic demonstrative style of acting" (1979, 38). Although I could agree with this conclusion to a certain extent, I believe that Benjamin's gloss of epic theater, despite its citation of Brecht, diverges from the playwright's own conceptualization of it. In effect, Benjamin functionally transforms it. It is Benjamin's conception of this theater that is of interest for my argument.

to take a certain amount of license in that he will tend to emphasize not the great decisions which lie along the main line of history but the incommensurable and the singular" (Benjamin 1992, 7–8). One of these details, as we shall see, is in the fold of the veil.

Karbala Drag Kings and Queens

According to Janet Afary and Kevin B. Anderson, the story of the martyrdom of Imam Husayn "sounds remarkably familiar" for those who were raised on the story of Jesus' crucifixion:

> If we compare Ta'ziyeh performances with the longest surviving passion play in Europe, the one that has been held in the village of Oberammergau (Bavarian Alps) since 1634, we find numerous similarities. The Oberammergau passion play centers on Jesus and his supporters, while the Ta'ziyeh centers on [Husayn] and his clan. Jesus is betrayed by those who are initially loyal to him, while [Husayn] is betrayed by the once-loyal Kufans. The Christian play is devoted to the "passion" of Jesus, meaning his suffering and gruesome death, just as the Ta'ziyeh is devoted to the tragic suffering and death of [Husayn] and his family. A significant part of both stories deals with the grieving, as well as the courage, of women, whether of Mary who mourns the loss of her son, or [Zaynab] who lives to tell the story of her brother's martyrdom. Both plays include flashbacks to the Old Testament stories, such as the expulsion of Adam and Eve from the Garden of Eden, Abraham's sacrifice of his son, and Moses leading the Hebrews across the Red Sea. (2005, 55)

Recalling a recent newspaper article about a clergyman who was admonished for his lecture on the Oberammergau passion, Arnold writes the following: "We have seen lately in the newspaper, that a clergyman, who in a popular lecture gave an account of the Passion Play at Ammergau, and enlarged on its impressiveness, was admonished by certain remonstrants, who told him it was his business instead of occupying himself with these sensuous shows, to learn to walk by faith, not by sight, and to teach his fellow men—to do the same" (1871, 669).

Indeed this admonition captures the very essence of clerical concerns with the *ta'ziyeh* drama in nineteenth-century Iran. "Mullas and regular ecclesiastical authorities," Arnold writes, "condemned the whole thing." And the reasoning struck a cord with Arnold, who was intrigued by the uproar surrounding the question of visual culture in England around the time of his speech. He observes: "The ta'ziyeh is an innovation which they [the Muslim clergy] disapprove and think dangerous; it is addressed to the eye; it departs from the limits of what is revealed and appointed to be taught as truth and brings novelties and heresies;—for these dramas keep growing under the pressure of the actor's imagination and emotion of the public and receive new developments everyday" (1871, 677). To elaborate on the drama, in this case the drama of the life of the holy family of the Prophet Muhammad, means to add to what has been established as the unalterable truth of history. This history is the holy and sanctified truth that imagination and public emotion pressures, elaborates, and projects into the visual realm. "Tazieh [*ta'ziyeh*] is no longer interested in a precise rendering of the story" (Wirth 1979, 38). It relies on the participant's knowledge of religious history. And whereas historical truth, which in this case is the Qur'an and the hadith,[9] is believed to inspire the inner eye and faith, spectacle only entertains vision. Spectacle thus functions no more in the cause of education than in the aid of historical reflection. So goes the argument.[10]

At high tide of the popularization of the *ta'ziyeh* in Qajar Iran, Shi'ite religious scholars were forced, albeit reluctantly, to deliver a decision on

9. The hadith are a collection of stories by the family and the close associates of the Prophet Muhammad. They describe the events and circumstances surrounding his life. The hadith that have a clear line of trustworthy narrators supply the basis for many Muslim laws and daily rituals.

10. This "erroneous judgment" on the part of the *ta'ziyeh*-loving populace as to where to direct their interest and enthusiasm for the religious figures of Islam is made even more profound when one notes that Persia was the only country in the entire Muslim world to nourish drama before the modern period. Persia, of all the hegemonic Muslim cultures, cultivated a deep attachment to figural representation, evidences of which we see in the prolific production of Persian miniature paintings, sculpture, carpets, and other visual arts (Chelkowski 1979, 4).

the religious drama. The first famous judgment was given by Mirza Abul-Qasem Ibn Hassan Gilani, who died about 1815–16. He was one of the most important religious authorities of the period and well-respected by the shah and his ministers. In answer to the question of whether it is "lawful on the days of Ashura to play the roles of the Imam or the enemies of the Family of the Prophet in order to induce the people to weep?" Mirza Abul-Qasem ibn Hassan Gilani issued the following *fatwa:*

> We say there is no reason to prohibit the representation of the innocent and the pure ones [The Fourteen Infallibles] and the generality of the excellence of weeping, causing weeping, and pretending to weep for the Lord of Martyrs [Imam Husayn] and his followers proves this. . . . Sometimes it is supposed that this dishonors the sanctity of religious leaders, but this supposition is invalid because it is not genuine identification, rather an imitation of form, appearance and dress merely to commemorate their misfortune. . . . Thus we answer . . . there is a time when it is among the greatest of religious works. And this which is merely to please God is a great *jihad.* (quoted in Baktash 1979, 107–8)

As a performance that takes license with historical materials, *ta'ziyeh* is, in the words of one of the leaders of religious thought, given full range on the condition that it causes weeping and pretending to weep for Imam Husayn and his family. License culled from the encouraging words of prominent religious figures such as Gilani creates the grounds for the emergence of sacred pictorial depictions in Persian art during the nineteenth century as well. "Once it had been accepted, to the dismay of the orthodox, that the roles of the martyrs and their adversaries were enacted by devout Muslims, the step toward the public's acceptance of religious paintings depicting the same narratives had already been made" (Peterson 1979, 75). "After hundreds of years of censure," writes Samuel Peterson about the advent of folk art in Persia, "during the nineteenth century there appear paintings of religious subjects which specifically were intended for the Iranian public at large" (1979, 75). The paintings depict the events of Karbala as *a translation* of the *ta'ziyeh* performances into the visual arts. The most significant of these "turns" can be seen in the sartorial details of the Karbala paintings. In the Qajar period the translation of history through the medium of the *ta'ziyeh* made the usage of veiling arbitrary in pictorial form.

Ta'ziyeh historians claim that the introduction of veils into the passion play was meant to cover the fact that only men and children took part in the representation of the Karbala tragedy. Women did not participate as role-carriers on the public stage. To depict female characters such as the daughter of the Prophet, Fatimih, mortal men donned the veil. This minor "twist" has had major consequences for the ancient traditions of painting in Qajar Iran. Samuel Peterson writes: "During the last half of the fifteenth century and until the Qajar period, the veil was an exclusive attribute of holy personages and was not used to cover the faces of women. However, once it became in ta'ziyeh productions a standard part of the costume of women—a sign of their modesty . . . it becomes in [Karbala] paintings a standard feature of Alid women. No longer used so consistently as the sacred symbol it formerly had been, in Qajar religious painting the veil is ascribed somewhat arbitrarily to holy figures; thus the faces of the [Shi'ite] Imams appear veiled and unveiled" (1979, 79).

On the stage, the tone of the voice and the presence of the veil worn by women came to determine the gender of the character in the *ta'ziyeh* performances. Young men with soft voices portrayed female characters; young girls performed certain minor female roles until the age of nine—the age of maturity.

It is said that one of the early Qajar performers of women's roles, Haji Mulla Husayn from Peek Zarand-Saveh, played female characters so well that each year he had to abandon his farm for the months of Muharram and Safar to perform at the Takiyeh Dowlat (Royal Takiyeh). In the late Qajar period, Mulla Farj'ullah Sangani, Haji Mulla Husayn, and Gholi Khan Shahi were three of the most famous female role-carriers and were specifically hired to play the role of Imam Ali's daughter, Zinat (Beiza'i 2000, 143–44). With the introduction of the gramophone to the court under the rule of Muzzaffar al-Din Shah (1896–1907), Gholi Khan Shahi's became one of the most recorded voices of the period (Rijai'i 1994, 29).

According to Bahram Beiza'i, the female role-carrier would wear a long black shirt, sometimes decorated with flowers, reaching down to the back

3. Ta'ziyeh *performance. The female character covered in a veil at the center of the tent and holding a piece of paper is played by a male role carrier. The "Western" male to the right of that figure may be a "farangi," a Christian figure in the story. Photograph by Antoin Sevruguin, courtesy of the Freer Gallery of Art and the Arthur M. Sackler Gallery Archives, Smithsonian Institution.*

of the role-carrier's leg. A second piece of black fabric would cover the head, the arms, and the hands of the role-carrier. A third would cover the face, so that only a sliver of the eyes and the fingertips of the actor would be visible. In the passionate reenactment of the historical battle between Imam Husayn and his archenemy, the female characters who belonged to Yazid's camp would wear the same costume, Beiza'i writes, but in red (2000, 145).

Western observers of the *ta'ziyeh* during the modern period—travelers and diplomats used to the European entertainment traditions—commented frequently on the lack of attention paid to the historical accuracy of costumes in the dramatic presentation of the *ta'ziyeh.* Browne observes, for example, that the performance of the *ta'ziyeh* on the seventh of Muharram 1888 CE was "spoiled in some measure by the introduction of a number of carriages, with pastilions barbarously dressed up in a half-European uniform, in the middle of the piece." He goes on to observe that this absurd piece of ostentation seemed typical of Qajar taste (1926, 604).[11] Writing in the 1850s, Eugene Flandin recorded that the role-carriers who represented Europeans on the stage borrowed the French troops' triangular hats and military uniforms in order to show themselves as real *farangis* (foreigners). Flandin was moved by the realism, if not the historical accuracy, of the *ta'ziyeh* performance, much like Gaspand Drouville who, some forty years earlier, could not fathom how the realistic and chaotic battle of four thousand performers left no one hurt or wounded (Beiza'i 2000, 119–20).

For Comte de Gobineau, however, the simplicity of clothing seemed to recommend itself to the production of the *ta'ziyeh.* This was a drama that relied on the marked contrast in clothing to convey a character's placement in the dramatic face-off between the forces of good and evil. In order for the spectacle to work, Gobineau maintained, the holy men wore turbans and the female characters donned the present-day veils used in Baghdad and Damascus (Gobineau 1900, 389). The *Ta'ziyeh of the Christian Girl* performed at the shah's Niyavaran palace and then at the Royal Takiyeh in Tehran, struck Gobineau as one of the most powerful *ta'ziyeh*s performed in the Muharram sequence. In this performance, the clothes of the Christian girl, played, as usual, by a man, are said to have been based on European paintings, so that in the passion play, the Christian girl appears as a stereotypical European woman in a straw hat, a country dress with a fanned skirt, and an apron, performing her part in tall black boots. It is here, precisely, that we find an example of the unembellished character of *ta'ziyeh* signifiers, and also of the cultural and sexual transvestism at the core of the performance.

The *Ta'ziyeh of the Christian Girl* (which Beiza'i writes may be the *ta'ziyeh* known as the *Majlis-i zan-i Nasrani*) is noteworthy because it is one of the few known mourning *ta'ziyeh*s with a female lead character. Its staging is uncharacteristic, too, in that it begins with a curtain around the otherwise

11. When the Qajar court acquired an automobile, for example, it was immediately used on stage in the *ta'ziyeh* performances in Tehran. The "foreign ambassador" at the court of Yazid wore tails in the time of Nasir al-Din Shah. The intention of contemporary splendor is in this way transferred to the historical sphere. For a summary of foreign sources on *ta'ziyeh* performances and *rauzeh khanis* see Calmard (1983).

open circular stage of the *ta'ziyeh*.[12] The scene is set on the barren plains of Karbala, and the coffins bearing the remains of the Third Imam, Imam Husayn, and his followers are visible. Lit candles atop a few of the coffins signify the holiness of the personages within. Weapons are scattered about on the ground, signifying the bloody end to a battle that has just been fought. In his description of the *Ta'ziyeh of the Christian Girl*, Gobineau muses that the staging gives the audience the sense that it can see both above and below ground (quoted in Beiza'i 2000, 141). The Christian girl enters with her entourage, riding a horse. Not knowing where she has arrived, she dismounts and asks her party to put up tents. But with every spike that penetrates the ground, blood gushes out as if from a fountain. Everyone in her party is perturbed. Eventually asleep in one of the upper rooms of the *takiyeh*, the girl has a dream in which Christ enters and tells the girl about the battle of Karbala. Meanwhile, an Arab thief enters the stage and, unaware of the Imam's station, opens his coffin. Looking for weapons and valuables, he disrespectfully searches the coffin. The Arab is so evil at heart, Gobineau observes, that he does not notice the candles or the doves that encircle the holy corpse. He is suddenly frightened by the voice of the martyred Imam, who speaks to him—and he is angered, too. After dismembering the Imam's body, the Arab thief leaves the scene. Then all the prophets of the past and the Fourteen Infallibles enter with veiled faces. They walk toward the Imam's corpse. As the performance ends, the Christian girl, moved by the tragic fate of the Imam, converts to Islam (quoted in Beiza'i 2000, 141–42).

As Mohammad Tavakoli-Targhi suggests, "Fascination with the non-Muslim woman has a long history in the Perso-Islamic literary culture" (2001, 70). The Roman/Greek Christian girl who seduces Shaykh Sanan, the elderly mystic and keeper of Mecca's holy places, is one example of this type in Persian mythology. But other representations of European women in Persian art and performance traditions express this Persian "imagination on the erotic and exotic" in relation to the European Christian woman (Tavakoli-Targhi 2001, 71). In the representation of the European women's eventual conversions to Islam, cultural productions articulated Shi'ite Iran's

12. The *ta'ziyeh* stage is generally an open circular stage without a curtain.

moral and ethical superiority against the economic and military threat of the West. But beyond this cultural and religious function, the *ta'ziyeh*s also play a fundamental political role in Iranian modern history.

As Calmard remarks, James Mourier's return to Persia in 1811, as the secretary of the British "Ambassador Extraordinary and Plenipotentiary" to the Persian court, dates to the negotiations on an Anglo-Persian treaty in which British military and financial support was expected by Fath 'Ali Shah Qajar. Calmard records the inclusion of the story of the European ambassador in the *ta'ziyeh* performance on perhaps the eighth night of Muharram. This performance insured that the audience was more favorably inclined toward the British presence, he writes (1983, 216). Under the reign of Muhammad Shah Qajar (1834–48) *ta'ziyeh* performances commonly included Russian and British missions in the audience. The diplomatic missions often contributed to the ceremonies with their patronage. The figure of the foreign envoy or ambassador, often referred to as *elci farangi,* figured in these performances, and, according to Calmard, "enhanced the diplomat's prestige amongst women," who, one Russian diplomat observes, would turn toward the foreign lodge every time the fictive ambassador spoke his lines (Calmard 1983, 218, 226n 40). By the time of Gobineau's mission to Tehran, the theme of the *elci farangi* was somewhat "eclipsed" by the new *Ta'ziyeh of the Christian Girl.*

The appropriation of the *ta'ziyeh* as a tool for revolutionary sociopolitical and cultural change suggests a core malleability that comes into relief with the appearance of female characters and European witnesses in the drama itself. This malleability, which Marjorie Garber calls the "transvestite effect," structures the *ta'ziyeh* as not only a nationalistic site for identification and disidentification, but also as an imaginary stage on which the culture of the other is donned and shed. Through the trope of the European woman, the *ta'ziyeh* provides a setting in which the category of gender can be boldly interrogated. This appropriation of the other's culture, and of other genders, points to "the centrality of the transvestite as an index of category destabilization altogether" (Garber 1998, 179). The *Ta'ziyeh of the Christian Girl* is only one example of the cultural and sexual transvestism at the core of the *ta'ziyeh* performance and a site in which the dress, the values, and the mores of others are tried on for size as the nation reaches for a definition of its modern identity. As one antimodernist cautioned: "[I]f Iranian women mingled with European women, they would be tempted to dress like Europeans, dance in public celebrations and gatherings, drink wine and sit with men on benches and chairs and joke with strangers. By becoming a 'land of freedom' *(vilayat-i azadi)* women of Iran would copulate with Europeans and no one would dare protest" (Tavakoli-Targhi 2001, 72). "This line of argument," Tavakoli-Targhi writes, "equated undesirable sociopolitical reforms with the Europeanization and Christianization of Iran" (2001, 72). The Western female and her unveiled presence represented a threat to some Iranian antimodernists. The feminization of power in the Iranian public sphere implied the threat of a heterosociality that was associated with the vices and mores of the West. The overwhelming enthusiasm surrounding the performance tradition during the reign of Nasir al-Din Shah Qajar thus situates the *ta'ziyeh* as a critical area for the study of perceptions of Otherness, as well as a location for evaluating emerging notions of modern selfhood in Qajar culture. On the *ta'ziyeh* stage men donned European women's clothing. Here role-carriers and *ta'ziyeh* participants could explore the possibilities of cultural emulation and political reform through performance and representation. As Jean E. Howard writes: "If a boy can so successfully personate the voice, gait and manner of a woman, how stable are those boundaries separating one sexual kind from another, and thus how secure are those powers and privileges assigned to the hierarchically superior sex, which depends upon notions of difference to justify domination?" (1998, 49). If a Persian man could don the skirt and apron of a Christian girl, how big are the differences between Iran and Europe? The *ta'ziyeh*'s "transvestite effect" located the place of women, European and Iranian, "at the crossroads of cultural change and contradiction" (51). As women's bodies factored incessantly in debates about the definition of the national identity, especially in late-eighteenth-century and nineteenth-century Iranian cultural productions, the *ta'ziyeh*'s promotion of male-female transvestism must be seen as trenchant ground for feminist research for its articulation of gender differences and the role of women in the construction of national and religious identity.

Beyond an implied gendered and cultural transvestism, *ta'ziyeh* performances involving foreign or European subjects, much like "the traveler's narratives" of the period discussed in later chapters, were used to situate independent witnesses to wrongs borne by the family of the Prophet at the hands of the Arabs. In the *ta'ziyeh,* the European foreigner or the *elci farangi* always corroborates the ethical and moral superiority of Iranian Shi'ism over Sunnite aggression. The foreigner's certain conversion at the end of the *ta'ziyeh* concurrently establishes the potency of Shi'ite Islam against Western political and industrial power. In the final slaughter of the foreigner (in the *Ta'ziyeh of the Arrival of the Family of the Prophet to Damascus,* for example), the performance ultimately suggests that the industrially advanced West (represented by the foreigner) and the emerging modern nation of Iran (as the sole national representative of Imam Husayn) are one under drag. One, at least, in light of the evil machinations of Iran's Sunnite neighbors. The beloved Shi'ite leader of Iran, Imam Husayn, and the *ta'ziyeh*'s representative of the industrially advanced European nations are thus both sacrificed at the end of the performance by the Sunni leader whose evil heart cannot recognize true worth.

Representing the Unpresentable

The staging of the *ta'ziyeh* during Muharram, on the first ten days of the Muslim year, is, as we have seen, meant to function as an annual reminder of the nation's religious history. But clearly, some of the events represented in the *ta'ziyeh* have no grounding in history and are created to stimulate an emotional response. Some stagings were in fact developed from shorter sketches whose function, as prologues, was to prepare the participants for the emotional range of the full-scale *ta'ziyeh* performance. Shorter dramas, called *gushes*, appeared at the beginning, middle, or end of the *ta'ziyeh* and often led to a heart-wrenching scene that encouraged and allowed the audience and the performers themselves to weep for the fate of those who suffered and died at Karbala. The *gushes* often focused on the meekness and righteousness of Imam Husayn and his family. They represented the Imam as the apotheosis of God's revelation, as the quintessence of divine miracles, and as the embodiment of the supreme power of the divine. *Gushes* were used to emphasize the importance of individual and collective sacrifice following the example of Imam Husayn.

Female characters appear more frequently as lead characters in *gushes* than they do in full-scale *ta'ziyehs*. In the *gushes*, they sometimes take on different characteristics and temperaments than those assigned to their role in the full-scale *ta'ziyeh*s. In the *Gushe of Panj Tan* (five beings), for example, Imam Ali's daughter, Zinat, takes a leading role. Zinat's representation in this *gushe* is significantly different from the assertive and stubborn role she plays at the court of Yazid in the known *ta'ziyeh* cycle. In the *Gushe of Panj Tan,* she is shown in a melancholic dream state, engaging in deeply affectionate dialogues with the Prophet Muhammad, his son-in-law Ali, and his grandsons Hassan and Husayn. The *Gushe of Panj Tan* ends with a reminder spoken by Imam Husayn that Zinat, too, will be present at the Prophet's heavenly banquet the following day. This is an ominous reminder not only of the tragic carnage in Karbala, but also of the subsequent fate of the women and young children in Damascus.

It is easy to forget that *gushe*s involving female characters were in some cases subject to such popular enthusiasm that they developed into full-scale *ta'ziyeh*s. The *Gushe of the Daughter of the Khatan Shah* is one such example. Its popularity, like that of certain other *gushe*s with female leads, affected the placement and importance of the more properly historical drama. In this way, the *Ta'ziyeh of the Martyrdom of Ali Akbar* became a *gushe* performed as prologue to the *Ta'ziyeh of the Daughter of the Khatan Shah.* Other *gushe*s were developed into completely independent *ta'ziyeh*s. The *Ta'ziyeh of the Children of Zinat* was a *gushe* performed as part of the *Ta'ziyeh of Ali Akbar.* A preserved historical script of the *Children of Zinat* suggests that a full-scale *ta'ziyeh* was later developed from the earlier prologue version (Fath-Ali Beygi 1992, 229–73).

The *Ta'ziyeh of the Indian Girl* is one *ta'ziyeh* that, like many of the *gushe*s discussed in this chapter, diverges from the historical tradition. It also demonstrates the ways in which the inclusion of female characters in the *ta'ziyeh* tradition allows for a meditation on everyday worldly concerns and desires. The *ta'ziyeh* begins with a conversation between a lover and his friend in which the lover discloses his passion for a beautiful Indian girl. The two friends decide to go to the home of the Indian girl to investigate the possibility of a union. They arrive at the girl's home to find that she is already married to an Indian man, and they conspire to murder the husband. Having beheaded the husband, the lover tries to woo the Indian girl. But in prayer, she begs Imam Husayn to bring her husband back to life. Imam Husayn arrives onstage to intervene prayerfully on behalf of the dead Hindu man. This loving gesture miraculously brings the husband back to life. Joyfully, the Indian husband and wife recognize the status of the Imam and convert to Islam. They return to their homeland to prepare a mourning *ta'ziyeh* for Imam Husayn (Fath-Ali Beygi 1990, 246). Dating to June 1855, this transcript of the *Ta'ziyeh of the Indian Girl* is a rare representation of desire of any sort in Iranian nineteenth-century visual culture.

In the painting tradition of earlier periods, we find frequent references to "the amorous couple" in which sexual desire finds modest representation. "Representations of young men in late Zand and early Qajar paintings include scenes of beautiful males, in particular representations of Joseph, or of young princes." We find, as well, representations of the male-female couple in this period. But by the late Zand and early Qajar periods, writes Afsaneh Najmabadi, male-male amorous couples disappear completely and, "we are left with only male-female couples," and "from early Qajar times on, there is a noticeable absence of amorous couples altogether" (2001, 92–93). It should be emphasized that until the late nineteenth century, as both B. W. Robinson and Najmabadi have remarked, "the beloved" could be represented by a youthful woman or a by young beardless man in literary or sometimes visual form. In the literature and paintings of the period, these narrow-waisted and cypress-statured beauties with crescent eyebrows and scented black hair were as often young beardless men *(ghilman)* as they were paradisiacal virgins (female *huri*s). Their eternally youthful bodies stood as metaphors for the paradisiacal pleasures described in sura 44 of the Qur'an, the sura of "Smoke."

In the *Ta'ziyeh of the Indian Girl* the lover shares his erotic desires with the audience as he describes his Hindu beloved to his friend in precisely those lyrical terms ascribed by poets to the male and female beloved in Persian poetry. There is no body more slender and no face more radiant than that of the Indian girl. Drawing on the tropes of Persian poetry in which ringlets of hair spill across the beloved's face, the lover tells his friend that his heart is entangled in the Indian girl's long dark locks. His very body is caught in those ringlets, which in the classical literary tradition represent both India and China. In the scenes that follow the murder of the husband, the staging of desire is further intensified as the lover asks the Indian girl to run away with him. Although this scene is set up in the narrative fiction as a heterosexual scene of desire, the transvestite effect provides the audience with an opportunity to contemplate and visually appreciate the features of the beardless man in drag, a man playing the role of a beautiful Indian girl. The *ta'ziyeh* drama, as Gobineau's repeated references to the male beauties appearing on the *ta'ziyeh* stage also emphasize, enables male-male gazing *(nazar). Nazar,* the gaze that is directed at the transvestite role-carrier in the *Ta'ziyeh of the Indian Girl,* is the same gaze that has the Indian girl herself as the object of its adoration. The interactive nature of the *ta'ziyeh* as a genre, a genre in which the viewer is always implicated as participant in the narrative, invites "the viewer to become an accomplice in the pleasure of the visual . . . to become actively engaged in the production and circulation of desire" both within and outside the performance (Najmabadi 2001, 96). Entangled in the web of desire for a transvestite subject in drag, both male and female audience participants of the *ta'ziyeh* performance cycle became party to what was seen by Western observers as the debauchery of Iranian modern culture. As the female character is played by a young beardless male role-carrier—one who represents himself, as he recites the part of his female character—the "amorous couple" on stage is simultaneously a "spectacle of heterosexuality" and a cauldron of homoerotic desires directed at the embodiment of the paradisiacal *ghilman*—the youthful beardless men who appear alongside female *huri*s in paradisiacal scenes derived from the Qur'an. This formal ambivalence, as Najmabadi notes, was critical to the constitution of the modern national identity: "Iranians became acutely aware that Europeans considered older man–younger man love and sexual practices very prevalent in Iran and that they considered it a vice. . . . While disavowal and homophobic retaliation may have been only one response to this scrutiny, dissimulation and 'cross-representation' could have been another" (2001, 99–100).

Such scenes in the *ta'ziyeh* cycle suggest that the homoerotic, which was an integral part of the *ta'ziyeh* participants' adoration and emphatic mourning for the male beloved, had to be covered and remade into a masquerade of heterosexual desire. As Najmabadi suggests, "one marker of modernity became the transformation of homoeroticism into masqueraded hetero-eros" (2001, 100). The young beardless beauty dressed in women's clothing was the embodiment of this recognition and its disavowal in the nineteenth-century *ta'ziyeh* cycle, which retained in its periodic restaging of antiquity the affective pleasure of object-ambivalent desire and the unshakable horror of such pleasure as vice. The staging of desire in the Muharram cycle and the reverberant horror of its pleasures plays a considerable role in my reassessment of Qurrat al-'Ayn Tahirih's representation in the early historical chronicles of her unveiling.

Women's *Ta'ziyeh*s

Although female lead characters in *ta'ziyeh*s were admittedly rare, their appearance on the public stage encouraged the impulse among the multitude of female *ta'ziyeh* enthusiasts to perform the *ta'ziyeh* cycle and to convene exclusive performances for women. One annual all-female event during the reign of Nasir al-Din Shah involved the restaging of the wedding of Fatimih's daughter-in-law. The annual performance was held on the birthday of Fatimih at the Munirieh palace, the residence of Munir al-Saltanah, who was one of Nasir al-Din Shah's wives. On this occasion a young woman would be selected to play the part of Fatimih's daughter-in-law. The assembled women would deck the halls and bejewel the actor and restage the wedding ceremony and celebration before an all-female audience. Munis al-Dawleh reports that among the women who gathered at the Munirieh palace were eager young girls who wanted to marry Nasir al-Din Shah; the young girls would commonly form a line to greet the shah when he entered. Nasir-al Din Shah would select two or three young women or girls from a crowd of two thousand as brides. As the shah and Kamran Mirza Nayeb al-Saltanih were the only two noncastrated men allowed at the all-female performance, court eunuchs would be ordered to transport the women swiftly on horseback to another room where a mullah would perform temporary marriage rites.

Before Nasir al-Din Shah's era, one of the daughters of Fath 'Ali Shah Qajar, Qamar al-Saltanih, arranged to have the full *ta'ziyeh* cycle performed at her house to an all-female audience in the first ten days of Muharram each year. *Ta'ziyeh*s were performed in the evenings following female *rauzeh-khanis*. In the *ta'ziyeh* performances that followed, female *rauzeh-khans* (eulogy readers) such as Mullah Nabat, Mullah Fatimih, and Mullah Maryam, would perform the leading roles. The Persian women of the day were largely illiterate, so the process of performing for the all-female *ta'ziyehs* was slightly altered. Unlike the men, who usually held slips of paper in the palms of their hands and looked down as if to remember their lines and to create with gestures a distance between themselves and the characters they played, women recited their lines from memory, making identification with the characters they played complete. Literate castrates would go to Muin al-Baka's home to learn the various lines by heart. They would also learn the musical scores for each part. The eunuchs would search the *andaruns* (home interiors) and harems and to collect a variety of female mullahs and then teach them their designated lines for the all-female *ta'ziyeh* performances. The eunuchs themselves would perform the music on stage, and at certain times a blind *kamanche* player, with the title "nadman-i koor," would also get onstage to play the traditional nineteenth-century Persian string instrument.

Munis al Dawleh relates that when Fath 'Ali Shah's daughter directed these all-female *ta'ziyehs*, she would typically appear onstage and give her directorial instructions to the musicians and the actors with a walking stick. When necessary, she would slap a mullah across the face in order to get the desired effect for the mourning *ta'ziyehs*. The performer would start crying, imbuing her part with a sense of reality (Munis al-Dawleh 2001 [1380], 105). *Ta'ziyehs* performed in these gatherings, though sometimes selected from among the more traditional scripts, were more often those with female leads. The *Ta'ziyeh of Shahr-banu* and *The Wedding of a Qurashite Daughter* were among the most popular female *ta'ziyehs*. Although the latter has some similarities with the *rauzeh* on Fatimih found in Kashefi's *Rowzat al-Shohada,* there are some fundamental differences between the eulogy and its staging as a *ta'ziyeh* for an all-female audience (see Aghaie 2005b, 49–50). Munis al-Dawleh's memoir tells us that *The Wedding of a Qurashite Daughter* was so popular that women came from faraway towns and villages to participate in it when it was staged in Tehran.

In this *ta'ziyeh,* the Qurashite women prepare a sumptuous wedding for an ugly, pimpled bride. They decide to invite Fatimih as a way of endearing themselves to the Prophet's daughter. Fatimih, busy at home with housework, decides that she neither has the time, nor the clothes, to go to a wedding. A tall female beauty bedecked with wings, representing the angel Gabriel, appears in the sky (or rather, on the roof of one of the nearby buildings) singing aloud to the *huri*s that they need to prepare and clothe Fatimih for the wedding. Each of the twelve *huri*s arrives at Fatimih's threshold, bearing gifts and treasure chests. We must assume that Fatimih is convinced that she can be appropriately dressed because she finally agrees to attend the wedding. At the sight of Fatimih's beauty, the ugly bride falls to the ground and passes out. The Qurashite women beg Fatimih to pray for the bride. She does, and the bride immediately comes to. The Qurashite women, idol worshipers one and all, convert to Islam (Munis al-Dawleh 2001 [1380], 105). Munis al-Dawleh writes that the more cheerful *ta'ziyeh*s, such as the ones representing *The Wedding of the Qurashite Daughter,* were performed in Rabii al-Awal, the month following the months of mourning, while mourning *ta'ziyeh*s by women and for women were more frequently produced in the months of Muharram and Safar. Women participated without the veil in these all-female performances, and female role-carriers appeared as lead male characters in drag and with applied facial hair. Playing male roles, women often carried swords and rode on horseback onstage. A particular breed of horse, writes Munis al-Dawleh, the *tatu,* was used on most occasion. Eunuchs walked alongside the *tatu* to guide the horse around the stage during the *ta'ziyeh* performance (Munis al-Dawleh 2001, 98).

Beiza'i maintains that performances by and for women not only showed women's appreciation of the art form but also their desire to gain the right to perform women's roles in the larger and more traditional all-male arenas. Women's *ta'ziyeh*s did not reach the public, however. Rare and poorly documented, they were only occasionally performed in larger private spaces, specifically in the homes of the wealthy and powerful, until the mid-1920s (2000, 151–52).

Messianic Time

In *Religions,* Gobineau presents several examples of prologues or *gushe*s to the *ta'ziyeh* performances witnessed during his residence in Persia. These prologues, he writes, provide the audience with a reason to watch the action that is about to take place on the stage. One of the prologues enacted on stage is the story of Joseph and Jacob. In his speech, Arnold provides a condensed version of Gobineau's description of this *gushe:*

> Joseph and his brethren appear on stage, and the old Bible story is transacted. Joseph is thrown in the pit and sold to the merchants, and his blood-stained coat is carried by his brothers to Jacob; Jacob is then left alone, weeping and bewailing himself; the angel Gabriel enters, and reproves him for want of faith and constancy, telling him that what he suffers is not a hundredth part of what Ali, [Husayn] and the children of [Husayn] will one day suffer. Jacob seems to doubt it; Gabriel, to convince him, orders the angels to perform the [*ta'ziyeh*] of what will one day happen at [Karbala]. And so the [*ta'ziyeh*] commences. (Arnold 1871, 673)

The formal qualities of this *gushe* capture the structure of time as it is appears in the *ta'ziyeh,* generally. Benjamin formulates this structure in his use of the phrase *"der jüngste Tag,"* which, in Ian Balfour's reading, can mean either the Last Day or "the most recent day," which is the proper object of a journal (Balfour 1991, 638). Although historically distant, two moments, the suffering of Joseph and the suffering of the family of the Prophet, are captured within the time frame of the present, disregarding the temporal impossibility of Gabriel's knowledge of a future event. As Chelkowski remarks on the function of such digressions from the main performance, it is through them that "all *ta'ziyeh* drama expands beyond spatial and time constraints to merge the past and present into one unifying moment of intensity that allows the spectators to be simultaneously in the performance space and at Karbala" (Chelkowski 2005, 23). The present moment grasps the antiquity of Islam and the antiquity of the world in one frame. The now of the stage forms a constellation with these doubled images rescued from the past. In constellation, these moments together create the stage as Judgment Day, where all people, past and present, are resurrected. The *ta'ziyeh* brings the Imams, the prophets, and the people together to revolutionize the Shi'ite consciousness of the present, the everyday.[13]

13. We find one example of this in month of Muharram, 1963. A few days before the 1963 riots against the shah, a *rauzeh* sermon was given by Sayyid Mahmud Taleghani during

The present moment of the Ashura as a time filled with the significance of all time dictates that all the important religious figures who predated and postdated the Karbala tragedy are added to the repertoire of Muharram drama (Chelkowski 1979, 4). Benjamin recognizes this model of the present as a model of messianic time and notes, "[A materialist historian] grasps the constellation into which his own era has entered, along with a very specific earlier one. Thus, he establishes a conception of the present as now-time shot through with splinters of messianic time" (Benjamin 2003a, 397). *Ta'ziyeh* participants and its role-carriers understand now-time as a snapshot of all time; a time in which mankind's full history is redeemed.[14]

As Beeman notes, oratorical skill for the performance of commemorative ceremonies during the Ashura involved a similar capacity, "the ability to make the events of [Husayn's] martyrdom seem immediate and relevant to the audience" (1982, 368).

> One *rauzeh* widely distributed on cassette tapes during the fall of 1978 when the revolution in Iran was in full swing was delivered by Ayatollah Kafi of Mashhad. In this *rauzeh* he calls Imam [Husayn] on the telephone, and cries out to him to quit the plains of [Karbala], because the greater enemy is in Iran in the person of the shah's regime. In this he duplicates the kind of telephone conversation that must take place

---

the Muharram. "In loud emotional voice, Taleghani turned to the audience and . . . quoting Husain said, 'You have written letters to me and promised to help me and stay beside me [referring to the people of Kufa]. If you are still willing to keep your promise, I am Husain, the son of Ali, and the son of Fatima who is the daughter of the prophet.' From the phrasing and particularly the direct quote from Husain in the present tense, there is little doubt in the mind of the audience what is being asked for . . . namely the support of the ulama (Husain's spiritual heirs) against an oppressive government" (Thaiss 1972, 360).

14. As Itzutsu notes, within the total Qur'anic context there are numerous semantic fields, one of which is composed of words relating to Resurrection and Last Judgment. "As is natural, an intense atmosphere of a very unusual nature pervades the whole field and reigns over it. Right into this atmosphere you put the word *yaum* with its proper neutral meaning of *day*, which it has in normal situations; at once you see a variety of conceptual associations formed around it, and the concept of day becomes tinged with a marked eschatological coloring. In short *al-yaum*—'the day' means in this particular field not an ordinary day, but the Last Judgment, i.e., the Day of Judgment" (Itzutsu 1964, 20–21).

> between separated relatives in Iran all the time. The pathos of the plea to Imam [Husayn] is accentuated by the contemporary setting given to the message. (1982, 368)

In *The Telephone Book,* Avital Ronell argues that the significance of telephonic logic means that "contact with the Other has been disrupted; but it also means that the break is never absolute. Being on the telephone will come to mean, therefore, that contact is never constant nor is the break clean" (1989, 20). Indeed, Ronell argues that Nietzsche's texts are telephonically charged in this way, as evidenced by his "telephone to the beyond" in the *Genealogy of Morals,* where the archaic past is both present and absent, as is the utopian beyond.[15]

The notion of the historical significance of the present, persistently retold and reenacted in the Muharram passion, transforms not only the time of the present into a messianic time filled with possibilities of revolutionary action and redemption, it transforms the stage apart into a public stage populated by the masses. "A [*ta'ziyeh*] actor," Wirth suggests, "cannot 'fall out of role' because he does not identify with it. . . . Therefore the 'role carrier' keeps his own identity intact and can react at anytime in his capacity as a non-performer" (1979, 38). Rebecca Ansary Petty confirms this observation with a slight twist. She suggests that "[i]n spite of the occasional instances when the characters briefly come to life, it is clear that the [*ta'ziyeh*] dramatists generally treat the protagonists and the antagonists as though they were opposing pieces in a game of chess" (1982, 325). The Nietzschian telephonic connection to the beyond, which in the *ta'ziyeh* is also the connection with the past, the future, and the present on the Day of Judgment, is a connection that, disrupted, is never constant, yet never entirely broken. Kafi's text shows that although the connection with the Imams of the past is disrupted, thus alienated, this disruption is temporary. There are still occasional connections between the believers and the Fourteen Infallibles, and it is this contact between the present and the past of Karbala that will bring the nation to the future Judgment

15. The first essay (sections 14 and 15) in the *Genealogy of Morals* (Nietzsche 1989) is illuminating in this regard.

Day. This day is *al-yaum,* the day on which all those resurrected with the Imams oppose a demonic Yazid. This understanding of the historical as the dramatization of the topical is evidenced by numerous recollections of *ta'ziyeh* performances under the Qajar reign.

"In a Ta'ziyeh performance," Wirth writes, "it is not unusual to see actors on stage drinking tea while waiting on their turn" (1979, 38). The role-carriers are one with the audience as they wait to speak their lines. As role-carriers, the *ta'ziyeh* actors connect and break from their characters at anytime, recognizing in gesture, a "now" shot through with the chips of all time. The audience, too, iterate from a position of spectatorship to that of Husayn's supporters in Karbala. As the representative of the people, the role-carrier becomes the telephonic connection between the past and the future on stage. This conception of temporality brings the past and the everyday together in a revolutionary conjunction that makes the everyday the site of the past, and yet also the unfulfilled utopian future returned. These temporal dimensions of the *ta'ziyeh* come to inform the tropes of reform thinking in historical tracts written during the late Qajar period, and they manifest as enunciative deictic markers in efforts to produce an emerging modern Islamic nation in postrevolutionary Iranian cinema, as well.

Judgment Day, the Everyday

One of the historical dramas performed during the month of Muharram is the episode of Fatimih. Fatimih is here depicted engaged in the daily routines of the home, washing the clothes of her young sons, Imam Husayn and Imam Hasan: "As she takes each small piece of clothing out of the washbasin, she identifies it and bemoans the fact that the child who wears it will one day be tortured and killed in the most horrendous way. She ends fainting in grief, her children's clothing spread around her" (Beeman 1982, 369). Fatimih, one of the Fourteen Infallibles, is here shown performing an everyday act of housekeeping. The routine of the act encroaches upon the divine. It does so to bring the historical message of redemption home to its audience. This engagement of the topical and the historical transforms the stage of the *takiyeh* into the site of the everyday. The everyday of the *ta'ziyeh* itself, in Benjamin's conception of *der jüngste Tag,* reenacts the past, sustaining a unique experience with messianic time. Its workings suggest the ambivalent status of the temporal and spatial on the *takiyeh* stage, an ambivalence that structures the everyday as the site of Judgment Day. The *takiyeh,* like the epic stage, is designed in fact "to enhance and preserve the dramatic interplay between the spectator and the actor," emphasizing, in the present, their mutual investment in the unfolding historical tragedy (Chelkowski 1979, 5). The theater becomes a space in which both actor and spectator relearn history in the enactment of the quotidian, the everyday.

Recognizing *ta'ziyeh*'s function as a communal event, each individual contributes according to means and ability (Chelkowski 1979, 8). Crystal lamps, mirrors, china, and tapestry are brought in to decorate the walls of the *takiyeh.* Arnold takes his cue from Gobineau when he describes the spectacle as "the effect of prodigality, color and sumptuousness," an effect that Arnold then relates to the "splendors of the Arabian Nights" (1871, 675):

> Up to a certain height these masts are hung with tiger and panther skins, to indicate the violent character of the scenes to be represented. Shields of steel and of hippopotamus skin, and flags and naked swords, are also attached to these masts. A sea of colour and splendour meets the eye all around. Woodwork and brickwork disappear under cushions, rich carpets, silk hangings, India muslin embroidered silver and gold shawls from Kerman and from Cashmere; there are lamps, lustrous coloured crystal, mirrors, Bohemian and Venetian glass, porcelain vases of all degrees of magnitude from China and from Europe. (675)

Such descriptions of the *takiyeh* interior, in stark contrast to the barren scene itself, underscore the investment of the community in the act of honoring the Karbala martyrs. Writing of his experiences in Tehran during his early travels to Persia between 1887 and 1888, Browne gives a description of the Royal Takiyeh in Tehran, a structure that he visited during the month of Muharram:

> The theatre is a large circular building—roofless, but covered during Muharram with an awning. There are boxes *(takches)* all round, which are assigned to the more patrician spectators, one, specially large and highly decorated, being reserved for the Shah. The humbler spectators

> sit round the central space or arena in serried ranks, the women and children in front. A circular stone platform in the centre constitutes the stage. There is no curtain and no exit for the actors, who when not wanted, simply stand back. (Browne 1926, 603)

Two or more corridors through the seating area to the back wall of the *takiyeh* enabled the bearer of messages, armies, and processions to move through the audience; actors in enacting their duels would plunge through the audience to gain central stage. Thus even in terms of spatial formality, the *takiyeh*s were designed to give the participant a sense that he or she was in fact on the plains of Karbala and encircled (in the central playing area) by the enemy. The *ta'ziyeh* in its permanent quarters thus established "a unique experience with the past" through spatial manipulation. It posited the present of the historical drama as the time of messianic happening.

As Beeman notes, the relationship between the *ta'ziyeh* audience and the performance is unique because the spectator must see him or herself both inside and outside the drama simultaneously (1979, 26). Temporal difference disappears and in terms of spatial positioning, the audience becomes both the force supporting Husayn in Karbala and mourners mourning the tragedy in the real time of the performance. This temporal cognition "comprises the entire history of mankind in a tremendous abbreviation" (Benjamin 2003a, 396). Beeman explains: "The liminal status of the audience as part of the dramatic action, and being situated both within its own community and on the plains of [Karbala] forms the central axis around which principles of representation are ordered" (1979, 27). Both time and space are rearranged in the meanwhile.

The circular brick structure mirroring the British concert hall was to be the grandest *takiyeh* in Persia during the Qajar reign. It provided a meeting ground, a public sphere through which contrary discourses of revolution and dynastic reverence, religious fervor and antidogmatic spectacle, the past and the present, the historical and the everyday merged. After the 1906 constitutional revolution had passed, Wishard proclaimed the death of the *ta'ziyeh:* "Everywhere these celebrations are becoming less popular, and as education and enlightenment come, we may expect their disappearance" (1908, 158). "From that period on one can see the trend of secularization within the framework of religious themes" (Chelkowski 1971, 127). The *ta'ziyeh*'s decline, it would seem, "was almost as rapid as its rise. After that," writes Chelkowski, "the ta'ziyeh troupes were mostly interested in the commercial value of the performance" (1971, 129). The impact of capitalism thus extended and further complicated the encroachment of the everyday upon the divine.

Ta'ziyeh Redeemed

The political versatility of the *ta'ziyeh* prohibited its performance under much of the Pahlavi rule. Its image was deemed not in keeping with the image of a modern state. After the Festival of Popular Traditions in Isfahan in 1977, attempts were made to lift the government ban on *ta'ziyeh* performances with the aid of the queen:

> She approached her husband on the matter, and he in turn consulted SAVAK. By that point the religious oppositionist fervor leading to the revolutionary events of 1979 had begun to make itself felt, and SAVAK recoiled in horror at the thought of hundreds of ta'ziyeh performances involving millions of persons being brought to an emotional pitch in a highly moving religious spectacle. Moreover they wished to pacify the conservative mullas opposing the government. Therefore SAVAK sternly advised the shah not to lift the ban and for the months of Moharram [Muharram] and Safar in 1977 a strict prohibition against ta'ziyeh performances was again announced. (Beeman 1982, 366–67)

Although the *ta'ziyeh* tradition lost the popularity it once had under the reign of Nasir al-Din Shah, the Islamic Republic of Iran found the dramatic performance a useful tool in religious, moral, and national regeneration. Not surprisingly, the spatial and temporal tropes of the tradition, and especially the *ta'ziyeh*'s focus on the recollection of the past in light of the quotidian present, seem to appear most forcefully on the screen of the postrevolutionary Iranian cinema. Bahram Beiza'i, whose earlier work for the theater was renowned for incorporating indigenous and Eastern dramatic techniques, has introduced some of these elements to his work for the screen. A *ta'ziyeh* performance appears, for example, in his *Legend of Tara* (1978), and a wrinkle in time awakens the dead for a festive wedding in the film *The Travelers* (1992). In the final sequence of *The Travelers,* the bride effectively enacts a gender reversal and plays the role of the bridegroom, Qasem, from a classical wedding *ta'ziyeh.* The bride's final decision to move forward with her wedding despite the mourning ceremony arranged for her sister's sudden death in *The Travelers* reenacts the key scene in the classical *Ta'ziyeh of Qasem* in which the bridegroom decides to move forward with his marriage in the midst of a wake. Mourning and celebration intermix in this *ta'ziyeh* just as mourning and joyous ululation fill the screen in the final sequence of Beiza'i's film.

The much-lauded tension between realism and illusion, which postrevolutionary Iranian cinema inherits from the *ta'ziyeh* tradition, is sustained by the *ta'ziyeh* performance's reflexivity. The tangible quotidian present and the antiquity of Islam, linked as they are in the *ta'ziyeh*'s deictics, its conception of time and space in recollection, call on the actors and participants of the drama to identify and simultaneously and self-reflexively to disavow their identity with the characters whose lives they perform. What takes place on stage is a happening in the now that is yet to come, a now that really only once may have become. The here and now, the there and then, the real and the imaginary displace each other constantly in the *ta'ziyeh* performance. These deictic shifts that give shape to the play of the real and the phantasmic are at the heart of *ta'ziyeh* dynamics and situate the ambivalent play of temporality and spatiality in some of the most prominent examples of postrevolutionary Iranian cinema. The shift in time and space as the structuring trope of the *ta'ziyeh* enters the cinema of the postrevolutionary period to configure its unique enunciation of time-space coordinates and the cinema's penchant for self-reflexivity: director Mohsen Makhmalbaf's *Moment of Innocence* (1995) and *Gabbeh* (1995), and Abbas Kiarostami's *Close Up* (1990), *Life and Nothing More* (1991), *Through the Olive Trees* (1994), and *The Wind Will Carry Us* (1999) are only some of the most marked examples of the ways in which postrevolutionary Iranian cinema gains in national character through its engagement with *ta'ziyeh* tropes. These deictic tropes are also used to sustain the national character of Iranian cinema against imperial encroachment by standardizing American values in film production in the postrevolutionary period. In the next three chapters, my attempt will be to illustrate the role that the *ta'ziyeh* has played in shaping Iranian cultural modernity by situating its sight lines, its mode of thinking in spatial and temporal terms, enabling it in this way to represent what is otherwise unpresentable. This attempt will also, in part, reveal how the tropes of the *ta'ziyeh,* imprinted as they are on the nation's historical and creative judgments, configure the formal structures that now inform postrevolutionary Iranian cinema, recalling Walter Benjamin's musing that "Modernity has antiquity like one has a demon, which came over it in sleep" (Benjamin 1999a, "Konvolute J").

3

Disciplining Babism

> [T]he "scientific" character of history as defined by positivism . . . is secured at the cost of completely eradicating every vestige of history's original role as remembrance [*Eingedenken*]. The false aliveness of the past-made-present, the elimination of every echo of "lament" from history, marks history's final subjection to the modern concept of science
>
> —Walter Benjamin, "Paralipomena to 'On the Concept of History'"

Chiefly interested in Sufi philosophy, Edward Granville Browne visited, one day in 1882, the University Library in Cambridge only to stumble upon Comte de Gobineau's *Les Religions et les Philosophies dans l'Asie Centrale.* Browne's fortuitous initial contact with Gobineau's *Religions* turned a budding medical student into the disciplinary heir of Western studies in Babism. "I took down the book," Browne writes, "glanced through it to discover whether or not it contained any account of the Sufis, and, finding that a short chapter was devoted to them, brought it back with me to my rooms. My first superficial glance had also shewn me that a considerable portion of the book was taken up with an account of the Babis, of which sect I had at that time no definite knowledge, save a general idea that they had been subject to a most severe persecution" (Browne 1891, ix–x). Browne describes Gobineau's portion of the book on the Babis as a "masterpiece of historical composition, this most perfect presentation of accurate and critical research in [the] form of a narrative of thrilling and sustained interest, such that one may, indeed hope to find in the drama or the romance, but can scarcely expect from the historian" (Browne 1891, x).

In light of so breathless a description, it seems obvious that this book had a profound effect on Browne, who after concluding his medical studies and his appointment at Pembroke College, pursued every trace of the Babi movement in his travels to Persia[1] and other sites around the world.[2] He devoted much time and much effort to collecting manuscripts,[3] translating early historical documents,[4] collating existing manuscripts held in various libraries in Europe and Russia, and writing lengthy articles to the *Journal of the Royal Asiatic Society* in Britain on the history and the doctrines of Babism in English.[5]

1. Browne's trip to Persia lasted from October 23, 1887, to September 27, 1888.

2. In spring 1890, Browne traveled to Famagusta, Cyprus, and Akka (St. Jean d'Acre), later Palestine. He went to Cyprus to visit Mirza Yahya Subh-i Azal, an early Babi and a half-brother of Mirza Husayn 'Ali Baha'u'llah who succeeded the Bab after his execution. From there Browne traveled to Beirut and then to Akka, during this time he met Baha'u'llah, the founder of the Baha'i Faith, and his son Abdu'l-Baha. He acquired on the occasion of his visit a manuscript of the anonymous history *A Traveller's Narrative.* This manuscript was later attributed to Abdu'l-Baha. (Its authorship confirmed as such, the manuscript original is in Baha'i hands). Browne visited Cyprus again in 1896. It was during this second visit that Azal produced for Browne's inspection a document that Azal maintained had conferred apostolic succession upon him after the cruel execution of the Bab (Browne [1918] 1961, 234).

3. See Browne and Nicholson (1932),"Shaykhi and Babi Mss," and also Browne [1918] 1961. Denis MacEoin gives a list of manuscripts presented to or purchased by Browne (MacEoin 1992, 29).

4. In all Browne published six historical documents on Babism: *A Traveller's Narrative Written to Illustrate the Episode of the Bab* (1891; the first volume of *A Traveller's Narrative* contains the Persian text, the second volume is the translation into English and notes); *Tarikh-i-Jadid or New History of Mirza 'Ali Muhammad the Bab* (1893; in translation with notes); *Mujmal-i badi' dar waqayi'-i zuhur-i mani' or Subh i Azal's Historical Narrative* (1893; published and translated as an appendix to *The New History of Mirza 'Ali Muhammad the Bab*); "Personal Reminiscences of the Babi Insurrection at Zanjan in 1850," translated into English and published in the *Journal of the Royal Asiatic Society* 29 (1897); the Persian text of the book he called *Kitab-i-Nuqtatu'l Kaf (Nuqtat al-Kaf),* attributed by him to Haji Mirza Zanjani (see Kashani 1910); the Arabic history written by Mirza Muhammad Jawad of Qazvin called "An Epitome of Babi and Baha'i History AD. 1898" was printed in *Materials for the Study of the Babi Religion* (1918).

5. On the project that Browne started on the Bab's *Persian Bayan,* left incomplete, and the six manuscripts used from various European and Russian libraries, see MacEoin (1992, 3n 5). A summary of the unfinished translation of the *Persian Bayan* is printed in Momen (1987). Excerpts from the text appear in *Selections from the Writings of the Báb* (Bab 2006, 99–146).

A Year Amongst the Persians, the detailed record of Browne's first travels through Persia and his search for the Babis between October 23, 1887, and September 27, 1888, is a tribute to the next-to-impossible task of finding accurate documentation on the Babis and the Bab himself, less than half century after the Bab's cruel execution in Tabriz in 1850.[6] In the course of his travels Browne met a few of the remaining Babis in Persia, many of whom had by then recognized Mirza Husayn 'Ali Nuri Baha'u'llah's leadership and who provided Browne with some early Babi and Baha'i manuscripts, which now make up part of a substantial Persian and Arabic collection at the Cambridge University Library in England.

Browne explains his reasoning for this avid search for answers on the Babis in a letter dated January 1, 1889, to a Persian colleague from medical school, "Mirza Ali":[7]

> I am very anxious to get as accurate an account of all the details connected with the Babi movement as possible, for in my eyes the whole

6. Four months after his initial entry to Persia, Browne meets one day "a vendor of curiosities" *(dallal)* who tells him that he knows the people Browne is seeking: "I was about to remind him that I had not asked him to come, and had only consented to examine his wares at his own request, and on the distinct understanding that by so doing I was not in any way binding myself to become a purchaser, when the younger *dallal* stepped up on to the platform where I was standing, put his mouth close to my ear and whispered, "You are afraid we shall cheat you. I am not a Musalman that I should desire to cheat you: I AM A BABI."

"To this day I am at a loss to account for the motives which prompted this extraordinary frankness. Perhaps some rumour had reached the man . . . that I was anxious to make acquaintance with the sect to which he belonged; perhaps he imagined that all Christians were better disposed towards the Babis than towards the Muhammadans. . . . Be this as it may, the effect produced on me by these words was magical. Here at last was the long desired opportunity for which I had waited and watched for four months.

"All my apathy was in a moment changed into eager interest. . . . 'You are a Babi!' I said, as soon as my astonishment allowed me to speak. 'Why, I have been looking for Babis ever since I set foot in Persia. What need to talk about these wares, about which I care little? Get me your books if you can; that's what I want—your books, your books!'" (Browne 1926, 223–24).

7. Mirza Ali Muhammad Khan (Muvaqqar al-Dawlih), who became the governor of Bushihr and the Gulf ports and later Minister of Public Works, was the father of the prolific writer H. M. Balyuzi, who was one of the biographers of the Bab. Mirza Ali died in 1921. He and his family were exiled to India in 1915 when the British occupied Bushihr.

> seems one of the most interesting and important events since the rise of Christianity and Muhammadanism. . . . I cannot rest till I have sifted the matter to the bottom. . . . I wish very much that while in Persia I could have seen anyone who had seen the Bab or conversed with him . . . if you could help me to collect any more detailed information about these matters, I should be very grateful to you, and I am sure you would be doing a most valuable work, and one which will get more and more difficult every year.—For suppose anyone could tell us more about the childhood and early life and appearance of Christ, for instance, how glad we should be to know it. Now it is impossible to find out much, but in the case of the Bab it is possible, and I feel that now that it is possible it may be neglected, and some day, when Babism has perhaps become the national religion of Persia, and many men long to know more of its Founder, it will be impossible. So let us earn the thanks of posterity, and provide against that day now. (Balyuzi 1970, 14–15)

Browne's untiring engagement with documenting Babi history earned, as we shall see, the respect and spurred the interest of many scholars of modern Middle Eastern and Ottoman history and literature—his methods infinitely emulated, his paths crossed and crossed again, and his work held up as a model by a multitude of scholars of Babi and early Baha'i history.[8]

During term breaks, Browne would travel abroad to collect materials for the historical and literary study of the Babi movement. During one of these trips, Browne journeyed to Cyprus and Akka in spring 1890. In Akka, Browne acquired an anonymously written history of the early Babis entitled *A Traveller's Narrative Written to Illustrate the Episode of the Bab,* which he immediately translated and published in 1891 through Cambridge University Press.

The book, not surprisingly, met with a tempered response in the academic community, which called into question Browne's own reasons and enthusiasm for documenting and translating Babi history. In 1892 Browne's translation of *A Traveller's Narrative* received this scathing review by *The Oxford Magazine:* "For, speaking candidly as a layman, we must

8. Refer to Cole (1998b) for a brief summary of such efforts.

own that the history of a recent sect which has affected the least important part of the Moslem world (nor that part very deeply) and is founded on a personal claim which will not bear investigation for a moment, seems to us quite unworthy of the learning and labour which the author has brought to bear upon it." The book, the reviewer goes on, is an "ex parte statement of trivial history" a "record of not very momentous experiences in easily accessible places like Famagusta and Acre." It is, the reviewer writes, "a laborious and indiscriminate collation of very recent evidence," which "smacks unpleasantly of book-making." Browne, according to the reviewer, "adopts a personal attitude almost inconceivable in a rational European, and a style unpardonable in a University teacher."

> We cannot find that Mirza Ali Muhammad had an Idea to reveal to mankind, any secret whereby Islam was to be rejuvenated: he claimed a "mission" and founded a mystic organisation and a secret society, facts sufficient in themselves to draw after him a crowd of devoted followers in the imaginative East. When examined, this "Bab" was found to be a commonplace pretender, very imperfectly cognisant of the Traditions and the Schools which he opposed: but the simple fact that he did oppose them and suffered martyrdom is enough for many thousand Persians and Mr. Browne. There are no signs that Mirza Ali Muhammad will leave any permanent mark on religious or political history; he has no claim to rank even with Wahháb or the Soudanese prophet; yet Mr. Browne can speak of him in terms not unworthy of the camel-driver of Mecca! Time may vindicate the author: but for the present we can only record our belief that the prominence given to the "Bab" in this book is an absurd violation of historical perspective; and the translation of the *Traveller's Narrative* a waste of the powers and opportunities of a Persian scholar. (Anon 1892, 394)

Time, as this anonymous reviewer writes, did indeed vindicate Browne, whose legacy—the interminable search for the "historical truth as fact"—reverberates in contemporary debates around the writing/righting of Babi history. Indeed, it is precisely his measure of historical perspective and the issues with which he engaged that inform the very paths traveled by many scholars of Babi history. Yet, gravely affected by the review, writes J. B. Atkins in his introductory memoir, Browne "worked off his feelings by constructing a hideous little image of cork which he placed on his chimney-piece . . . and for some time pouring upon it daily execrations" (Atkins 1927, 40–41). The attacks of the reviewers and the pressure by influential people to drop the whole subject matter, coupled with the exceedingly convoluted circumstances and problems preventing Browne from sifting "the matter to the bottom," finally disillusioned Browne to the extent that he dropped publishing work on the movement and left the collation of available Babi manuscripts unfinished.[9]

Certainly one of the most difficult problems was that of acquiring enough material to do a thorough study of the movement's brief history. But the most intricate problem and perhaps the most complex debate, which the legacy of Browne left behind and which still appears to be relevant to scholars of Babi history, is grounded in two very distinct, yet related, set of questions. The first is the validity of academic approaches to Babi history, centering on the issue of disciplinary verses doctrinal interpretation of "given facts" and hence the effort to view the subject of Babi history from either a politicized or a theological perspective. The second is a related issue and perhaps the most involved: the authentication of manuscripts, their authorship, and the valuation of certain historical documents over others. Although serious attempts have been made by partisans on both sides of the debate, neither side seemingly manages to work outside the historically situated positions of disciplinarity on the one hand and dogma on the other, or to attempt in some way to free up the field for a study from within a broader spectrum of cultural and literary criticism. This is an analysis that, in my opinion, the Babi movement deserves, not only because of its relevance to Islamic and Near Eastern studies, but because of Babism's undeniable influence on and role in the production of Iran's modernity.

My attempt here is to trace the legacy of Browne's work in current Babi historiography and, in doing so, to situate the disciplinary mark left

9. See Browne (1892, 706) and also Browne's introduction to Kashani (1910, lii). MacEoin is now completing the translation of the *Bayan*. Parts of these translations are available on the H-Bahai publications website. Excerpts from the text also appear in *Selections from the Writings of the Báb* (Bab 2006, 99–146).

by Browne on the field of Iranian Studies. I will attempt to signal the ways that Browne's early encounters with the Babi materials and his relation to the academy shifted the ground for the academic study of Babism. I argue that this relationship to disciplinarity has constituted the study of the texts relating to the Babi movement as a battle over fact and myth—a battle, in other words, based on the distinctions made between disciplinarity and doctrinal beliefs. This unresolved dispute has for over a century overshadowed nearly every approach to the three major Babi texts published by Browne, with the notable exception of Juan Cole's close reading of *A Traveller's Narrative* in *Modernity and the Millenium* (1998a). The dispute has otherwise hindered a serious study of the Babi movement in ways that would explain its comprehensive engagement with Iranian modernity.

I will attempt to outline a significantly different approach to the study of the "Browne chronicles" and argue for a different intellectual agenda as signaled by the practices of the Babi intellectuals themselves. The concerns I raise will then set the ground for an alternate study of the Babi texts—a study founded on the antidisciplinary site of culture and cultural practice, rather than in doctrine and disciplinarity. In an attempt to free up the field of Babi studies from the disciplining of the text, I will pursue the cultural specificity of the "Browne chronicles" to gain an understanding of their global claims. I pursue this project more rigorously in chapter 4, where I suggest that the cultural specificity of these texts locates an 'otherness within,' an otherness that is the index of the abject in Iranian modernity. It is this index against which postrevolutionary Iran focuses its struggle for identity in the realm of culture and especially in its national cinema. This recognition suggests the global claims that are made possible by reorganizing the terms of the study of Babism from within the field of Babi studies itself. With that in mind, let us turn our attention to the current state of Babi studies and the work of its contemporary Western scholars.

Babi Scholarship Today

In the past three decades numerous books have been published on the subject of Babi history. Two historians following the peregrinations of

Browne have focused their energies on the unearthing of manuscripts and documents related to the Babi movement. Moojan Momen, on the one hand, confident that Western sources may cast a more impartial light in accounting for the events surrounding the early days of the Babi movement, edited in 1981 a weighty collection of Western accounts in the chapter "The Ministry of the Bab (1844–1853)" in *The Babi and Baha'i Religions, 1844–1944: Some Contemporary Western Accounts.*[10] The book is a valuable source of observations by mainly Western commentators either on diplomatic duty or otherwise engaged in work, travel, or research in Iran. In addition, the collection samples a variety of articles on the nascent movement in European papers and journals. On the value of these sources for the discipline of history, Denis MacEoin is correct in observing that the diplomatic dispatches reproduced in this collection refute the common slander that Babism was a subversive movement "created by Western imperialists to destroy Islam in Iran from within. These accusations," MacEoin goes on, "are still repeated in Iranian and Arab polemical literature and amount to something very like blood libel used to justify arrests, confiscations and even murder. None of the materials discovered in Western archives show anything but puzzlement or curiosity as to the origins, purposes and ideas of the Babis" (1992, 133).

The second of those two prominent British scholars, Denis MacEoin, claims for himself the legacy of Browne's unfinished study of Babi history

10. In the preface to this text Momen accounts for the interest and importance of these documents: "(1) They are independent of (and in the case of the earlier accounts, written before the establishment of) mutually opposed and irreconcilable positions of Baha'i, Azali and Muslim scholars. (2) Particularly with regard to the diplomatic records, there can be no justification for statements that the material, once received, has been tampered with or altered—an argument only too readily used about much of the primary historical material that exists. . . . (3) Since, particularly in the case of the diplomatic records, the accounts were written within a short period of the events they describe, they are invaluable for determining the dates of the events. . . . Much of what was written in the way of historical accounts was recorded many years after the events took place. Thus most of *Nabil's Narrative* is the record of what Nabil and his informants at a relatively advanced age could remember of events that had occurred in their youth" (1981, xvi–xvii). Incidentally, for a complete list of *Nabil's* informants see MacEoin (1992, app. 9, 220).

as the grounds for his own scholarship.[11] He has made a number of significant contributions to the field of Babi historiography and has written a more or less comprehensive survey of currently known manuscripts of the works of the Bab, his early followers, and some of the movement's chronicles. This book, published by Brill, is entitled *Sources for Early Babi Doctrine and History: A Survey* (1992). Predictably, MacEoin takes on one of the most provocative and difficult tracks traveled by Browne in the course of examining and translating several of the early and later Babi historical documents. Recognizing the major inconsistencies in Babi historical and theological texts with respect to the questions of historical facts, of their authorship, and of their reliability for historical study, MacEoin's *Sources* supplies a discussion of the available manuscripts in libraries in Iran and abroad. In a lengthy discussion of what MacEoin entitles "Sources for Babi History," he enters into a century-old debate around "the questions of the identity, reliability, and authenticity of" *Nuqtat al-Kaf*.[12] This is followed by a structural comparison of *Nuqtat* and *Tarikh-i-Jadid or New History of the Bab*—the latter a text that is claimed to be a revision of the earlier one. My concerns regarding the continued attempt to "discipline" Babi texts and Babism as a historical movement demands the following background to the debates continued in MacEoin's work.

Besides *A Traveller's Narrative Written to Illustrate the Episode of the Bab*, the authorship of which, he later was assured, belonged to Abbas Effendi

11. See his introduction to *Sources* (1992, 1–7) and his article "Baha'i Fundamentalism and the Academic Study of the Babi Movement," for his response to the refutation of his recent work in the journal *Religion*.

12. McCants and Milani (2004) continue this project by attempting to verify the redaction history of the published version of *Nuqtat al-Kaf* by comparing it to a manuscript of the *Nuqtat al-Kaf* found in Princeton's collection of Babi works. The book was part of Dr. Sa'id Khan Kurdistani's collection. Kurdistani studied as a doctor in Hamadan. He was a Sunni Muslim convert to Christianity who commissioned copies of a number of Babi and Baha'i books. Kurdistani did not recognize his copy as Browne's printed volume entitled *Nuqtat al-Kaf* and instead recorded it as yet another history of Babism. Kurdistani's collection of Babi manuscripts was purchased and later donated to Princeton by William Miller, a Presbyterian missionary in Iran. For more on Kurdistani, see Miller (1969) and McCants and Milani (2004).

Abdu'l-Baha, Browne struggled to find conclusive documentation on the sources for, and authorship of, his two other major "finds" and translations of Babi historiography. In the investigation of these issues, Browne conjectured to provide a means of assessing the date of their completion and thus their value as eyewitness or near-eyewitness sources. Two things stood in Browne's way. First, the authors, fearing for their lives or the public ridicule of their arguments, had been unwilling to acknowledge their contributions.[13] And second, the process of transcription often folded into a process of rewriting, alteration, and thus an unintended coauthorship, which hindered for all intents and purposes the final judgment on who wrote what, when, and under what circumstances. Partisans, immersed in the events of these turbulent times in Iran and in exile elsewhere, attributed various opposing intents to each historical document, further muddying the pristine waters of academic Orientalist research.

The history of the problems associated with two chronicles that were successively published by Browne as *Tarikh-i-Jadid* (1893) and *Kitab-i-Nuqtatu'l Kaf* (1910) have been adequately discussed in great detail, not to mention with great adamancy since before the turn of the twentieth century. These disputes are the subject of MacEoin's review of the "Historical Sources on Babism" as well. The *Tarikh-i-Jadid* (New History), which as its title suggests is a new history of Babism, was supposedly based on an older history of the Babi movement. The latter was written, or so it is argued, by one of the early adherents of the Bab prior to the imprisonment and bloody executions of Babis in Tehran in 1852.[14] This new history and its relation

13. On this subject MacEoin writes: "In a *risala* written in reply to points in the Persian introduction to Browne's edition of *Kitab-i-Nuqtat al-Kaf,* Sayyid Mahdi Dahaji remarks that the early Babi period was so confused that no-one had the leisure to sit down and write a narrative of events as they were occurring. He goes on to say that, after these events, not only had the majority of the main participants perished, but the survivors tended to be reluctant to set down their memoirs for fear of distorting the facts" (1992, 132).

14. A well-documented persecution of the Babis occurred mainly in Tehran in 1852 following the attempt on the life of Nasir al-Din Shah. Browne (1910) indicates the merchant Mirza Jani as the author of the older volume, *Kitab-i-Nuqtat al-Kaf* (3–4). McCants and Milani confirm that the Baha'i scholar Mirza Abu'l-Fadl Gulpaygani attributes the text to Mirza Mustafa, a Babi scribe living in Tehran (2004, 431). McCants and Milani suggest that Mirza

to *Nuqtat al-Kaf* presides at the center of the controversy.[15] Is *Nuqtat al-Kaf* the old history and therefore the source of the new one? Is it something entirely different—perhaps a combination of several texts by different authors? (Cole suggests the latter; see 1998b) Is it a forgery and therefore not really an early eyewitness account? At risk in the debates that followed the unearthing of these documents is the question of the authorship of the texts and the actual dates of their completion, which, according to the participants in the debates, who were divided along partisan lines, would determine the value of the texts as historical sources for the Babi movement prior to the definitive break between the surviving Babis into Azali and Baha'i camps.[16] As William McCants and Kavian Milani argue,

> Dating the text and determining its redaction history is important since it determines how historians can use it. If it was written in the early 1850s and underwent little redaction, then it is one of the earliest internal histories of the Babi movement as well as a valuable window into the confused state of the community during the time it was composed. If it was written later or heavily redacted, then it may be the product of the animosity between the partisans of Mirza Yahya (known as Azal or Subh

---

Mustafa did indeed prepare a copy of the text in his own hand but that he derived his corrections to the manuscript from Browne's published version of *Nuqtat al-Kaf.*

15. An able account of the controversy and further speculations on the directions one could take in order to verify the dates and authorship of these sources is found in chapters 6 and 7 of part 2 of MacEoin (1992, 129–61) and McCants and Milani (2004). Browne takes up the debates in the introduction to *Tarikh-i-Jadid,* (1893, xii, xxxiv–xlvii) and in the introduction to *Nuqtat al-Kaf* (1910, mxii–xx and xxxiv–xlvii). *Kashf al-Ghita 'an hiyal al-a'da* written by mirza Abu'l-Fadl Gulpaygani and completed after his death by his nephew Sayyid Mihdi Gulpaygani, is devoted entirely to resolving the problems and exposing the distortions and discrepancies of *Nuqtat al-Kaf.* In an attempt to do so, Amanat claims (1989, 423–24), it creates more of its own. Again, see further discussion in MacEoin (1992) and McCants and Milani (2004).

16. An Azali is a follower of Mirza Yahya Subh-i-Azal, the half-brother of Mirza Husayn 'Ali Baha'u'llah. Mirza Yahya Subh-i-Azal was regarded as head of the community after the Bab's execution. Baha'u'llah was to establish a new world religion, the Baha'i Faith in the mid-1860s. Azalism was a development that, unlike the Baha'i Faith, was not a new religion but an attempt to preserve Babism with limited changes.

> Azal), the head of the Babi community nominated by the Bab, and those of his half-brother Mirza Husayn Ali (known as Baha' or Baha'u'llah), who began to establish a new religion in 1863. As such, it would be less valuable as a source for the early Babi history, although it could be used to gauge later communal tensions. (2004, 432)

It is the particulars of these debates, buried nearly half a century, that reemerged as a modern battle over the text on the pages of the journal *Religion* almost exactly a century after Browne's initial contact with Babi materials and the decision to pursue a historical line of inquiry. In 1982 and 1983 (issues 12 and 13 of the journal *Religion*) MacEoin published two articles on Babi history making a case for the concept of jihad (holy war) in Babi practice. He grounded this discussion of jihad in one of the early works of the Bab himself entitled *Qayyam'ul Asma* (commentary on the sura of Joseph).[17] In the articles MacEoin attempts to establish links between the ideals laid out in this exegesis and the practice of defensive jihad by the Babis during the Babi struggles in Mazandaran, Zanjan, and Nayriz between 1848 and 1850.

Refutations of the article followed by two Baha'i writers, Muhamad Afnan and William Hatcher, in 1985, in one of the subsequent issues of *Religion,* culminating in 1986 in a rivalrous duet of response to their refutations by MacEoin and a restatement of their position by Afnan and Hatcher. While Afnan and Hatcher maintain that the link established between the text (the Bab's *Commentary on the Sura of Joseph*) and the practice of the Babis during the uprisings in MacEoin's essay is untenable, MacEoin categorically states that Afnan and Hatcher are, in fact, in no position to make that determination. Their article, he says, is motivated "not by strictly academic criteria, but purely theological consideration." MacEoin, in a long litany against his interlocutors, indicates their nonqualification to enter the debates and points to their general and respective academic weaknesses as not having "carried out any independent research," "not having

17. This is, incidentally, one of the early texts of the Bab, translated by Qurrat al-'Ayn Tahirih into Persian (Rabbani 1970, 23). Todd Lawson (1987) includes *Qayyam'ul Asma* as an appendix to his doctoral thesis.

made serious contributions to the field," and "having no understanding of methodology employed in academic work."[18] Taking the attacks one step further, MacEoin points out that Afnan is a professor in clinical bacteriology and infectious disease and that Hatcher is a professor in mathematics. Leaving aside the rather ironic fact that Browne, to whose legacy MacEoin attaches his own, had no modern historical training as such, we could sum up MacEoin's distinctions between his work and that of Afnan and Hatcher as a distinction between the criteria for writing academically on the history of the Babi movement and what is termed by MacEoin the "Baha'i Fundamentalist" attitudes toward "non-hagiographic" readings of Babi history.

In my view, of course, the problem is disciplinarity itself, and a problematic that in different ways informs both approaches to the historical material. MacEoin's perspectives on contemporary academic discourse on Babi history derives its strength, admittedly, from Browne's early attempts to respond to his critics in order to bring academic dignity and acceptability to his line of inquiry. This is a line of inquiry initially inspired, as we recall in Browne's own words on Gobineau, by "a narrative of thrilling and sustained interest, such that one may, indeed hope to find in the drama or the romance, but can scarcely expect from the historian" (Browne 1891, x). This attempt to bring disciplinary criteria and values to Babi historiography has enmeshed the task of modern historians in a web of questions and considerations related to political and doctrinal bias and time-line analyses, relegating Babi historiography to the realm of the age-old tradition of the man and his works.

The limits of this attitude toward history in general have been discussed by Hayden White in several articles. In a 1976 article entitled "The Fictions of Factual Representation," White argues that historical works that claim to represent the bare facts of past events are mere "fictions of factual representation" in the extent to which the discourse of the historian and that of the writer of imaginative fictions overlap, resemble or correspond with each other (21). White argues that if we view histories and novels simply as artifacts, they would be, as Browne's own insights on Gobineau's

18. Juan Cole's Research Note (1998b) includes a similar attack on Douglas Martin.

Religions demonstrate, indistinguishable unless approached with specific preconceptions about "the kinds of truth that each is supposed to deal in" (22). Historicizing the writing of history in the eighteenth century, White argues that the crucial opposition was not between fact and fancy, but between truth and error: "many kinds of truth, even in history, could only be presented to the reader by means of fictional techniques of representation. These techniques were conceived to consist of rhetorical devices, tropes, figures and schemata of words and thoughts . . . identical with the techniques of poetry in general. 'Truth' was not equated with 'fact' but with a combination of fact and the conceptual matrix within which it was appropriately located in the discourse" (24). Based on this historization of historiography, one could argue that rhetorical devices and tropes associated with dramatic epics and epic poetry could be considered part of the rhetorical schematic and conceptual matrix from which many eighteenth-century histories were told.

History as a scholarly discipline in the West took shape in the nineteenth century against "a profound hostility to all forms of myth." Obviously that is the context out of which the *Oxford Magazine*'s criticism of Browne's translation of *A Traveller's Narrative* emerges. And it is well worth noting that contemporary academic dismissals of the text as "hagiographic" and of "little value to the knowledge of history" must be understood in terms of a profound skepticism toward its narrative style and mythologizing bent. There is a rampant dialectic of sorts in these accounts, for while these "myths" constitute the very grounds on which the academic study of the movement must be accomplished, it is the mythic and the poetic approaches associated with it—the unpresentable of academic historiography—that is disregarded by the historians. The academic historiography of Babism has erected its rhetoric behind the veil of scientific knowledge, making its "object"—the text—answerable to a disciplinary discourse incommensurate with it. As John Mowitt suggests with regard to the structural character of texts and the antidisciplinary stance that can be taken in relation to them: "By virtue of its ambivalent structure, the text insists that artifacts mean both what we make them mean and what others might make them mean if we stopped trying to represent their interests for them. Of course, we are in no position to know what this might be, and we have to structure what we do so that it might be pirated by those whose struggle against disciplinarity might well be unrecognizable to us" (Mowitt 1992b, 46).

In "Fictions of Factual Representation" White, further arguing for the similarity between the tropics of the novel and historiography, writes, "Novelists might be dealing only with imaginary events whereas historians are dealing with real ones, but the process of fusing events whether imaginary or real, into a comprehensible totality capable of serving as the object of representation, is a poetic process. Here the historian utilizes precisely the same tropological strategies, the same modalities of representing relationships in words, that the poet or novelist uses" (1976, 28). Nineteenth-century and by default the early-twentieth-century Western historical method, as Browne's own practice is a witness, consists of "'little more than the injunction to get the story straight' . . . and to avoid both conceptual overdetermination and imaginative excess . . . at any price." Avoidance of both, as noted by White, has led to a repression of the conceptual apparatus and the poetic moment in historical writing (1976, 30). A symptomatic reading of contemporary work on Babi history suggests the repression of the mythic in historiography. In the works of the most well-established Babi historical scholars, early and late historical Babi works as well as the oeuvre of the Shirazi prophet (the Bab) are scanned to discover "traces of historical specificity." Who wrote, when? What events took place, where, and when? As one may infer from the McCants and Milani article (2004) on the Princeton manuscript of *Nuqtat al-Kaf,* the answers to these questions are thought to get one to "the real truth of the Babis" from which an objective historical narrative can emerge.[19]

Without categorically dismissing these serious and valuable contributions to the field of Near Eastern and religious studies to which my own work is greatly indebted, I will briefly observe that perhaps the main problem with this dream of scientific inquiry in historical discourse is not that these data are not available through this kind of reading, but that the

19. McCants and Milani ultimately argue that a redaction history such as theirs may suggest whether a text is a more or "less valuable source for early Babi history" (2004, 432).

answers to these questions are already caught in a fabricated, mythical web that suggests their relationships. Not surprisingly, Denis MacEoin deems *A Traveller's Narrative,* "on the whole, of extremely limited value to the student of early Babism. . . . The style is of course, hagiographic and rather loose, yielding little in the way of solid information and nothing that seems to be based directly on documentary or eye-witness evidence" (1992, 170). Abbas Amanat comments that "it adds little fresh information to the knowledge of the early [Babi] period. Perhaps more significantly, from the viewpoint of style and approach, it was an effort to write an account that could justify the Baha'is' stand while avoiding the highly committed language of other Baha'i polemics" (1989, 424). In other words, the early Babi historical narratives themselves reside within a web of traditions whose "fresh information" to quote Amanat, cannot be separated from their polemical, poetic, dramatic, mystic, partisan, or hagiographic styles to which historical scholarship has objected. It is my argument that this "constitutional instability" of texts must be allowed to pressure the discipline beyond its current limits.[20]

One of the most stirring passages in the early historical narrative *Nuqtat al-Kaf* will allow me to demonstrate this argument more adequately. In the appendix attached to his translation of *Tarikh-i-Jadid,* Browne half translates and half paraphrases, in his typical style, a passage on the activities of Qurrat al-'Ayn in Karbala, Iraq, in 1845. He does this to somehow supplement *Tarikh-i-Jadid*'s inadequate reading. This passage recalls the period after Qurrat al-'Ayn's acceptance of the Bab's early claims during a time in which she was actively engaged in lectures presumably on her understanding of the Bab's mission. The passage, which reads true to the *Nuqtat al-Kaf*'s Persian version, goes as follows:

20. John Mowitt defines cultural artifacts as texts in as much as they are "constructs of the interaction between a signifying practice and a methodological field." The text "arose at the point where several disciplines sought to reorganize themselves around an object which eluded each of them in different ways." This alterity present within the text suggests its ambivalence as an object. "The text is simultaneously shared by several disciplines, while also exposing those disciplines not merely to the borders they share, but to their limits as formations of disciplinary power" (1992b, 44–45).

> Her lectures at Kerbela [Karbala] were attended by women as well as men, the former being admitted within a curtain which separated her from the male portion of her audience. . . . It appears that it was not so much the scruples entertained by her and her followers as the legality of meats procured from the bazaars . . . that attracted the attention and called down the disapprobation of the Turkish Government, as the claim advanced by Kurratu'l-'Ayn that she was a "manifestation" *(mahzar)* of the Prophet's daughter Fatima *and that any unclean thing was rendered pure by being submitted to her gaze.* It appears also that (probably as a consequence of these pretensions) the chief Mufti of Baghdad nearly determined to put her to death. (1893, 356; my emphasis)

What is interesting about this passage is that it contains numerous possible historical "facts" about Qurrat al-'Ayn Tahirih's popularity among the followers of the Bab and about her new students in Karbala; students who were, importantly, part of a heterosocial group. Further, the passage shows that she spoke, in this period, from behind a curtain that enshrouded herself and other women, separating them from the men who also attended her lectures. The passage elaborates on Qurrat al-'Ayn's claims regarding her own identity as the "manifestation" of Fatimih. The text maintains that a ceremony of ritual purification was held in order to clean the meats purchased by the Babis at the public bazaars. Clearly these are "facts" that an able historian could reconfigure into a historical narrative that elaborates on Qurrat al-'Ayn Tahirih's practices and early claims in the Babi community.

Abbas Amanat reads the original of this passage for these facts and produces the following narrative:

> Qurrat al-'Ayn's actions complemented her theoretical position. On the one hand, she questioned and in many instances rejected the soundness of the practices of past generations in the matter of legal injunction *(furu)*; on the other, by emphasizing the imminent advent of a new prophetic cycle she sharpened the distinction between believers and denouncers. In what amounted to a symbolic protest, she enjoined her followers not to buy food from the market, because people who denounced the Bab were infidels and therefore eating their food was unlawful—no doubt a

> defensive response to the pressure on the Babis, who were now rejected as unbelievers. She justified her new prohibition on the basis of the Bab's assertion that since in the state of "initial truth" of the Fourteen Infallibles she stands as the manifestation of Fatima . . . her sight is purifying. She ordered the Babis to bring all the food to her, so that by her purifying sight she could make it suitable for use. (1989, 303–4)

Using the same source, MacEoin argues for the historical significance of Qurrat al-'Ayn in Babism's abandonment of entrenched Shi'ite and, more broadly, Islamic practices and finally the abrogation of the Shi'ite *shari'ah* (religious law) itself in Badasht.

It seems, however, that no matter how much the issue is rationalized in terms of doctrinal or chronological evidence (which, as I have argued, has been the basis of much modern academic research on Babi history) the fact remains that neither the *Nuqtat al-Kaf*'s version of the events in Karbala nor the modern narratization of it will explain the past to us free of poetic license. The citation of its "truths" remains imbedded in a web of traditions and poetics.[21] (Did her gaze really have magical powers? To what extent did she believe herself to be the reincarnation of Fatimih?) I submit that the historical sources that provide different descriptions of past events cannot be weighed, judged, or accepted purely on the basis of factual reliability. In fact all sources, however contradictory, would make claims regarding what they report to be the truth about what happened. But what is fundamental to the understanding of these texts (I am referring to primary sources, but this applies to the modern readings of them as well) is that rather than explaining the past to us with a list of facts, their narratives *organize* our field of vision and place us in a position from which the writers or recollectors themselves understood the events that they thought were taking place. It is not that certain events did not take place, but that their telling for the presence of writing must

21. And this regardless of McCants and Milani's verification that whereas "the exact identity of the author and the scribe" of the *Nuqtat al-Kaf* copy found in the Princeton Babi collection "is still a mystery," this text, which is of an early provenance, is not "drastically different from Browne's published text" (2004, 449).

by necessity represent that "taking place" through a poetics of reckoning (or discourse).

In his discussion of this act of ritual purification in Karbala, Amanat suggests that the "eyesight of the clan of God, is symbolic of their will, upon which rests the prohibition or confirmation of religious command" (1989, 304). With regard to this specific passage, why not then consider this mythic context for the understanding of Qurrat al-'Ayn's role and presence in Karbala as understood by the author(s) of *Nuqtat al-Kaf*? Would this not be more "factual" in describing the way in which the author(s) directs our attention and constructs our methodological field, that is, not to what actually took place (which in any event remains subjective), but to how what might have happened in Karbala was perceived by the author or authors or by others like them?

From the perspective suggested by Amanat, we could infer that those with a claim to divine inspiration are thought to create purity or goodness through their will. Persian literature is full of the idea of good created through the operation of (divine) will. This will is actualized as a gaze, a touch, a word, a dream, and so forth. Specifically related to this passage is the poet Hafiz's celebrated verse: "Those who turn soil to elixir with their gaze / would they gaze upon us from the corner of their eyes?"[22] In this historical context where the gaze is understood as the expression of divine will, and in a time and place where this idea literally consumes classical literature, it is expected and not merely understood that anyone with a claim to divine inspiration, such as Qurrat al-'Ayn, would allege (however poetically) to possess such a purifying and regenerative gaze.[23]

In reading early narratives and recollections of the nascent Babi movement, it is impossible to miss the propensity among writers to use dramatic stylistic tools to describe the events that they experienced.[24] Mulla

22. There are similar verses by Abu-Sa'id Abu'l-Khayr as well as other Sufis. My thanks to Ahang Rabbani for drawing my attention to this poem.

23. The Bab substantiates this stance in his much-circulated work *Furu al-Adliyya* translated into Persian in the Karbala period by Qurrat al-'Ayn herself (his statements regarding the power of the gaze appears in chapter 7 in Arabic, and in chapter 13 in Persian).

24. White, of course, points toward the poetic moment in historical writing. I use his argument here to write about the dramatic tradition. The *ta'ziyeh*, which is fundamental to

Muhammad Shafi' Nayrizi's memoirs provide one such instance. The poetic moment in this Babi chronicle places the historical. The memoir spans the childhood recollections of Nayrizi and his family's involvement in the two Babi upheavals in the city of Nayriz. Here the cultural discourses of the month of Muharram (the *rauzeh,* the *ta'ziyeh,* and the processions) flow through his text, position it, and validate it as legitimate history.

In this chronicle, Nayrizi is operating on the basis of a culturally accepted norm—a norm disseminated through the dramatic performance of the *ta'ziyeh* passions and the *rauzeh*s. Nayrizi's chronicle can be understood if we accept the premise at work throughout the narrative: that one may, in the historical representation of recent happenings, draw poetic parallels with events that have taken place in the past. (This past for Nayrizi and his contemporaries is the heroic antiquity of Islam.) Further, one may see oneself, one's activities, and those of others in one's company as a reenactment, a return or a resurrection of past characters, past happenings and past tragedies. These allegorical tools create synthetic confluences between the past and the present. These spatiotemporal confluences are implicit deictic elements of the *rauzeh*s and of the *ta'ziyeh* dramatic structure. Mulla Muhammad-Shafi' Nayrizi, as a chronicler of the Nayriz uprisings, is operating on the fundamental assumption, then, that his readers know the function of some basic cues, namely that history can and does repeat itself, and that the past can put on the garb of the present and in this way enliven the present moment.

One of the common tropes and cues of the *ta'ziyeh* performance is, in fact, the putting on of the burial garb by the actor who plays Imam Husayn. Ritually, when this actor puts on his white shirt in the course of the *Ta'ziyeh of Imam Husayn,* the crowd starts to mourn. This gesture, not the actual slaughter of the character, Imam Husayn, is the climax of the performance and the signal to the audience that Imam Husayn is making the ultimate sacrifice on behalf of the pious Muslim (Wirth 1979, 36).

Nayrizi's narrative rhythmically marks the pages of history with signs that have profound meaning for participants of the *rauzeh khani*s and the

---

my analysis of Babi history, is recited almost completely in poetic meter. Fittingly, only villains, the supporters of Yazid, speak in prose.

spectators of the *ta'ziyeh* stage, namely his contemporary readers. This marking is made apparent in the segment of the narrative where he writes about his hero's entry into Chinar-Sukhtih quarter, where the Babi leader, Vahid, gives a speech at the Masjid-i Jami'. In response to Vahid's moving speech and in acknowledging his warnings about the dangers involved in responding to his battle call, Nayrizi records the following dramatic event: "the crowd (as a mark of willingness for self-sacrifice) spontaneously placed burial garbs over their shoulders, unsheathed their swords and readied the guns."[25] For the informed reader, the death of Vahid's supporters is made inevitable and imminent through the poetics of the text. In this passage the Babi leader, Vahid, like the legends of Imam Husayn as reenacted in the *ta'ziyeh,* foresees the future of his actions. Prophetically, he warns his companions of the consequences. Thus, by activating narrative cues, Nayrizi's recollections of the Nayriz uprisings create direct cognitive links between the early history of the Shi'ites and the history of the Babi movement, mimetically in fact, in a nonteleological manner. Just as Imam Husayn's small clan is cut off from water by his enemies, so are Nayrizi's heroes. The text goes further to designate the key players of the Nayriz tragedies as the reenactors of the characters who suffered great losses in the catastrophe at Karbala.

Witness, for example, the following passage, where Vahid is negotiating with the enemy troops: "'However as you have cut our access to the water, should you immediately relinquish control (over the flow), then all is well. Otherwise, be warned, that this very night I will see to it that water should flow freely.' (In reply,) the Khan sent a second messenger, saying, 'If you are the Prince of the Martyrs [Imam Husayn], then I am . . . Shimr. I will not allow you or your companions a drop of water.'"[26] Nayrizi does not merely imply a conjunction between the antiquity of Islam and the historical present, he puts the words of recognition in the dialogues exchanged between the warriors of his dramatic history. The Karbala traditions, then, are fundamental to grasping the context in which the Babi events were understood. They supply the times and

25. The Nayrizi passages are from chapter 5 of Ahang Rabbani 2007.

26. Note that "Shimr" here is the name of Caliph Yazid's representative at Karbala.

places toward which the recollectors of the Babi events aim to direct their reader's gaze.

It is with an understanding of the prevalence of these cultural, deictic, and allegorical tropes of the Karbala drama and the cultural representations associated with the passion play that I will read the "Browne chronicles." I aim to locate the recollections of Qurrat al-'Ayn's unveiling in Badasht within them.

Qurrat al-'Ayn's unveiling in Badasht emerges as a mythic moment that only exists in the fragments of other historical manuscripts as remnants of shock or utter disgust, but that nonetheless suggests a significant revolutionary potential in the guise of poetic license, pious reverence, or psychological torment. Qurrat al-'Ayn Tahirih emerges in later narratives and references (1873–93) to this period as the prototype of Iranian modernity in her discourse, in her interpretation of Bab's work, and in her characteristic attempts to break from the confining limits of Shi'ite Islam. In my reading, I will note the absence of the moment of her unveiling in the "Browne chronicles" and attempt to situate the reasons for it.

My aim in this admittedly limited project is to show the ways in which the reform-oriented chroniclers of Babi history orchestrate a device that cues the subject toward a specific position from which the otherwise anamorphic image of the past is momentarily resolved. They do so by the citation or rather by the siting of the temporal index embedded in the past. In reading the Browne manuscripts, I use the term "anamorphism" to account for the orchestration of sight lines and lenses, which align and focus the encounter between the historian and the image of the past.[27] In Walter Benjamin's essay "On the Concept of History" (2003a), such a historical orchestration aims at a momentary resolution of visual ambiguity by means of epistemological and spatiotemporal privileged points

27. The term "anamorphism" is used by extension of its historical sense in Western painting, where it refers to the incorporation within the composition of a painting of a blurred or distorted section that, when viewed from an oblique perspective, resolves into a figural image of some type. The momentary resolution of the image takes place at the site of the reckoning subject. This implies the fundamental relevance of the moment and place of the encounter and its critical urgency for the present.

(not unlike anaphora) that must be grasped in a flitting flash—as if with the click of a camera. The resolution takes place in the writing and in the process of coping with the particular and arrested moment of the past and the index within it that is destined for redemption.

If for Benjamin, as Ian Balfour has argued, reading and citation are the modes for understanding history, this reading of the past is a particular kind of reading. It is actualized in the writing of the historian who, in that encounter with the past, grasps with it a present that is inseparable from it. For Benjamin the past cannot be read from the standpoint of progress in which time parades in the figure of a homogeneous empty time. It must be reckoned with, performed, and actualized, as the present ("now-time") that is shot through with chips of messianic time. In this reading of history, the past carries with it an index that has a claim on the present. This index is the cite or site—the anaphoric point—through which the sight lines of the historian are focused from a particular and critical spatiotemporal positioning and through which the image of the past gains clarity. The gesture of representation does not reduce the past to a finite citation that gives the past its clarity for all time. The image remains blurred. It is the historian's position in relation to that index that clarifies its urgency by constituting its particular link to the present and, in the present, to an unforeseen future. It is in reckoning with this infinite sense of urgency in the present that every moment of the past becomes citable for a redeemed mankind. In reckoning with the past, the newest day of the chronicle becomes the awaited Day of Judgment. As my discussion of the *ta'ziyeh* has emphasized, this historical perception filters through the drama's own. As such, this perception of the historical plays a vital role in the constitution of the methodological field that is the study of Babi history.

The Future of Babi Studies

In my discussion of the debates surrounding the Babi texts, I have implied that the field of Babi studies is in need of a different kind of intellectual and a different sort of "historical" practice. While my conception of this historiography is informed by Benjamin's anaphoric temporality, a temporality I associate with the Karbala passions, I take my cues from Foucault on the kind of new intellectual I envision. I acknowledge, of course, the problems associated with this affiliation.

Writing against the contemporary practices of historiography, Foucault brings discontinuity to the writing of history. He spatializes history and sees breaks where others would produce continuities. In 1966 Jean Paul Sartre discredited Foucault's *Order of Things* as the work of a structuralist enemy of history. Sartre argued that Foucault's archeological labor was unable to explain how people move from one thought to another. In order to explain that phenomenon, Foucault would have to allow "praxis and thus history to intervene, and that's precisely what he refuses to do" (Flynn 1997, 324n. 9). Foucault rejected Sartre's labeling and claimed *contra* Sartre that his aim was "to substitute *different types of transformation* for the abstract, general, monotonous form of 'change' which so easily serves as a means for conceptualizing succession" (Foucault 1991, 56). Foucault argued that he was instead "substituting for the theme of *becoming* an analysis of transformations in their specificity" (56). Benjamin's historical approach "resolves" the dispute between Sartre and Foucault through the "dialectical image" as a model for history, a model that deals with the temporal without resorting to teleological progression. In this regard Keya Ganguly writes that for Benjamin:

> dialectical images performed an anaphoric function in that they made it possible for the historian to signify history and its inscription. In this conceptual scheme, the burden of representation is on intuiting "possibility" rather than establishing "truth." Reckoning with history is a mode of reading, of shuttling between constitutive and constituted discourses. That such a system of relay is brittle or disjunctive is evoked by the severity of Spivak's image of "violent shuffling"—the figurative tenuousness of the "Third World woman" located between disappearance and presence, historical possibility and factitious objectivity. (1996, 171–72)

Historical thinking for Benjamin assumes image form. Its model is the photographic image that in his view assumes "a magical value, such as a painted picture can never again have for us" (1999b, 510). In such pictures, Benjamin finds "the tiny spark of contingency, of the here and now with which reality has (so to speak) seared the [the photographic] subject." In this spot, he locates the index of the past, "where in the immediacy of the long-forgotten moment the future nests so eloquently that we, looking back, may rediscover it" (1999b, 510). This past that reveals itself to technology and that inscribes itself on glass plate or paper is an inconspicuous site—an index—revealing a space in which "human consciousness gives way to a space informed by the unconscious" (1999b, 510). Thus, historical writing, focused as it is on the momentary clarity of a flitting image, reveals, like the photographic image, "image worlds, which dwell in the smallest things," making as Benjamin points out, "the difference between technology and magic visible as a thoroughly historical variable" (1999b, 512). The written historical moment is a moment grasped—a moment in which the ur-past and the present form an urgent configuration beyond the horizon of continuity and progress, not unlike the forms captured by Karl Blossfeldt, who, in his plant photographs, Benjamin remarks, "reveals the forms of ancient columns in horse willow, a bishop's crosier in the ostrich fern, totem poles in tenfold enlargements of chestnut and maple shoots, and gothic tracery in the fuller's thistle" (1999b, 512). The spatialization of the temporal in history informs a practice to which Foucault might attribute an antidisciplinary stance, and it is within this stance that he would locate the figure of the specific intellectual.

In a 1976 interview entitled "Truth and Power," Foucault gives shape to his vision of the new intellectual (which is distinguished from the Gramscian organic intellectual) in his discussion of the "specific" (as opposed to the "universal") intellectual. He claims in the interview that it is in part the confrontation with the judicial and police apparatuses that creates a new configuration of contact and affinity between the intellectual and the proletariat. This conjunction in the conditions of interest between the two classes gives the specific intellectual a new revolutionary significance (Foucault 1980, 126–27).

Foucault dates the emergence of the specific intellectual to World War II and the scientific work of Oppenheimer, but in the figure of Darwin he acknowledges the possibility of the existence of the specific intellectual prior to this moment (1980, 129). Regardless, what Foucault is eager to develop is the specific position of the intellectual within the local conditions of his/her field of study and his/her link to "the general functioning of the apparatus of truth" (132). The urgent task facing the intellectual based on his/her specific position in society, according to Foucault, is the reorganization of the systems of power and knowledge that enable the production, regulation, distribution and the operation of statements. Foucault sees the task of the intellectual as one involved in the reconstitution of the systems of power that reify the hegemonic production of truth. Recognizing truth as an antidisciplinary object, this is a task with global consequences. It affects, through the institutions and the technologies that hold them together, the very specificity of the local field of investigation, as well.

My understanding of "antidisciplinarity"—a term elaborated by John Mowitt in several of his texts—arises out of this discussion of the specific intellectual. As I have already indicated, the term antidisciplinarity defines a practice that is involved in the transformation of the intellectual's approach to knowledge through the specificity of his /her objects of research. Antidisciplinary practice, according to this formulation, transforms not only the field of study and its techniques, but constitutes a critique of "disciplinary reason as such" (Mowitt 1992a, 185). As "a critical practice seeking to problematize the cultural work effected by the disciplines," the practice of the specific intellectual in approaching his/her object of study involves a disruption that makes the object "oppose the discipline(s)that made it" (Mowitt 1992b, 14). Recognizing that the specificity of a practice "derives from the institutional field that surrounds it," antidisciplinary research, Mowitt predicts, "requires that readings reach from within artifacts to the paradigms that govern their interpretation and beyond these paradigms to the structures of disciplinary power that support them" (1992b, 216–17). Antidisciplinary work involves the specific object in the reconfiguration of the global field.

There are many examples in the history of the Babi movement that point to antidisciplinary practice on the part of its most notable membership and its intellectuals. Before I move on to elucidate some of these activities and discuss their relevance to the study of Babism, I would like to recall the image of Shaykh Ahmad Ahsa'i and the Shaykhi school that in reality served as a center from which the Bab drew his earliest disciples.

Shaykh Ahmad (1753–1826) was a native of Eastern Arabia, educated in Bahrain and the theological centers of Najaf and Karbala in Iraq. He also lived and traveled in Iran, where he received the patronage of the Qajar princes. He was invited by Fath 'Ali Shah to reside in Tehran, but he feared that his commitment to justice for ordinary people would eventually lead to him conflict with the court (Cole 1997, 2). In her biographical study, Mangol Bayat underscores Shaykh Ahmad's propensity for solitude and meditation (1982, 37). Shaykh Ahmad's theological knowledge, his dreams, and his mystical relation through them to the Imams, were a source of attraction for his followers. In Najaf and Karbala the leading *mujtahid*s awarded him a license to teach and to function as a spiritual guide. While dispensing with much within traditional conceptions of Shi'ite Islam, Shaykh Ahmad maintained "an extremely complex relationship with his immediate intellectual heritage" (Cole 1997, 2). This positions him at a crisis point between the position of the old "universal intellectual" and the constitution of the "specific" one.

It is in the figure of Shaykh Ahmad that we begin to see a very peculiar move within the scholarly circles of Shi'ite Islam—a move away from a desire for universal knowledge and disciplinary involvement, toward a certain form of expertise. The shaykh's biography underscores his persistent refusal to learn the traditional sciences necessary for him to have a position within the priestly class. The Bayat biography stresses, in particular, the shaykh's rejection of the study of grammar and philology in order to concentrate on theology proper (1982, 38). This categorical rejection of the basic disciplinary rules for access to theology in Shi'ite Islam suggests that already in the faint beginnings of the Babi movement there was, within its future membership, a concentrated resistance to the disciplinary structures informing the theological practices of the time.

Although not formally a student of the shaykh, the Bab himself became a victim of relentless criticism on the basis of his nondisciplinary learning. One of the reasons for the rejection of his claims among the leading *ulama* was his lack of traditional disciplinary knowledge and his failure to follow the rules of Arabic grammar. In part, this claim arose from the Bab's interrogation in Tabriz, where representatives from the clergy and the government were present. The purpose of the trial was to discredit the Bab and to demonstrate the heretical nature of the movement to the public.

According to the documents available on the "consistory," the Bab opened the session by proclaiming his Mahdihood and proceeded to solicit the allegiance of the trial's participants to his cause. This infuriated the *mujtahid*s (scholars of Islam), who began an aggressive line of argumentation. The *mujtahid*s asked him for his miracles and proofs, to which the Bab responded that his proof was his word and went on to extemporize a passage in Arabic. The tribunal's report to Muhammad Shah records this unexpected recital with awesome irony and self-aggrandizement:[28]

> Then I asked him "What hast thou of signs and miracles?" He replied, "My miracle is this, that I can cause verses to be revealed for my staff," whereupon he began to recite the following words:
>
> *In the Name of God the Merciful the Forgiving. Glory be to God the holy the Glorified, Who created the Heavens and the Earth as He created this staff, as one of His Signs.*
>
> But according to the rules of [Arabic] grammar he wrongly vocalized the word Samáwát (Heaven) as Samáwáta. They said: "Make its [final] vowel i." Then he recited the word al-Ard (the Earth) also with the [final] i. (Browne [1918] 1961, 254)[29]

28. Of nine sources consulted by MacEoin, six claim that this incident happened. Apart from the Bab's claim to Mahdihood (nine out of nine), this is ranked high in plausibility by MacEoin (refer to MacEoin 1997b for a list of sources).

29. Mamaqani's *Namus-i Nasiri* gives a slightly different account (quoted in MacEoin [1997a, appendix]): "My late father said: 'Your name isn't unique to you. On the strength of what you say, shouldn't anybody called 'Ali Muhammad or Muhammad 'Ali be considered a Lord apart from God?'

"No reply could be heard. Then he put his hand to his ear and said: 'Listen. I shall reveal a verse: "Praise be to God Who created the heavens and the earth,"' putting the vowel 'a' at the end of the word 'heavens' *(samawat).*

"His majesty said: 'You don't even know the rules of Arabic grammar. "Whatever takes its plural in ta' and alif is vocalized with 'i in both accusative and genitive."'

"Bab: 'Listen: "And he made the sun and the moon,"' vocalizing the shin of shams [the sun] with 'i.

"The onlookers exclaimed: 'You've made a mistake. Why do you put the vowel "a" where you should have "i"'?"

MacEoin writes the following about the Bab's Arabic and the answers he gave on this occasion: "No-one who has read his books and letters in that language will deny that the

Having ridiculed the Bab for his failure to master Arabic syntax and orthography, the official report claims that the tribunal proceeded with the interrogation, asking questions on the hadith (Islamic traditions) and jurisprudence, including questions, as Amanat notes, on "some ludicrous problems of sexual purification."[30] Numerous questions on geography, astronomy, and medicine followed (1989, 391). The Bab apparently answered some questions with a declaration of ignorance; others he plainly ignored.

Browne's documents on the Babi religion include a copy of a fatwa addressed to the Bab sometime after the trial. The fatwa establishes the Bab's apostasy on the ground of the charges admitted by him at the trial. It closes with these words that question the Bab's sanity: "[The] only thing which has caused the postponement of thy execution is a doubt as to thy sanity of mind. Should this doubt be removed, the sentence of an incorrigible apostate would without hesitation be executed upon thee" (Browne [1918] 1961, 259).

The official report on the Bab's trial, despite its significant divergence from other reports, flags the issue of disciplinarity in bright colors. The triumph of disciplinary power, as we have learned from Foucault, lies in its ability to define subjects intimately on the basis of their specific features and to situate them along a normalizing scale, open to infinite judgment.[31] The official report to Muhammad Shah also makes it clear that

---

Bab's Arabic was idiosyncratic; nonetheless, they are very far from being the products of someone who could not decline *qala* (or even says *'qala*? What *qala'*?) or vocalizes *al-samawati* as *al-samawata*. The Bab had a relatively sophisticated grasp of Arabic, and it is hard to imagine him mumbling and stumbling his way through a series of easy questions on grammar."

30. Mamaqani's *Namus-i Nasiri* reports the following: "Nizam al-'Ulama' said: 'You, sir—what's the meaning of these words of 'Allama: "If a man should have intercourse with a hermaphrodite, or a hermaphrodite with a woman, ablutions are obligatory for the hermaphrodite, but not for either the man or the woman." Explain the mode of this ruling, and what was 'Allama's thinking.'

"Bab: 'I've already said that I have not studied religious law.'" (quoted in MacEoin 1997b, appendix)

31. For Foucault's definition and discussion of disciplinary power refer to his *Discipline and Punish* (1979), but also his significant later articles and interviews (1980, 1981, 1991).

from the standpoint of both the theological and the dynastic institutions, the Bab's claim can only be judged on the basis of its proper functioning within the dynamics of this web of power/knowledge, that is, his insertion into the classical disciplinary scene. In the scene of the examination, any claim to Mahdihood must encompass and surpass what is considered documentation of higher learning, namely, the *mujtahid*'s own. For what use is a Mahdi, if he cannot produce any miracles besides the word? If the claim to Mahdihood is not followed by signs of disciplinary reason and documented in describable form, it must be marked as apostasy and its bearer's sanity put to question. Reason, if we are to derive it from the case made against the representative of its other (i.e., the Bab), is imbedded in the sciences of Arabic grammar, geography, astronomy, and medicine. The failure to perform within the constraints of this disciplinarity would by necessity demand a judgment of insanity.

Rather than look at this episode from the psychologizing perspective of the Bab's failure to perform within the set directives of disciplinary power and reason, as some have done, or even simply to place this event within a corresponding logic of victory and loss, I think it is more fruitful to discuss the events within the dynamics of antidisciplinarity. For it is, after all, disciplinarity more properly that is at stake. In what follows, I will argue that the kind of linguistic combat witnessed in the descriptions of the trial are linguistic manipulations played out on an uneven playing field of syntax. For let us recall the following: during his trial the Bab performs the proof of his claim by speaking a phrase in Arabic. Midway through his sentence he drops the 'i' at the end of the Arabic word for Heaven, committing a strict error in classical Arabic grammar. His questioners correct his mistake, but in correcting himself, the Bab persists to add an 'i' where it does not belong. In this sense, from within the proper field of Arabic, the Bab makes a tactical move that disrupts the disciplining and disciplinary field of Arabic grammar, questioning the relevance of disciplinarity itself on a more global scale. Syntax becomes a weapon in and indispensable part of an antidisciplinary combat. Most of the Babi partisans explain these "errors" in terms of the Bab's disinterestedness in worldly knowledge. They maintain that the power of his verses, despite his lack of institutional learning, is proof of the miraculous coming of the

Mahdi. Setting aside these claims, however, the semiotic mishaps at the Bab's trial can be read as fragments of a more general combat played on the field of Arab hegemony. As "ways of speaking" they signal, in Michel de Certeau's terms, "a way of operating" within and against the general domain of Shi'ite discourse (Certeau 1988, 39). MacEoin, in fact, compares the proceedings to an elaborate game:

> But it is equally easy to see that we are, in fact, witnessing the acting-out of a sort of unrehearsed play, or the playing of an elaborate game. The Bab's behaviour, even as reported by the hostile accounts, may have been deliberately designed to convey a range of symbolic meanings. Here, for example, is someone claiming to be the Mahdi, yet his opponents insist on his declining Arabic verbs or answering questions about veterinary medicine. A dignified silence, or perhaps a statement to the effect that he had studied some grammar as a child but since forgotten it might well be seen as responses designed to point up the inappropriateness of the line of questioning being taken. And we should not forget that the Bab himself, taking his cue from popular notions of the Prophet Muhammad's illiteracy, made a point of saying he was a merchant by training, not a divine. Hence the difficulty of interpreting almost anything the Bab is reported to have said and done during this session. (MacEoin 1997b)

A game, perhaps, but my argument is more pointedly that whereas under conditions of danger and fear some Babis seem to give up combat and resort to a game of *perruque,* a practice that Michel de Certeau exemplifies in terms of a worker doing his or her own work on company time, a kind of chameleon camouflage that is similar to the traditional Shi'ite practice of *taqiya* (dissimulation), at other times they do not. In my reading, Babi tactics seem to get their strength not, as de Certeau (1988) might claim, from within a biological context of camouflage, a weapon of the weak, but from within their specific locations, their situation or position as intellectuals within the apparatus of power and knowledge—a situation that they eventually confront, affecting in this way a global configuration of power and knowledge. In taking this position, I implicitly support Foucault's later discussions of power, and especially his American essays and interviews (such as "The Subject and Power"), in which he clearly defines disciplinary power not as a repressive instrument, but as a predominantly productive one. Power, defined by Foucault as "actions on others' actions," presupposes, rather than annuls, the capacity of agents, and acts upon and through them to construct an open set of practical and perhaps even ethical possibilities within the field of power.[32] This formulation enables a discussion of the Babi intellectuals' antidisciplinary practices from within the Foucauldian *dispositif*, from within the apparatus of knowledge and power itself. This said, let us return to the field of antidisciplinary combat.

One substantial attack on Arab and Shi'ite hegemony by the Babis from within the apparatus of Islamic knowledge and power must be characterized as a combat of time over space typified by the adoption by the Babis of a new calendar. During his brief career, the Bab introduced a new calendar that his followers appropriated as a replacement of the old Islamic one. The Babi year, divided into nineteen months of nineteen days, celebrated the first day of the spring as the New Year—the ancient equinox observed by Persians since pre-Islamic times (Browne 1926, 367). In adopting this new calendar, the Babis reinscribed the revolution of time in terms of ancient Persian astrological beliefs, situating the subject's activity within a new logic of Persianness. In this calendar each of the nineteen days were given a separate name, thus circumventing and "bungling" the traditional relation between everyday practice and time's unfolding. This was a specific transformation on the level of personal practice that influenced the global perceptual field.

In addition to the reinvention of time, the Bab substituted the old Islamo-Arabic understanding of space with a new Persianness. The old centers of pilgrimage in the Arab world were replaced by new ones in Iran (Bayat 1982, 108). His residence at all times became the *qibla* toward which his followers turned in prayer. Such a substitution reoriented the pious body and situated it within new geographic boundaries.

The Bab wrote many books, including letters of advice, mystical poems and prayers, and a number of treatises in which he elucidated religious

32. For a thorough reading of Foucault's discussion of power after *Discipline and Punish,* consult Gordon (1991).

questions of the past and prophesied the coming of "Him Whom God Shall Make Manifest" *(Man Yuzhiruhu'llah).* Yet the *Persian Bayan* was adopted by the Babis as the Most Holy Book, preferred over all other texts written by the Bab in the Arabic tongue (Bayat 1982, 108). Writing, that is, the repository of memory and tradition and theological knowledge, was thus imbued with a new, specifically national air. Browne cites that in one of his many encounters with the Babis during his travels in Persia, a group of Babis showed him samples of a new script developed by the Babis themselves. Browne calls this new script the *Khatt-i-badi* or "new writing." This new writing, he claims, "bears some superficial resemblance to the Armenian character. Each letter consists of a thick oblique stroke descending from right to left, to which are appended various fine curves and flourishes, all thick lines being parallel and equidistant (1926, 359–60).

In these three examples of antihegemonic, and more specifically antidisciplinary, combat, two very distinct moves can be suspected. The first is a move away from hegemonic and specifically Arab practices and toward a local substitution: toward a Persian definition of time, a Persian constitution of sacred space, a specifically Persian form of writing. Significant here is that all three practices played a decisive role in the articulation of Iran as a nation and made claims in the nationalist discourses of the Constitutionalist movements around the turn of the century. Here are specific transformations activated within the field of disciplinarity with global effects.

The second move in each example demonstrates a transformation and a fixation of the first in a different register. Time is rerouted on a particularly local, Persian, calendar, but it is altered to activate another dynamic. The body is reoriented in space. It is relieved of its fixed directionality toward the *qibla* and, owing to the Bab's constant movement, given an almost nomadic quality within a given, more properly Iranian, geographic boundary. Writing and memory are detached from their hegemonic relation to Islamic Arabic and situated in the context of the national. As such, both writing and memory are then fixed within a separate, new, Persian script.

These simple but strategic attacks on Islamo-Arab hegemony provide us with a context for studying the ways in which particular Babi intellectuals intervened in the structures of power and knowledge in order to dismantle, from within their own specific areas of expertise, what they considered an imperiled disciplinary hegemony.

Among many of her self-dictated agendas, for example, Qurrat al-'Ayn Tahirih took on the task of confronting the Shi'ite traditions. On several occasions she is said to have ridiculed her fellow Babis' practice of *taqiya* (dissimulation), claiming that this practice was motivated by fear (Bayat 1982, 111). Mulla Muhammad Khurasani recalls a conversation with Qurrat al-'Ayn Tahirih in which she makes an unequivocal statement regarding her views on *taqiya:* "She asked me 'Do you know why I summoned you?' I replied 'No.' She said 'I was previously given the responsibility for the authority *(wilaya)* of Mulla Baqir, and I made it incumbent upon all of you to accept it. Yet no-one accepted it from me, with the exception of fourteen individuals, seven men and seven women. Now I shall present you with something else.' I said 'What is that?' She replied 'It has come upon me, through the tongue of my inner mystic state *(bi-lisan al-bal),* not through physical speech, that I wish to remove all concealment *(taqiya)*" (quoted in MacEoin 1979, 214).

This tradition of dissimulation in Islam, *taqiya,* a practice I earlier related to de Certeau's notion of *perruque,* was thought of as a means of concealing one's true views. It was considered by theosophers as the "highest and most necessary of virtues," not unlike the practice of female veiling. The Shaykhi school where Qurrat al-'Ayn had received part of her training taught that the practice of *taqiya* was necessary, owing to the limited capacity of the ordinary believer. The secrets and true meanings of religion, the school argued, could not be grasped by the ordinary individual (Amanat 1989, 56).

Qurrat al-'Ayn's extraordinary refutation of *taqiya* was not only aimed at Shi'ite orthodoxy but was also directed at the democratization of attitudes within the heterodoxy from which she emerged as an intellectual. It arose from a set of local and specific interests and preoccupations, yet it had significant importance on the global scale. In waging an antidisciplinary struggle within the specificity of her own intellectual interests, Qurrat al-'Ayn Tahirih's attack on the hegemonic traditions of Shi'ism converged with the interests of the "universal." Her rejection of the practice of religious dissimulation confronted the lines of power separating "the ordinary believer" from statements that, because of their linkage within systems of power—to disciplinarity, in other words—were only accessible to the religious intellectual. This kind of practice (Qurrat al-'Ayn's) is attributed by Foucault to the practices of the emergent "specific intellectual"—a scrupulous antidisciplinary stance on the part of Qurrat al-'Ayn.

In one of her well-known poems, Qurrat al-'Ayn Tahirih envisions her own project (what I have identified as that of a specific intellectual) of antidisciplinarity in relation to the systems of power and knowledge:

> Truly, the Morn of Guidance commands the breeze to begin
> All the world hath been illuminated; every horizon; every people
> No more sits the Shaykh in the seat of hypocrisy
> No more becomes the mosque a shop dispensing holiness
> The tie of the turban will be cut at its source
> No Shaykh will remain, neither glitter no secrecy
> The world will be free from superstitions and vain imaginings
> The people free from deception and temptation
> Tyranny is destined for the arm of justice
> Ignorance will be defeated by perception,
> The carpet of justice will be outspread everywhere
> And the seeds of friendship and unity will be spread throughout
> The false commands eradicated from the earth
> The principle of opposition changed to that of unity.
> (Translation by Susan Stiles Maneck and Farzad Nakhai in Afaqi 2004, 260)

Similarly, in an address to her comrades on the issue of religion and justice, Qurrat al-'Ayn is said to have emphasized the importance of human responsibility for change in similar terms: "O people, there is no resurrection except that resurrection which you institute in the way of truth [or regaining rights or administering justice]. Paradise and hell for you are in this world" (Fischer and Abedi 1990, 231).

The Babi intellectual discourses, such as those of Qurrat al-'Ayn Tahirih, suggest that the movement's appeal relied on its membership's constant effort to wrest knowledge from its entanglement with a disciplinary and hegemonic system of power. Its appeal, though specific to the constitution of Shi'ite Islam in Iran, was one of political and intellectual urgency, as significant to the field of Babi studies today as it was to the Shi'ite society it confronted in the nineteenth century.

There is a great lesson here for those of us who in the study of Iranian modernity must encounter issues that have emerged within Babi historiography as part of modern Iranian history. This lesson must necessarily push the scholar well beyond the vale of historical facts and figures and the verification of some truths over others. One part of this lesson is precisely that the Babi scholars of Shi'ite Islam and of the Bab's texts approached their specific area of knowledge in a way that had global consequences for the circulation of knowledge and power. These effects in turn reflected on how the Babi intellectuals themselves continued their specific studies of the Bab's text and formed their practice of Babism. They studied their objects in a way that reconfigured the study of Shi'ite Islam, indeed did so in ways that breached the established disciplinary system of power and knowledge (the *shari'ah*) and rooted knowledge in completely different channels. Time, space, writing, even the traditional practice of *taqiya* were reconfigured or abandoned. These antidisciplinary labors had consequences for how the Babi intellectuals defined the study, the recognition, and the practice of the Bab's own work.

In my view, current scholarship dedicated to the study of Iranian modernity, of which Babism is a core component, must learn from its "object," so as not to re-erect the disciplinary and rhetorical "veils" that have proven themselves ineffective over time. I see the early presence of these veils in Browne's blindness to what was going on in his own objects, that is, in the works that he himself translated and published around the turn of the century. It is clear that although he saw these texts as narrative histories, the texts themselves constituted emergent visions of reform in Iran by attaching themselves to the revolutionary tropes of the *ta'ziyeh.* Throbbing with life, these reform tracts envisioned new political and social systems and were grounded in expansive landscapes that revaluated intellectual practice. Browne's insistence on principles of disciplinary conformity is, without doubt, responsible for the century-long oversight of the significance of the labor in these texts. It is the lack of attention to the antidisciplinary labor within the texts and within the antidisciplinary practices of the specific intellectuals who made up the nascent Babi community that has made Babi studies a battleground over the authentication of the text on the one hand and the authenticity of its authority on the other.

In the chapter that follows I attempt to outline the cultural context for some of the earlier narratives translated and published by Browne, trying in this way to wrest the field of Babi studies from the stranglehold that disciplinarity has had on an essentially antidisciplinary object. It is to culture, then, that I return, as it is this site that has been cleared so that particular disciplinary and doctrinal studies of the movement could flourish. My attempt will be to unpack the ways in which each of the Browne narratives orchestrate the reader's sight lines. I will then show how each narrative, in its particular and topical articulation of the Babi movement, saw in it an index that bore an urgent relevance to the conditions of the time—an index by which it was referred to the redemption of Iranian modernity. This gesture recognizes a significant difference in historical practice, one rooted in the concept of redemption. In my own historical practice, then, I adopt the redemptive model that is deeply upheld by the *ta'ziyeh*'s historical articulation and recalled—redeemed, in fact—by the early chroniclers of the Babi movement to capture the present of Babi action. To reenvision the field, I return to the "Browne chronicles" in search of a practice appropriate to the field from within the texts themselves. That this gesture of antidisciplinary "rewiring" has global consequences implies that contemporary hegemonic representations of Iranian identity are at stake.

4

Resurrection, Return, Reform, Revolution

> For Benjamin, the truth of history does not involve the representation of an "eternal past" but rather the production . . . on an image. This truth of history is performed when we take the risk of making history rather than assuming it to belong only to the past. It happens, in other words when we understand historicity as a kind of performance.
>
> —Eduardo Cadava, *Words of Light*

Although the title of this chapter is inspired by the title of Abbas Amanat's now classic history of the nineteenth-century Babi movement, its concerns are in essence different. Its aims, rather than being a discussion of the history of Babism itself, are to reflect on the theoretical conditions or modes of witnessing that, I will argue, structured the engagement with that history by some of the movement's contemporaries and early inheritors. This chapter assumes that historiography is a representation of events, but one informed by what Walter Benjamin called "the idea of redemption." A redemptive history recognizes that "[t]he past carries with it a secret index by which it is referred to redemption" (Benjamin 2003a, 390). Redemption informs historiography because that known, that desired, or that vision of a utopian future already understood underlies the writing of the past. The past thus returns in recollection only in the guise of the known but unredeemed past, not in the robe of the unknown. For what can a chronicler of history say of a series of events that to him or her are like no other? The chronicler can represent the occurrences of his or her time only in so far as he or she can cast them in the mold of a previously known time—one envied or desired—or in the shape of experiences in which the chronicler has already been embroiled.

This conception of the temporal is precisely the reason for the use of the persistent prefix "re-" in the chapter title. It is there to signal that sense of taking place again, of a repetition of an action, but also of that ambiguous notion of "making," "turning or converting into," "fitting," or "furnishing" the possibility of something else inherent in the etymology of the prefix. Thus to *re*present is to make the past present again, as a *re*-turn, a *re*surrection, a *re*form or as a transformation of the old by way of a *re*volution. For most of the early Babi chroniclers, the stage of the *ta'ziyeh,* as the copied form of the Karbala plains, furnished the possibility for representing—for making present—Iranian modernity's unpresentables in embodied form.

Ta'ziyeh, the spectacular dramatic performance of early Muslim history, which reached the height of its popularity during the middle of the nineteenth century, supplied the model for the witnessing of the Babi chroniclers' present. It was an annual cultural occurrence by which the revolutionary claims of the Babi movement were understood. In this chapter I will argue that the *ta'ziyeh* as a mode or limit of the historically understood furnished the conditions for the representation of the Babi movement's essential features in early Babi historiography. Though concerned to elaborate on the details of the events that took place under the auspices of Qurrat al-'Ayn Tahirih in Badasht and the movement's ultimate break with the *shari'ah* in that garden landscape, we will note that most chronicles fall silent, marking the historical unpresentability of her acts. The central question of this chapter is then: How did these chronicles represent the unpresentable?

Three particular texts are of interest here, all of which were published thanks to the persistence of the British orientalist Edward Granville Browne: the *Nuqtat al-Kaf, A Traveller's Narrative Written to Illustrate the Episode of the Bab,* and *Tarikh-i-Jadid* (known as *New History of Mirza Ali Muhammad—the Bab*). These three texts, although supported by the history of the Babi movement, use the narrative of its history to argue for various social, political, and moral causes in constituting Iranian modernity. The texts engage current literary tropes to cope with the past and make it legible for the present. The literary tropes that inform this manner of thinking out and coping with the past in the present of writing articulate the redemptive and abiding sense of the present as the reenactment of a sacred or secular history. This notion is more specifically evident in a style of writing, whether political, historical, or theological, in the period immediately following the execution of the Bab and of the killing and violent persecution of the majority of his followers. In particular, one would want to point to writings of some of the greatest reformist thinkers of the era, such as Mirza Fath 'Ali Akhundzadih, Mirza Husayn 'Ali Baha'u'llah, Muhammad Hasan Khan Itimad al-Saltanih, and Abbas Effendi Abdu'l-Baha, who in the four decades between 1850 and 1890 time and again modeled their reformist writings along the formal lines of the popular *ta'ziyeh* drama and the Karbala eulogies. Although different in their suggestions for reform, each reflect on sacred or secular histories to promote their vision of change for modern Iran. These modern reflections adopt a model for the witnessing of historical events that recall earlier times, redeeming them in order to reflect on what "could have happened if not . . . ". What could have happened *now* if the message of Imam Husayn to the people of Kufa had not been intercepted? What could have happened if Imam Husayn had won the struggle with Yazid's troops in the plains of Karbala? And also, what could have happened if Iran had not accepted Islam? What could have happened if Persia had followed the route of France? The *ta'ziyeh* structure, in reflecting on the past in the present, redeems the past in light of the cultural variables of its time. The *ta'ziyeh*'s structure, its temporal and spatial modes, more than its historical contents, produce this effect. While casting the audience as the mourners, mourning the events of the past, the eulogies' temporal and spatial tropes fit the *ta'ziyeh* participants into the mold of the supporters of Imam Husayn in the present and everyday. In redeeming the past in this way, the *ta'ziyeh* performance transforms the audience into the promoters of a new revolution in thought and calls on them as activists in the reform of the present nation.

Ta'ziyeh as a Model for Historiography

Resurrection

Of the Babi historical narratives that Browne published, *Nuqtat al-Kaf* (literally, *The Point of K*) is considered the earliest record of Babi historiography and therefore perhaps one of the first Babi records of the momentous break with the Shi'ite *shari'ah* at the Badasht Conference.[1] Recognizing the present as the Day of Judgment, *Nuqtat al-Kaf* reviews Islam's antiquity and the Shi'ite traditions. It thus proceeds to examine the prophesies related to the Day of Resurrection. The text provides proofs of their fulfillment in the historical and heroic acts of the Babis. Hence, the text engages for the most part in an effort to elaborate on the Qur'anic verses, exegesis, and hadith related to the traditions of Resurrection and Return before pursuing an elaborate chronicle of Babi history. The literary style of *Nuqtat al-Kaf* on the history of the Babis is characteristic of the dramatic resurrection of the historical messianic time and space of the early days of Islam. The text casts the Babis as actors in the tragedy of Imam Husayn as represented in the popular style of the Karbala eulogies.

Written circa 1852, the *Nuqtat al-Kaf* renders Babi history as a resurrection of the Karbala story. Every moment of the Babi present is shot through with the chips of messianic time. *"Al-yaum,"* the Arabic word for "the day," "the present," the most recent day, becomes the subject of a day prophesied—the Last Day, or the Day of Judgment. Browne takes note of the stylistic devices employed by *Nuqtat al-Kaf* in the following account: "Teheran is compared to the capital of the wicked Mu'aviya and his yet more wicked son Yazid; while Mulla Husayn is likened to the martyred Imam Husayn, Sheykh Tabarsi [Shaykh Tabarsi, the site of a bloody battle between the Babis and the Qajar troops] to the immortal plain of Kerbela and Barfurush whither the Babi captives were brought after the conclusion of the siege to Kufa" (1893, xvii; my addition). Recognizing the significance of historical happening in the Babi present, the *Nuqtat al-Kaf* situates within the past the index from which it can be understood as having been resurrected in a potent and revolutionary present. Ignoring the specificity of geographic frontiers, frontiers that later became important to land-based debates among reformers and intellectuals who were preoccupied with the fate of Iranian modernity, *Nuqtat al-Kaf* notes, "whenever the banner of the Truth is set up, summoning men to defend it, and the people of Truth are gathered together, and the word of Love and Emancipation *(fená)* is spoken, there is the land of Kerbela" (Browne 1893, 337; 1910, 170).

1. Refer to Juan Cole (1998b) and to McCants and Milani (2004).

In recognizing the moment that is indexed for redemption (the time of the raising of "the banner of Truth"), the text casts the Babis as its redeemers: Karbala, detached from its grounding, returns in the phantasmatic time and space of the present (Browne 1910, 169–71). The Prince of Martyrs (Imam Husayn) himself is returned in the Babi figure, Mulla Husayn, as on the reputed Day of Resurrection. He, on that day, arises to be denied once again by the evil opposing troops. The hidden Imam, the Mahdi, too, arises to champion the meek Imam for the last time on Judgment Day.

Historically, this stylistic device has been a feature of the *ta'ziyeh* drama and the Muslim eulogies that disperse versions of the Karbala tragedy throughout the body of the nation during the month of Muharram. In casting the modern Shi'ite Muslim in the mold of the past, these narratives, not unlike the *Nuqtat al-Kaf,* call for revolutionary and redemptive acts by the Iranians. "In the course of the agitation which led to the granting of a constitution in 1906, the Qajars were sometimes compared to or even identified with the hated Umayyads, while the struggle for a constitution was decreed as being 'like a Holy War under the command of the Hidden Imam,'" writes MacEoin (1982, 100). Similar moves are evident in descriptions of the *rauzeh-khanis* (eulogy readings) held under the Pahlavi rule close to a century after the collapse of the Babi movement:

> A few days prior to the 1963 riots and demonstrations against the Shah a rauzeh sermon was given by Sayyad Mahmud Taleghani during the Muharram. "In loud emotional voice, Taleghani turned to the audience and . . . quoting Husain said, 'You have written letters to me and promised to help me and stay beside me [referring to the people of Kufa]. If you are still willing to keep your promise, I am Husain, the son of Ali, and the son of Fatima who is the daughter of the prophet.' From the phrasing and particularly the direct quote from Husain in the present tense, there is little doubt in the mind of the audience what is being asked for . . . namely support of the ulama (Husain's spiritual heirs) against an oppressive government." (Thaiss 1972, 360)

In establishing the Islamic Republic, Khomeini likewise played on the temporal tropes of the Karbala eulogies to form his legitimacy as the ruler of Shi'ite Iran. As early as the 1960s, Roxanne Varzi explains, Iranians were preparing for the Islamic revolution in anticipating the return of the hidden Twelfth Imam on Judgment Day: "many in the general public were convinced that the nation must rise up and prepare for the coming of the imam, even if that imam was not officially the hidden imam [the Imam Mahdi]. Khomeini played on the popularity and expectation of the hidden imam to derive legitimacy directly from the people. Eventually, Khomeini allowed his proper name to be replaced with the title imam, and it was this title that he took to his grave. He did this by redefining the modern Shiite conception of imam, by first demystifying it and later by picking up on the mythic and mystic notion to give himself absolute power" (Varzi 2006, 37–38; my addition). While these gestures involved the reinterpretation of the *shari'ah,* they also required the more important temporal link to Shi'ite antiquity and the mimetic return of the sacred body of the Mahdi in the present and in the figure of Khomeini.

Given the historical persistence of this temporal maneuver, we can safely claim that the Karbala story constitutes the traditional context for revolt and popular uprising in Shi'ite Iran. Its comparatively meager basis in histories such as that of Tabari, and its elaborate development into *rauzeh*s and Muharram passions in Iran seem to provide a uniquely national character to the story that appeals to the national conscience (Browne 1924, 188). Its retelling signals the urgency of the present. The temporal configuration produced by its repetition calls its audience to collective and national action. It gives the promise of the ultimate redemption to those who support and rectify the wrongs suffered by the meek Imam (Imam Husayn) and also to those who grieve his worldly defeat in the present. *Nuqtat al-Kaf* understands the Babi instance of messianic "return" in terms very similar to the contemporary understanding of *ta'ziyeh* dramatic practice and the *rauzeh* in the middle of the nineteenth century. Like the *ta'ziyeh* role-carrier, who denies his direct association with the characters he plays as he portrays them on stage, the *Nuqtat al-Kaf* defines the Babi return negatively as being neither incarnation *(hulul),* nor absorption *(ittihad),* nor transmigration *(tanasukh)*; "it is as it is, and none knoweth it save those who have returned" (Browne 1893, 338; 1910, 170).

The sense of "return" in the text points up the ambiguity in the etymological roots of the word "return" as an act of coming back, a fact of recurring, or coming around, a renewal of a condition that is neither an absorption of nor an incarnation of the past, but rather, in geographical terms, a bend, which brings one back to a prior place. What this notion of "return" in *Nuqtat al-Kaf* suggests is a sense of return associated, in contemporaneous culture, with the dramatic *reenactment* of history in the final sequence of the *ta'ziyeh,* when all things manifest themselves in their perfection (Browne 1910, xviii). The history in *Nuqtat al-Kaf* functions as a witness to a theatrical reckoning with previous historical events and constructs from this positioning a theory of the Babi movement's urgency in the present. The author writes that Mulla Husayn, like Imam Husayn, knew of his death before he died (172); that "[t]he one who arises after 1000 years demands of the people to avenge the blood of Husayn" (171); and that in Shaykh Tabarsi, the Babis did what they did in Karbala (171). As such, *Nuqtat al-Kaf* posits Babi history as a Resurrection of Shi'ite Islam's antiquity.

Return

The *Tarikh-i-Jadid,* Browne's second translation of Babi history, dates to 1879,[2] twenty-nine years after the Bab's execution. According to Denis MacEoin's discussion of its recensions, this history was based on "an early version written by one or more persons based on an 'old history' (i.e., *Nuqtat al-Kaf*) and borrowing devices of writing under the persona of a foreign traveler in Iran from Akhundzadih's fictitious correspondence between the imaginary princes Jamal al Dawla and Kamal al Dawla" (1992, 159). As such, the author of *Tarikh-i-Jadid* posits his identity in numerous, sometimes contradictory terms and implies in various sections that he is a Christian (Browne 1893, 3), a European (17) a Frenchman (318), and not a Persian (23). His expressions sometimes imply that he is a Babi but claims that he utilizes the titles used by the Bab's followers as a way "to show respect" for one who "suffered martyrdom by reason of his love for his nation and his attempts to admonish and regenerate them" (30).

2. Browne claims an earlier date, 1873 (1893, xxxiii). I am basing this date on MacEoin's discussion of the text's recessions.

At one point, the author describes himself as a geographer who travels to various cities and villages to describe the geographical features of each (24). The text foreshadows in this remark a development within reform circles that were focused on national frontiers, a development that was inaugurated by the court luminary I'timad al-Saltanah and his interest in Iranian geography and territory in the 1890s in *Durar al-tijan fi tarikh bani ashikan.*[3] The author of *Tarikh-i-Jadid* also identifies himself as a religious scholar, recording doctrines and principles (Browne 1893, 26). Finally, he claims to be an unprejudiced historian who seeks accurate information of circumstances, practices, and doctrines of any sect (27).

In the preface to this text, the author, identified as a foreigner not unlike the fictional Kamal al-Dawla, proceeds to recount the ills of the nation. He contends that the problems of the nation are fostered in the bad habits in which the Persians "are rooted and which are against their nature." *Tarikh-i-Jadid* catalogues these habits as falsehood, hypocrisy, and injustice (Browne 1893, 5–8). The author argues that "if they [the Persians] desire to please God and his prophets, regenerate their faith, restore to their creed its pristine lustre and if they are to render their country and state once more free" and to prevent decline and remove the obstacles to progress, efforts must be made to improve on their habits (5–8). The *Tarikh-i-Jadid* bases its arguments on the Qur'an and the traditions. Referring to these texts, it argues for the reproachability of contemporary national habits. The text also compares the illness of Persia with the ills of some of the European nations in the past. It notes that Italy was recently similarly afflicted and indeed sought and found a solution to the problem. The men of learning assembled to deliberate on their plight and to "investigate the cause" of their affliction (6). "After due thought and deliberation," *Tarikh-i-Jadid* notes, "they discovered that this [affliction] was wholly traceable to the influence of the Pope, who in their country represented the supreme spiritual authority, declaring himself to be the vicar of Christ. He, like the divines of Persia, withheld men from acquiring useful arts and accomplishments or amassing wealth by senseless injunctions, in proof of which he would adduce sayings of great and holy men whereof he had wholly

3. See Firoozeh Kashani-Sabet (1999, 40–41).

failed to apprehend the true purport" (6). The text claims that despite the Pope's admonitions against material and worldly preoccupations, the people of Europe developed astronomical instruments and tables and saw remote "celestial orbs," which they beheld "with the eyes of sense":

> [H]owever, when the wise men of Europe and the people of Italy had proved the extent of His Holiness the Pope's hypocrisy, guile and deceit, they exerted all their energies, and notwithstanding all his power and the subjection in which he had hitherto held all the sovereigns of Europe, so effectually deposed him and his children and grandchildren that naught remained of him but the name and appearance, nor did anyone thenceforth pay the slightest heed to a single word which he wrote. After this they employed themselves in spreading the triumphs of Art, Commerce, and Political Reform, until in a little while they became objects of emulation to all their fellows and contemporaries. (7)

Drawing on a fictive history of a Europe that was distinguished for its progress, the preface implicitly calls for a similar strategy of change in order to confront the problems now embroiling Persia: to overthrow the clergy, the main inhibitors of the cause of progress in Iran, and to implement political and social reforms.

Situating a humanist rhetoric alongside medical and scientific prescriptions elaborated to rid the national body of its ailments, the text attributes Europe's progress to the apprehension by the wise of the virtues of affection and concord that has "devoted [them] to the devising of such appliances as may serve to lessen the sufferings of God's creatures or conduce to their prosperity and comfort, whereby also the glory of the State is increased" (15). Among these "appliances," the *Tarikh-i-Jadid* suggest the invention of the steam engine and a mechanism for the administration of justice:

> Thus was the power of steam discovered, whereby thousands of factories of different kinds were set in motion, many precious and wonderful goods produced, and prodigies of workmanship hitherto undreamed of accomplished. The land was delivered from the thraldom of desolation and disorder, the people were freed from sloth and poverty, the nation

> waxed rich and the state strong. Governments ceased to depend on oppression and injustice as a means of acquiring revenue and the practice of extorting money by threats and promises fell into disuse. Every effort was made to secure equal justice for all, and every exertion put forth to perfect the mechanism of the administration. . . . Thus they made progress in every direction and became objects of emulation to all around them. (15)

The railroad, as one of Europe's inventions, is hailed by the *Tarikh-i-Jadid* for bringing prosperity to the country and freedom to the people, "leaving none within its sphere of influence poor or unemployed" (16). The *Tarikh-i-Jadid* suggests that the prime minister of Persia had recently decided to introduce this means of progress to his nation. However, "in this design he was vigorously opposed by the doctors of religion, who stirred up people against him by telling them that the increased influx of Europeans which would result from the proposed innovation would infallibly bring about the spread of infidelity and the downfall of religion "(16). In fact, the author claims, these statements against the railroad were actuated by the clerical fear that the people would become acquainted with the world around them, and thus would not obey the clergy blindly.

Distinct historical circumstances, writes Kashani-Sabet, gave shape to many such humanist tracts in nineteenth-century Qajar culture. "Though influenced by Enlightenment and Positivist models, Qajar intellectuals created a unique vocabulary of humanism that derived also from their country's specific experiences, especially its religion and its sociopolitical climate. They stressed fields such as hygiene, medicine, and geography in their desire to learn about themselves and their evolving society" (2000, par. 4). Drawing on examples from Mirza Aqa Khan Kirmani's *Sih Mktub* (Three treatises), a text composed in the late nineteenth century and one that illuminates *Tarikh-i-Jadid*'s search for "a civilizing process" in Iran, Kashani-Sabet argues persuasively that "the themes of humanism and civilization often went hand in hand [in Qajar political discourse]. Humanism became the catchphrase for pursuing progressive reforms aimed at restoring what was seen as Iran's pride and former grandeur" (par. 7; my addition). Thus the *Tarikh-i-Jadid* concludes that if the author dwells on the praises of Europe, "it is from no mere desire to extol his compatriots

[Europeans] but in hope that thereby I may arouse the spirit of emulation in these people [Persians], incite them to acquire these good qualities and induce them to desist from injuring and destroying their fellow countrymen" (Browne 1893, 17).

Having encouraged its readers to act on the European prescriptions for progress, the text suggests that the claim the Bab advanced was "a great one" and notes that the Bab was a man of great heritage, "of illustrious descent and a Sayyid of the people." He was a man who suffered martyrdom because of his love for his nation and his attempts to "admonish and regenerate them" (Browne 1893, 30). In the name of progress and in a move to associate the Babis with such regenerative values, the author maintains that "in Europe the name of such a man is not mentioned slightingly, but accounted worthy of honour" (30).

In the body of the text, *Tarikh i-Jadid* casts the activities of the Babis in a mode similar to that of *Nuqtat al-Kaf.* More preoccupied with the bloody confrontations between the Babis and the government armies, *Tarikh-i-Jadid* draws on the stories about the battle between Moses and the pharaoh as represented in the verses of the Qur'an to elucidate the events that took place in the Mazandaran uprising. In a letter said to have been written by Mulla Muhammad Ali Barfurushi (known as Quddus) in response to Prince Kuli Mirza,[4] Quddus calls for a reasonable discussion and argument to settle their difference. If this is deemed unacceptable by the prince, Mulla Muhammad Ali Barfurushi Quddus suggests a *mubahilih.* Finally, he is said to write: "if this content them not, let us kindle a fire and enter in to the midst thereof, that the truth or falsehood of either side may be made apparent without the shedding of blood or the slaughter of God's servants" (Browne 1893, 61).[5] Three distinct suggestions regarding the resolution of the problems are made in this letter, mimicking very

4. Based on a copy of the manuscript in his possession, Dr. Ahang Rabbani claims that this letter was actually written by Mulla Husayn.

5. The call for a *mubahilih* is as follows: "If not, then let us invoke God's curse on whomsoever is in error, leaving to Him the decision" (Browne 1893, 61). For the significance of *mubahilih,* see Corbin (1971–72, 210–13). The ordeal by fire is a pre-Islamic tradition that is found under the episode of Siyavush in the *Shah-namih.*

distinctly the manner in which *Tarikh-i-Jadid* itself produces its suggestions for reform: (1) enlightened discourse in the European manner; (2) *mubahilih,* a traditional religious resolution of problems by drawing on the wrath of God; (3) pre-Islamic traditions of ordeal by fire. Through this letter, the author calls on Prince Kuli Mirza to deal justly with the Babis, as the pharaoh did with Moses, implying that the Bab and the Babis are the return of the prophets of old (61–62). This reference to Moses in particular seems to be a rather palimpsestic reference that situates the Babis as Moses and his people, in his defiance of the pharaoh as a civil authority, as well as the pharaoh's priests (clerical authority).

The author then maintains that the Babis were misrepresented to the government because of the false ideas promoted by the Muslim scholars of the time. Adopting devices commonly employed by the *ta'ziyeh* cycle, the *Tarikh-i-Jadid* recounts the historical confrontation between the government troops and the Babis in Shaykh Tabarsi with the following: "Mulla Husayn began to fight even as Husayn fought at Karbala, and to mete out to the enemy the recompense for what they had done" (Browne 1893, 68). Because of the use of this stylistic device, the revenge, it seems, is not only cast as one directed at the present-day troops of Prince Kuli Mirza, but is portrayed as a retribution claimed for the wrongs that Yazid's army inflicted on the Imam Husayn and his family. The text thus situates Babi history within what one might call "a fold in time." Its implications for the contemporary audience of *Tarikh-i-Jadid* is evident: the injustices rained on the Babis as the return of the people of the third Imam, Imam Husayn, must have significant national consequences for a people whose religious conviction and national distinction defines them as opposed to those who stood by the unjust Caliphs. In the *Tarikh-i-Jadid,* then, the Babi period as a return of antiquity is inserted into an unfolding Shi'ite history. The Babis role is to replay, once again, the scenes in Karbala and to appeal from this position to the injustices inflicted on the people of the Imam. This appeal calls directly on the nation, whose national identity as Shi'ite is constituted as the supporter of the meek Imam (Imam Husayn) against the unjust Caliph. Even when claiming to quote directly from the *Nuqtat al-Kaf,* the *Tarikh-i-Jadid* makes an effort to insert instances that emphasize the Bab's intuitive powers and premonition, constructing the

Bab's identity as a man of miracles.[6] This is seen as an important quality for a man who claims to be the Mahdi (the return of the twelfth Imam, to whom Imam Khomeini attached his own title). Doubly ensuring the applicability of the appeal to the reform-minded and popularly engaged Shi'ite population, the *Tarikh-i-Jadid* expounds on the story of Karbala and the sacrifices of Imam Husayn. A speech attributed to Mulla Husayn clearly suggests his return as the Prince of Martyrs, Imam Husayn, the most honored of Shi'ite martyrs:

> For this it was that the Chief of Martyrs, together with his supporters and adherents, stood firm in the plain of self-sacrifice, and bore active witness to the truth, for the guidance of mankind and the establishment of the faith; whereby, long years after the consummation of their martyrdom, the Law of the Prophet matured, and the ordinances of his holy religion established. And now we likewise, for the awakening of our fellow-men, be they rich in virtues or beset with faults, intelligent or heedless, wise or simple; for the removal of the doubts and objections of the obdurate; and for the admonition of the careless and indifferent, are constrained by the good pleasure of the Beloved to bear witness by our deeds to the truth of this new revelation, to prove our sincerity by disregarding all earthly considerations, to undergo sufferings transcending human imagination and endurance, and to lay down life itself for the establishment of this great truth and the perfecting of the proof to our perverse and benighted opponents. Know, then, for a surety, that once arrived in Mazandaran all paths of escape will be closed to us; that we shall without doubt be slain with most grievous torments; and that the land beyond Barfurush shall be dyed with the blood of these our comrades. Indeed our supreme object is pressing forward to the goal of this our journey of woe is naught else than to bear witness to the truth and attain the lofty rank of martyrdom. (46–47)

The *Tarikh-i-Jadid* here draws an analogy between the present of the Babi resistance to the evil Qajar forces and compares the struggle in Mazandaran to the tragedy of Imam Husayn in Karbala. In this scenario, as is the

6. See for example Browne (1893, 34 and footnote).

case with the participants in the *Ta'ziyeh of Imam Husayn,* Mulla Husayn's companions weep and agree to endure the ultimate sacrifice in his path (47–48). Comparing the persecution of the Babis with the plight of Imam Husayn in Karbala, the *Tarikh-i-Jadid* notes that in previous ages, seventy to four hundred doctors declared Imam Husayn a heretic. Now after a thousand years, they recognize their wrongs "and vainly beat their breasts and heads in mourning for that broken troth and the desertion of the holy one whom they left alone in the plain of Kerbela, crying out continually, 'O would that we had been you!'" (1).

The history of the Babis in *Tarikh-i-Jadid,* thus framed within the narrative of Karbala, is supplemented by the appeal to emulate European progress and technology. It calls for the overthrow of the Shi'ite clergy and encourages a move toward the acceptance of European ideals of justice and technological advance. It hails a reform-minded nation to join the Babis in the overthrow of the outdated and hypocritical limits of the Shari'ah by the clerical class. Important to this framing is the equation drawn between the Persians and the enlightened Italians, an equation that is seamlessly coupled with an appeal to the nation's constitution as the first supporter of the meek and martyred Imam. The identity of the Iranian people is thus dually framed along the lines of the identity claimed by the fictional author himself—as a fictive European and a pious believer versed in the Muslim and Shi'ite traditions. Babism's historical present fluctuates in this text between the mythologized history of premodern Islam, the demands for the miraculous performance of the prophets of old, and the enlightened history of Europe.

Reform

A Traveller's Narrative, the first of Browne's translations of Babi histories, uses much the same stylistic device employed by Mirza Fath 'Ali Akhundzadih's critique of modernity in 1863–64. Written in 1886, the author of *A Traveller's Narrative* employs the persona of a traveler who recounts the episodes of the Babis. In the work the author presents himself as an observer who in his own words "sought out with utmost diligence during the time of [his] travels in all parts of Persia, whether far or near, from those without and those within, from friends and strangers" in order to recount the history of the Babis from the point of view of "that whereon the disputants are agreed . . . so that the summary of the facts of the case may be at the disposal of those who are athirst after the fountain of knowledge" (Browne 1891, 2). The book captures the essential highlights of the history of the Bab: his trial in Tabriz; his subsequent imprisonment; and the Mazandaran, Nayriz, and Zanjan clashes, downplaying in each case the role of the unified governing body in the decision to persecute the Bab's followers. *A Traveller's Narrative* attributes the subsequent persecution of the Babis wholly to the work of the clergy and the bloodthirsty Prime Minister Mirza Taqi Khan, Amin Nizam (48–49). It considers the prime minister: "a person devoid of experience and wanting in consideration for the consequences of actions; bloodthirsty and shameless; and swift and ready to shed blood" (32). Relieving Nasir al-Din Shah of all responsibility, the *Traveller's Narrative* further asserts the following about Amin Nizam:

> [A]s His Majesty the King was in the prime of youthful years the minister fell into strange fancies and sounded the drum of absolutism in [the conduct of] affairs: on his own decisive resolution, without seeking permission from the Royal Presence or taking counsel with prudent statesmen, he issued orders to persecute the Babis, imagining that by overweening force he could eradicate and suppress matters of this nature . . . whereas [in fact] to interfere with matters of conscience is simply to give them greater currency and strength; the more you strive to extinguish the more the flame be kindled, more especially in matters of faith and religion, which spread and acquire influence so soon as blood is shed, and strongly affect men's hearts. These things have been put to the proof, and the greatest proof is this very transaction. (33)

A Traveller's Narrative thus addresses a directive to the people of Persia and an admonition to the government to stop the intolerance and molestation of the Babis.[7] It argues that cruelty ultimately appeals to the conscience of humanity and only works to increase the numbers of the Bab's followers.

7. Juan Cole (1998a) deals with the question of humanism and tolerance in the writings of the author of *A Traveller's Narrative*, Abdu'l-Baha, in greater detail.

Interference in the conscience of individuals by the rulers firmly establishes the Bab's movement in Iran.

Appealing to the nation's desire for its previous power and political grandeur in the world, *A Traveller's Narrative* goes on to maintain that interference in the conscience and beliefs of people is "an obstacle to the expansion of the kingdom, an impediment to the conquest of other countries, an obstruction to multiplication of subjects and contrary to the established principles of monarchy" (160). Humanist sentiment is, in this text, associated with fluctuating frontiers, as territory becomes "the source of Iranian, as opposed to Persian, identity" (Kashani-Sabet 1999, 10). As Kashani-Sabet notes, Iranian nationalism "promoted land and geography as compelling criteria for Iranianness," mourning Iran's past grandeur in terms of its territorial expanse (10). Conditioned by the emerging rhetoric of its time, the text appeals to the models of Iran's pre-Islamic historical and territorial superiority, so endeared to the people by other modernist reformers. At stake is the recognition that interference with the conscience of the people has direct results in the loss of empire.

In recollecting the greatness of Persia during the ages when the government did not interfere in the affairs of its people, the author notes that many provinces and vast territories lived under the just rule of its administration. Interference in men's conscience, therefore, diminished the empire of Persia. To support the argument, *A Traveller's Narrative* points to examples of more recent revolts leading to the independence of Afghanistan and the revolt of the Turkmens as evidence of such repercussions (Browne 1891, 161). As Juan Cole suggests, constitutional, parliamentary civil government was viewed as desirable by many later Babis and Baha'is in exile, and the belief in the Shi'ite *ulama,* in the Imam's theocracy, did not fit the picture. Hence the *Traveller's Narrative* selects and reads specific instances of confrontation between the Babis and the population, downplaying the role of the administration in the brutalities and decisions that led up to them. In historical terms and especially owing to the text's positive outlook on the initiatives of the Bab, the *Traveller's Narrative* supports the claims forwarded by Akhundzadih that the Muslim clerics are responsible for the backwardness of Iran. In so doing, the text ensures a scenario in which the government and the people are minor players in the dramatic repression of Babi sentiment and are more or less free of responsibility in the attacks against the Babis. The text thus implicates the *ulama* as the major agitators.

Some Conclusions

What emerges from a perusal of these narratives is that the *ta'ziyeh*'s vision of time and space as a formal mode of witnessing the past makes Babi history understandable to the audience and promotes a theory of reform easily grasped and already understood by the witnesses of the *ta'ziyeh* drama. In *Nuqtat al-Kaf,* where the urgency of the present is located in its association with the Day of Resurrection, that is, Judgment Day, the association between the Babis and the main figures of Shi'ite antiquity, namely the Fourteen Infallibles, is mimetic and direct. It justifies Babi claims vis-à-vis the Shi'ite populace and hence calls on their support, just as they support Imam Husayn and his people. In *Tarikh-i-Jadid* the mode of representation is more comparative; the Babi return serves as a wrinkle in time that associates the urgency of the present with that of the past. The present state of corruption is thus informed by the corruption of the early Muslim community by the Caliphate. As such, the text hails the Persian populace to rebel with the Babis against the injustices of the government and the priestly class. While significantly different in its approach, *A Traveller's Narrative* uses the same temporal maneuvers as the *ta'ziyeh* and *rauzeh* eulogies. The Babi moment is represented as every other moment in which interference in the conscience of the Persian populace has resulted in the downfall of the country and, importantly, the loss of empire. It calls for a fundamental reform in the government's approach to its subjects and promotes the idea of an atheocratic state—one that leaves the conscience free to pursue its ideals.

The *ta'ziyeh* as a dramatic, but historical, genre is formative of a temporal and spatial model for the telling of Babi history in the "Browne chronicles." It functions as a significant and popular mode for the communication of the urgency of the present. Its mimetic and comparative maneuvers are utilized in order to call on the populace (as supporters of the Imam) to redeem the nation from the hands of the evil contemporary

Yazid and to join forces with the present army of Imam Husayn. Babi history functions in all three texts to remind the nation of what may befall it, if it fails to rise to its destiny—a destiny that the fate of Imam Husayn has written for all Shi'ites for all time.

Qurrat al-'Ayn Tahirih in Badasht

Representing the Unpresentable

The infamy that Qurrat al-'Ayn Tahirih's gestures at the Badasht Conference enjoy in popular Qajar rhetoric differs significantly from the narrative representation of the event in the three texts recovered by Browne. The 1858 history by Riza Kuli Khan, the *Rawzatu s-Safa* (volume 10), mentions the proceedings of the Badasht Conference (Browne 1891, 188). Sipihr's *Nasikh at-Tavarikh* (volume 4) records Qurrat al-'Ayn Tahirih's address at that conference (Sipihr 1353 [1958], 57) and remarks at one point earlier in the text that she discarded the veil and openly preached the new doctrine (Sipihr 1353 [1958], 46). Abu Turab (quoted in Nabil's narrative [Zarandi 1996]), Samandar (1991), and Baghdadi (1991) include at least a passing reference to the incident.

The *Nuqtat al-Kaf* mainly refers to Qurrat al-'Ayn Tahirih in two instances: the first is a reference to her genealogy in contemporary culture—her family, her breeding, and her role as agitator of innovations (inspired presumably by the Bab's own writings) in Karbala. The author of *Nuqtat al-Kaf* writes that she attracted the attention of the Turkish government in Karbala (where she was residing immediately before and immediately after her recognition of the Bab's claims) by asserting that she was a "manifestation" *(mazhar)* of the Prophet Muhammad's daughter, Fatimih. As such, any unclean thing was rendered pure by being submitted before her gaze (Browne 1910, 141; 1891, 356). In this way, the author constructs his understanding of the present of Babi activity in light of the claims of its key players. This claim to being a manifestation of Fatimih, the author of *Nuqtat al-Kaf* maintains, was the reason behind the lapsed decision by the Mufti of Baghdad to put Qurrat al-'Ayn Tahirih to death. Denis MacEoin traces the origins of the Qurrat al-'Ayn Tahirih's claims to be "the incarnation of the holy Fatimih" in *Nuqtat al-Kaf* with the following: "originally the followers of Qurrat al 'Ayn practiced extremely severe forms of asceticism." He goes on to note, basing this reading on some of the early exhortations of the Bab found in his writings, "this situation continued until the Bab's *Risala furu al-Adliyya* reached Karbala. In this it is stated that the glances of Fatimih and the Imams *(al Allah)* were among the agents whereby impure and forbidden *(haram)* materials could be rendered lawful" (1979, 206). The entry of a much circulated and translated text of the Bab into the Karbala community, MacEoin claims, thus transformed the discourses of the community and its praxis. The Babis once again started commerce with the non-Babis resident in Karbala but mediated their activity through the purifying gaze of one who was understood to be the return of Fatimih. MacEoin translates the relevant passage of the Bab as follows: "And among the purified substances in certain verses are those which have fallen beneath the gaze of the Family of God even though none of the ulama have mentioned this nevertheless, the decision rests with him whom God has caused to witness the creation of the heavens and the earth" (Bab n.d., Arab. chap. 7, 94; Persian chap. 13, 130; see MacEoin 1979). In a later text, the *Persian Bayan,* the Bab writes that the Imams have "returned to the Life of the World"—presumably in the persons of the first to accept the Bab's claims (1987, 323–24).[8]

Regarding the Badasht Conference, *Nuqtat al-Kaf* notes that the rumors of the event that took place at that conference, "partly true, partly false," preceded the conference participants wherever they went, causing great clamor and dispute in the towns and villages to which the Babis traveled. One is to wonder then at the gravity of the events that were rumored to have taken place because in each instance, after the conference, *Nuqtat al-Kaf* reports that the Babis were molested and attacked by villagers and by the army.

According to Amanat's reading of the original sources, the Babi conference in Badasht was held for three weeks in June and July of 1848. Mulla

8. Although the *Persian Bayan* is one of the Bab's last known written works, it is obvious that the belief that these figures had returned in the persons of such Babi leaders as Qurrat al-'Ayn Tahirih and Mulla Muhammad Ali Barfurushi Quddus was commonly held long before the dissemination of this work.

Muhammad Ali Barfurushi Quddus (one of the first people to join the Babi movement) and his companions, who were among the conference participants, had intended to raise the Black Standard in Mashhad.[9] They were, however, forced out of the city of Mashhad because of heightened anti-Babi fervor and were traveling on horseback in the northeastern corner of Iran. Qurrat al-'Ayn Tahirih and her companions, traveling from Tehran, were on their way to the region of Khurasan to join Quddus's forces and to ride under the Black Standard. They met the group of Babis en route on the Mazandaran-Khurasan road and from all accounts decided to change their destination. Despite the turn of events, the two groups joined and decided to rent three gardens in which they could contemplate their fate and review a range of questions regarding the identity of the movement and its future strategy.

The group's charismatic leader, Sayyid Ali Muhammad, the Bab, had claimed (in 1844) to be "the Gate" to the Qa'im, who would usher forth a new era in religious history. Owing to his claim, which traditionally would imply the imminent relinquishment of power by both the Shi'ite clergy and the Qajar dynast, the Bab was imprisoned by the authorities in a remote castle prison in Azerbayjan. The prime agenda of this group of eighty-one Babis, therefore, was the plight of the Bab. They were anxious to find a way to rescue him. Any effort in this direction, Amanat writes,

9. In July 1848, the Babi leader Mulla Husayn Bushru'i raised the Black Standard in Mashhad and rode westward. The implications of this gesture for the government and the religious hierarchy alike, were obvious. In Shi'ite Islam, there is a well-known hadith attributed to the Prophet Muhammad that suggests that should one see the Black Standard coming from Khurasan, then one should go to it. The Mahdi will be there. More important, however, the raising of the Black Standard in Khurasan was an act imbued with historical and contradynastic significance. The raising of the Black Standard is historically known as the gesture that inaugurated the final overthrow of the Umayyad dynasty by the Abbasids. This symbolic act signaled an impending attack on the existing religious order by the coming of the Mahdi. It also posed a definitive threat for the existing dynasty. Although, ironically, the importance of this challenge got buried under the confusion of the government over the death of Muhammad Shah, the populace in Barfurush confronted the Babis, who were traveling under Mulla Husayn's banner, forcing them to take up positions around the Shrine of Shaykh Tabarsi. The conflict between the two groups lasted from mid-October 1848 to early May 1849 (See Momen 1983).

was contingent on a plan of future action. "Moderation and prudence in the face of mounting hostility, radical Babis argued, could lead only to further suffering. Yet the final Insurrection against the forces of oppression would materialize only if the Qa'im made his advent unequivocally apparent" (1989, 325). This raised the question of the Bab's precise claim and the nature of his mission. Who was the Bab? Was he the Qa'im, the Messiah whom they had been expecting for hundreds of years? Was his message a rejuvenation of the Islamic truth? Or did he intend to establish a new and independent religion? These pressing questions were meant to establish the status of the movement and the identity of its members. Sources reveal a factional setting in which the nature of the present and the identity of the movement was debated. According to historians of the period, there is evidence to suggest that there were three factions, the supporters of Qurrat al-'Ayn, the supporters of Quddus, and those who were neutral, yet it is unclear who asked which questions and with what gains since "the most obvious outcome of the Badasht debate was . . . the prevalence of Qurrat al-'Ayn's views" (Amanat 1989, 328).[10]

According to *Nabil's Narrative,* of the three gardens, one was assigned to Qurrat al-'Ayn—surnamed Tahirih (The Pure One) at the conference. The second was assigned to Mulla Muhammad 'Ali Barfurushi Quddus. Mirza Husayn 'Ali Nuri Baha'u'llah, who had rented the gardens, occupied the third. The rest of the participants camped on the grounds surrounding these Babi leaders.

The more detailed narratives and histories of the events differ slightly in their accounts of the manner in which the events took place. According to Amanat, most agree on the following points: (1) that the poet/leader Qurrat al-'Ayn Tahirih appeared unveiled before the conference participants;[11] (2) that she argued for a definite break with the tradition of Islam;

10. Historians have chosen to represent the debates differently for different religious, moral, or political gains. The compilation of historical writings on Tahirih Qurrat al-'Ayn edited by A. Q. Afnan (1991; see for example, Samandar and Baghdadi in that volume) demonstrates these differences quite clearly in one place.

11. Some of these sources use very vague language that could allow for an interpretation of her action as the gesture of physical unveiling, or of the unveiling the truth of

(3) that confusion and contention followed, leading to the denial of faith on the part of several of the participants; and (4) that the gathering affected the further development of the movement and effected a radical change in the rituals and actions undertaken by its participants.

Amanat maintains that Qurrat al-'Ayn Tahirih took on the leading role at the conference, arguing for a definitive break with the Islamic Shari'ah (religious law). Some sources maintain that Quddus rejected her as a radical and "the author of heresy." She, on the other hand, questioned Quddus's claims to leadership because he failed to raise the banner of Babi revolt in Mashhad (Amanat 1989, 326). This radical split between the two leaders is claimed by historians to have determined the dynamics of the Badasht Conference. That is the image that emerges of the conference from a historian's perusal of several contemporary sources. The account given by *Nuqtat al-Kaf,* however, is somewhat different.

The Badasht Conclave in *Nuqtat al-Kaf*

Without giving a detailed account of a dispute between the Babi figures, *Nuqtat al-Kaf* records a speech delivered at the Badasht Conference. Browne notes that because of corruption in the manuscript, he cannot say whether this speech was delivered by Quddus or Qurrat al-'Ayn Tahirih (Browne 1893, 357). Browne reports on the nature of the speech in *Nuqtat al-Kaf:*

> Its length, and the amount of commentary required to make clear certain obscure points of doctrine which it raises, render it impossible for me to attempt a full translation of it here, but certain obscure points demand notice. The doctrine of "Return" *(rij'at)* is treated of at some length. . . . The outward forms of religion (prayer, fasting, pilgrimage, and alms) are all explained allegorically, after the fashion of the Isma'ilis. All men's

---

a matter, or of the unveiling one's true intentions. That makes the issue somewhat more ambiguous but underscores the fact that the veil is not simply an item of clothing. The problematic of veiling and unveiling and the government injunctions to abide by publicly enforced laws on the question of veiling is capably discussed for the contemporary period in Naghibi (1999).

> goods are declared to be the property of the "Point" (i.e. the Bab). The abrogation of the laws of the previous dispensation is announced, and laws in general are declared to be necessary only till such time as men have learned to comprehend the "Doctrine of Unity" *(Tawhid)* by which is meant the recognition of the true nature of the "Point" or Divine Manifestation of the age. (Browne 1893, 357; 1910, 151–52)

The reintroduction of the doctrine of the Return into the *Nuqtat al-Kaf* narrative (regardless of who may have introduced it) concurs with other chronicles on the point that a break with the laws of the Shi'ite Shari'ah occurred in Badasht. The speech, which according to Browne could have been delivered by the poet Qurrat al-'Ayn Tahirih at the conclave, reiterates the significance of the break in terms of a Return:

> It is declared in many traditions touching the religion of the Ka'im [Qa'im] that it shall abrogate all [previous] religions, for *"the perfection of the doctrine of Divine Unity is of all predicates from Him,"* and *"mankind shall become a single church,"* and He will make all religions one. Now His ordinances are esoteric ordinances, and when the esoteric comes, the exoteric order must needs depart. . . . And should men not be able to receive the doctrine of the Unity at the beginning of the Manifestation, ordinances and restrictions will again be prescribed for them, till they acquire such power, when these in turn will be abolished. But during the continuance of the Return the veils will gradually be lifted, till the verities [of religion] be established and men learn to explore the Prophetic Mystery, which is the Paradise of Primal Unity [*Jannat-i-Ahadiyyat*]. Of this there is no occasion to speak at present, and I have only submitted to you these remarks that, when people say, "A company [of Babis] went to Badasht and conducted themselves in an unseemly fashion," you may know that they were persons of no mean quality, but the elect of the world; that they did a great work; and that when men heap curses and censures on them, it is because of their own benighted condition. For there is a tradition that "when the standard of Truth appears, the people of the East and of the West shall curse it." (Browne 1893, 357–59)

Having constituted the grounds for the legitimate severance of the Shari'ah supported by a commentary on doctrine and the traditions of the Day of Resurrection, *Nuqtat al-Kaf* proceeds to allude to the tradition of the four standards. Unlike the cautious tone of *A Traveller's Narrative,* this tradition, read into the charts of the Babi figures, is construed by *Nuqtat al-Kaf* as a final and physical attack by the Babi leaders on the royal dynasty. Rayat-i-Yamani (whom the author equates to the Bab); Rayat-i-Husayni (Mulla Muhammad 'Ali Barfurushi Quddus); Rayat-i-Khurasani (Mulla Husayn Bushru'i), and Rayat-i-Talikani (Qurrat al-'Ayn Tahirih): these four stand opposed to the Rayat-i-Sofyani, who the author claims are the royal ensigns of Nasir al-Din Shah (Browne 1893, 359; 1910, 152–53). As such the Babi leaders are set up by *Nuqtat al-Kaf* as forces opposing the royalist camp.

Concluding his report on Badasht, *Nuqtat al Kaf*'s author claims that the noise and clamor of the conference attracted the people from the neighboring villages and areas. It records that Quddus had foretold an uprising and that he had counseled them to not take up arms. Accordingly, the uninvited visitors attacked the conference participants overnight and took them for everything they had. The assemblage dispersed (Browne 1910, 154). No further mention is made of the role of Qurrat al-'Ayn Tahirih in this conference, except to identify her as one of the four forces confronting the ensigns of the Shah.[12]

The Badasht Conclave in the *Tarikh-i-Jadid*

Drawing from *Nuqtat al-Kaf, Tarikh-i-Jadid* claims that at Badasht, Quddus announced himself as the Qa'im and "in brief spoke words that the Qaim must speak" (Browne 1893, 282). "Then Jinab-i-Tahira [Qurrat al-'Ayn] ascended into the pulpit and exhorted the believers, setting forth the Mysteries of the Divine Unity and the renewal (of all things)" (283; my interpretation). The author goes on to claim that "[t]hereafter so great a mass of writings, comprising prayers, homilies and doctoral treatises emanated from that much wronged woman that the eye of time never beheld anything like it" (283). Following another paragraph expounding on Qurrat

12. In a later passage *Nuqtat al-Kaf* calls her "The Mother of the World" *(An Madar-i-Imkan)* (Browne 1893, 241).

al-'Ayn Tahirih's scholarship and eloquence, *Tarikh-i-Jadid* writes that on the dispersal of the assembly at Badasht she was taken prisoner to Tehran. There she is said to have foretold her own cruel execution. Arrayed in a white dress, she was taken to the place of her strangulation in Nigaristan. As if to reject all accusations of her improper behavior, the *Tarikh-i-Jadid* then records, "As she would not suffer to remove the veil from her face (though they repeatedly sought to do so), they applied the bow-string over her veil, and thus compassed her martyrdom" (284). Characteristic of all three texts, which tend to regard the tale of the great poet as a digression, *Tarikh-i-Jadid* writes: "We must however, return to our previous topic, lest the thread of our proper narrative be unduly prolonged" (284).

Qurrat al-'Ayn Tahirih in *A Traveller's Narrative*

A Traveller's Narrative likewise deems the details of the events at Badasht irrelevant and assigns only a minor, passing reference to Qurrat al-'Ayn Tahirih herself. The text takes note of her heritage as the daughter of Haji Mulla Salih of Qazvin and recognizes her talent and eloquence with these words: "She according to what is related was skilled in diverse arts and amazed the understanding and thoughts of the most eminent masters by her eloquent dissertations on the exegesis and traditions of the Perspicuous Book [Qur'an], and was a mighty sign in the doctrines of the glorious Shaykh of Ahsa [Shaykh Ahmad Ahsa'i]" (Browne 1891,30; my additions). The *Narrative* goes on to record what may strike one as an apologia for her rumored behavior: "She had a brain full of tumultuous ideas and thoughts vehement and restless." Speaking of her charms, charisma, and engaging character at a wedding party in Tehran, the *Traveller's Narrative* concludes: "In short in elocution she was the calamity of the age and in ratiocination the trouble of the world. Of fear and timidity there was no trace in her heart, nor had the admonition of the kindly-disposed any profit or fruit for her. Although she was of (such as are) damsels (meet) for the bridal bower, yet she wrested pre-eminence from stalwart men, and continued to strain the feet of steadfastness until she yielded up her life at the sentence of the mighty doctors in Teheran. But were we to occupy ourselves with these details the matter would end in prolixity" (32). According to the *Traveller's*

Narrative, the order for her execution is said to have come directly after the attempted murder of Nasir al-Din Shah by a Babi. It was during the 1852 bloodbath that many of her compatriots were either exiled or brutally murdered by the masses on the order of his court. The poet's sentence, according to the text, is dictated by the priestly class, "the mighty doctors."

Such gestures to remove any sentence against Nasir al-Din Shah in this document is very typical of the reformist intentions of the document. As noted earlier, the shah was known to have asked Tahirih for her hand in marriage. Her acts against the nuptial dreams of the shah undercut her role in the project that promoted civil government in Iran. It was therefore undoubtedly wise to note her resistance to marrying *any* man and to assert her devotion to the Bab and to the scholastic enterprise. The *Narrative* seems to be more broadly interested in establishing the compatibility of the *millat* (Iranian populace) and the *dawlat* (state) with one another, encouraging both to work together.[13] The centrality of the unveiled woman to occidental discourse, and its fluctuating appropriation by opposing factions, would risk the loss of this cooperative spirit. The *Narrative* thus takes a more conservative route, emphasizing what could establish a common interest between the people and the ruling monarchy.

If the three texts recovered by Browne seem merely to hint at the events that took place in Badasht and the role of Qurrat al-'Ayn Tahirih in them, then by contrast Shaykh Abu Turab, Nabil's informant, seems to have a lot to say.[14]

13. An earlier text by the same author, Abdu'l-Baha, entitled *The Secret of Divine Civilization* (1981), was only the second of a number of major reformist books written in Persian in the late 1860s and 1870s. It was completed in 1875 and published in Bombay in 1882. As noted by Juan Cole (1996) this treatise was written in response to the period of cabinet and other reforms in Iran in 1871–73. The book urges Qajar Iran to adopt European technologies on purely pragmatic grounds. As we have already noted, the *Tarikh-i-Jadid,* in passages praising European humanist values as the force behind many of the greater European technological advances, argues similarly for the eradication of fanaticism and for the benefits of adopting progressive technology for the good of the nation and its consolidation (Browne 1891, 15–17).

14. Amanat gives the following description of *Nabil's Narrative* in *Resurrection and Renewal:* "Another attempt at writing a general history of the early years was that of the early

Qurrat al-'Ayn Tahirih's Unveiling

The recollector of Qurrat al-'Ayn's unveiling in Badasht, Shaykh Abu Turab, emerged from the Shaykhi school, not unlike the majority of the early adherents of the Babi movement in Iran in the middle of the nineteenth century. The school, as we have noted, was situated in Karbala (Iraq), a city that was a major center for Shi'ite religious training. The Shaykhi school, associated with Shaykh Ahmad Ahsa'i, was known for its progressive teachings and reformist attitudes. A significant number of the early adherents of the Bab had received six to nine years of formal religious training at the school. Indeed much of their thinking about the day of Resurrection, the advent of the Mahdi, and the theory of prophetic cycles came from their contact with the instructor and later leader Sayyid Kazim.[15] After the death of Sayyid Kazim, many of them found the fulfillment of their teacher's promises of the return of the Mahdi in the message and the personage of the Bab. Typically, the Shaykhi-Babis opposed the corruption of Shi'ite doctrine within Shi'ite orthodoxy and had a strong awareness of the way in which it accommodated the needs of the Qajar rule.

---

convert Shaykh Muhammad Nabil Zarandi, known as Nabil Azam, by far the most complete of the general narratives. Written in its final version between 1305/1888 and 1308/1890, Nabil's narrative was based not only on his own personal observations but on the oral and written memoirs of many early Babis, to whose authority he refers throughout. He also benefited from the assistance of Mirza Musa Nuri, brother of Baha'u'llah. Nabil Zarandi's work covered the history of the movement up to the time of completion. An articulate writer, he was able to compile his history in a systematic and chronological order" (1989, 424–25). Amanat mentions a number of deficiencies in the text, one of which is Nabil's relative distance from the events. This distance caused considerable gaps in the narrative for which Nabil compensated by adding elements of the marvelous and the mysterious. Amanat objects to Nabil's melodramatic language, and bias because of his devotion to Baha'u'llah. He notes that the original manuscript in Persian is unavailable, but that the translation into English by Shoghi Effendi (Baha'u'llah's great-grandson) corroborates the facts supplied by earlier accounts of the Babi movement.

15. *Kitab-i Nuqtat al-Kaf* reviews these aspects of Shaykhi thought in great detail. Compare Juan Cole's three papers on Ahsa'i (1993b, 1994, 1997). Cole (1993a) pursues these themes in some detail in the work of Baha'u'llah in "'I Am All the Prophets': The Poetics of Pluralism in Baha'i Texts."

Shaykh Abu Turab, whom the Babi historian Nabil introduces as the "best-informed as to the nature of the developments in Badasht," is reported to have related the following incidents:

> Illness, one day, confined Baha'u'llah to His bed. Quddus, as soon as he heard of His indisposition, hastened to visit Him. He seated himself, when ushered into His presence, on the right hand of Baha'u'llah. The rest of the companions were gradually admitted to His presence, and grouped themselves around Him. No sooner had they assembled than Muhammad-Hasan-i-Qazvini, the messenger of Tahirih, upon whom the name of Fata'l-Qazvini had been newly conferred, suddenly came in and conveyed to Quddus a pressing invitation from Tahirih to visit her in her own garden. (Zarandi 1996, 293–94)

Quddus refused the invitation, but was soon hailed by a messenger with another urgent message from Tahirih insisting on his visit. When Quddus persisted in his refusal, the messenger "unsheathed his sword" and begged Quddus to either follow him or to cut off his head. Shaykh Abu Turab continues:

> Muhammad-Hasan [the messenger], who had seated himself at the feet of Quddus, had stretched forth his neck to receive the fatal blow, when suddenly the figure of Tahirih, adorned and unveiled,[16] appeared before the eyes of the assembled companions. Consternation immediately seized the entire gathering. All stood aghast before this sudden and most unexpected apparition. To behold her face unveiled was to them inconceivable. Even to gaze at her shadow was a thing which they deemed improper, inasmuch as they regarded her as the very incarnation of Fatimih, the noblest emblem of chastity in their eyes. "Quietly, silently, and with the utmost dignity, Tahirih stepped forward and, advancing towards Quddus, seated herself on his right-hand side. Her unruffled serenity sharply contrasted with the affrighted countenances of those who were gazing upon her face. Fear, anger, and bewilderment stirred the depths of their souls. That sudden revelation seemed to have stunned

16. This formulation presumably means that while she appeared without a veil, she had decorated herself with jewels.

> their faculties. Abdu'l-Khaliq-i-Isfahani was so gravely shaken that he cut his throat with his own hands. Covered with blood and shrieking with excitement, he fled away from the face of Tahirih. A few, following his example, abandoned their companions and forsook their Faith. A number were seen standing speechless before her, confounded with wonder. Quddus, meanwhile, had remained seated in his place, holding the unsheathed sword in his hand, his face betraying a feeling of inexpressible anger. It seemed as if he were waiting for the moment when he could strike his fatal blow at Tahirih. His threatening attitude failed, however, to move her. Her countenance displayed that same dignity and confidence which she had evinced at the first moment of her appearance before the assembled believers. (Zarandi 1996, 295; my addition)

Such is the report provided by Shaykh Abu Turab of Qurrat al-'Ayn Tahirih's unveiled appearance before an assembly of some eighty-one men. Later historians fascinated by the cite/sight of Qurrat al-'Ayn Tahirih's "unveiling" have either applauded this gesture in Shaykh Abu Turab's narrative as the originary moment of women's liberation in Iran or, in absolute disgust for this act of heresy, claimed this gesture to be the foundation for, as well as the fundamental proof of, the deserved ill-repute and false motives of the Babi movement. Seldom have they stayed to bear witness to what Shaykh Abu Turab claims followed:

> A feeling of joy and triumph had now illumined her [Tahirih's] face. She rose from her seat and, undeterred by the tumult that she had raised in the hearts of her companions, began to address the remnant of that assembly. Without the least premeditation, and in language which bore a striking resemblance to that of the Qur'an, she delivered her appeal with matchless eloquence and profound fervour. She concluded her address with this verse of the Qur'an: "Verily, amid gardens and rivers shall the pious dwell in the seat of truth, in the presence of the potent King." As she uttered these words, she cast a furtive glance towards both Baha'u'llah and Quddus in such a manner that those who were watching her were unable to tell to which of the two she was alluding. Immediately after, she declared: "I am the Word which the Qa'im is to utter, the Word which shall put to flight the chiefs and nobles of the earth!" She then turned her face towards Quddus and rebuked him for

> having failed to perform in Khurasan those things which she deemed essential to the welfare of the Faith. "I am free to follow the promptings of my own conscience," retorted Quddus. "I am not subject to the will and pleasure of my fellow-disciples." Turning away her eyes from him, Tahirih invited those who were present to celebrate befittingly this great occasion. "This day is the day of festivity and universal rejoicing," she added, "the day on which the fetters of the past are burst asunder. Let those who have shared in this great achievement arise and embrace each other." (Zarandi 1996, 295–96)

The days that followed revolutionized the habits of those assembled:

> Their manner of worship underwent a sudden and fundamental transformation. The prayers and ceremonials by which those devout worshippers had been disciplined were irrevocably discarded. A great confusion, however, prevailed among those who had so zealously arisen to advocate these reforms. A few condemned so radical a change as being the essence of heresy, and refused to annul what they regarded as the inviolable precepts of Islam. Some regarded Tahirih as the sole judge in such matters and the only person qualified to claim implicit obedience from the faithful. Others who denounced her behaviour held to Quddus, whom they regarded as the sole representative of the Bab, the only one who had the right to pronounce upon such weighty matters. Still others who recognised the authority of both Tahirih and Quddus viewed the whole episode as a God-sent test designed to separate the true from the false and distinguish the faithful from the disloyal. (Zarandi 1996, 295–98)

Abu Turab's detailed recollection of the moment of Qurrat al-'Ayn Tahirih's assumption of power is unequaled in the annals of early Babi historiography.[17] Stunning in its rhetoric and its representation of Qurrat al-'Ayn Tahirih's actions, Shaykh Abu Turab's recollection "cuts" (to evoke Michel Foucault) the contemporary knowledge of Islamic history and disarms its notion of a unified subjectivity and historical continuity.

17. Although this same word-for-word rendition can be found in Fadil Mazandarani's *Tarikh-i Zuhur al Haqq* Volume 2.

It is against these discourses associated with continuity and identity that Shaykh Abu Turab's recollection of Qurrat al-'Ayn Tahirih's radical critique seems to be aimed. Fundamental to this critique is the codification of historical recollections related to the early days of Islam and the historical relation of Islam to questions of spatiality. A brief digression will facilitate a deeper understanding of the terms of the critique.

Islam and Spatiality

It is said that in the early days of the religion of Islam, the Prophet Muhammad used space and orientation as a way to establish the fundamental nature of Islam. He did this first to distinguish his newborn religion from paganisms by aligning it with other extant monotheistic religions. Every day he would turn in prayer toward Jerusalem—the *qibla* of Judaism and Christianity. For the followers of the new religion, this corporeal gesture became a sign of difference from the surrounding religious practices, affiliating the religion of Islam through the orientation of the body in space with the other two monotheistic religions. Then one day, it is said, his followers realized that he no longer was turning in that direction, but that he now was turning toward Mecca, changing the direction of his prayer in order to establish the unique and independent nature of Islam within the context of monotheism (Mernissi 1987, 65–70). Spatiality thus gained relevance for the identity of the pious Muslim through these doctrinal and ritual practices of the body.

Spatial discourses in most Islamic societies today function similarly to constitute a national and/or a personal identity. They are enforced to distinguish the realm of the public from the private. Spatial discourses directly superimpose the differential place of women and men upon this private/public split. These distinctions are justified on the basis of interpretations that find grounding in verse 53 of sura 33 of the Qur'an on the *hijab,* which in Arabic literally means to hide something from sight, to separate or establish a threshold, or to forbid. Thus linked, the verse of the *hijab* is construed as a prohibition that concerns space and is more commonly associated with the practice of veiling. Verse 53 of sura 33 of the Qur'an reads as follows:

> O ye who believe! Enter not the dwelling of the Prophet for a meal without waiting for the proper time, unless permission be granted you. But if ye are invited, enter, and, when your meal is ended, then disperse. Linger not for conversation. Lo! that would cause annoyance to the Prophet, and he would be shy of (asking) you (to go); but Allah is not shy of the truth. And when ye ask of them (the wives of the Prophet) anything, ask it of them from behind a curtain. This is purer for your hearts and for their hearts. (Mernissi 1987, 85)

Traditionally, when the question of the relevance of a certain verse arises, Islamic scholars turn toward memory or recollection. The hadith have constituted this memory for posterity through the (re)collection of the various stories told by the associates and the family of the Prophet. Among the thousands of these hadith there is one that relates to the Qur'anic verse on the question of veiling and that, according to Fatima Mernissi, gets lost in the shuffle. This misplacement in the processes involved in the codification of Muslim laws, processes that should more relevantly be called "dissimulation" (because of the word's close association with the act of veiling), has, according to Mernissi, instituted a rather skewed impression of the context of the verse and suggested that the Prophet Muhammad ordered the separation of the sexes with it.[18]

According to Mernissi's reading of sources from this period, the political and cultural context for the verse on the *hijab,* as constituted by al-Bukhari's version of Anas's recollections of this incident, would prove such a view far from the mark. In his collection of hadith, the historian al-Bukhari writes that on the night when he celebrated his marriage to Zaynab, the Prophet Muhammad became frustrated with his guests. The whole city of Medina had been invited to the celebrations and, despite the show of impatience on the part of the Prophet, the guests would not leave. Finally, standing on the threshold of the wedding chamber he recited the verse of the *hijab* (quoted above), while drawing a curtain between himself and his companion, Anas (Mernissi 1987, 100). In effect, this act of drawing

18. For other references to *hadith* related to this verse, consult chapter 3 in Ahmed (1992).

the curtain not only separated the space between the sublime and the profane (the space between the Prophet and his disciples), but also the space *between two men.* This act and the verse of the *hijab* situated, above all, the identity of the two men as separate and established a hierarchical division of power between the two through a spatial division.

Mernissi notes that in the period that followed, the verse uttered on the Prophet's wedding night became a handy tool for a confused community in civil war in Medina. The wedding of Zaynab and the Prophet took place during a period of instability in which the Prophet attempted to gain a foothold in Medina. The Muslims were constantly under attack by the surrounding community, and it was obvious that one of the most powerful ways to weaken an already unsettled community was through attacking the Muslim women. The verse of the *hijab* gave the Muslim community a solution to a whole network of problems, argues Mernissi (1987, 92). The act of veiling was introduced into the Muslim community as a way to distinguish between the wives of the Prophet (to whom the Medinese were forced to show respect) and the female slaves.[19] Veiling, then, derived from the act of drawing the curtain *between two men,* was introduced into the Muslim community in Medina as a sign of hierarchical differentiation between men and women and among women. In the midst of civil war, the wives of the Prophet adopted the veil to protect themselves from molestation and to secure the community from vigilant attacks. During this war, the streets of Medina, that is, public space, became male space, and if women of higher status wanted to enter into this space, they were to do so on the condition that they pull a piece of clothing over their heads and bodies.

Deriving her arguments from later codifications of the hadith and interpretations of the Qur'an, Mernissi maintains that the institution of this act in the Medinese period marked the beginning of women's repression in Islam—a religion which from its inception, she argues, was conceived as an egalitarian community.[20] Be that as it may, in order to support this

19. Ahmed suggests other circumstances for the institution of the veil, drawing from Ibn Sa'd's (re)collections. See Ahmed (1992, 54).

20. Fatima Mernissi suggests this event as a symbolic expression of "regression on sexual equality" commingled with a "regression in social equality," but the coincidental

position, one would have to disregard the more recent history of Muslim women who, in the struggle for independence in the Algerian War of Independence (1954–62) and in the struggle against imperialism in Iran during the Iranian Revolution (1978–79), chose to don the veil as a gesture of defiance of and resistance to colonial and imperial powers.[21] Indeed, for a generation of largely upper-class, urban, educated female writers who were born before the establishment of the Islamic Republic, the female body and its compulsory veiling appear as an over-determined site for the articulation of the sociopolitical tensions, as a law enforced in the years immediately following the Iranian Revolution simulated the effects of an earlier legislation in 1937 by the Pahlavi regime by which women were prohibited from appearing veiled in public (Naghibi 1999). The *hijab*, which was enforced in the new republic to represent the integrity of the nation and to protect and preserve the purity of its women, is described in the semibiographical texts of Gelareh Asayesh (1999), Marjane Satrapi (2003), and Azar Nafisi (2003), for example, as "stifling" and "unnatural." Yet the Iranian *chador* (veil) in these texts stands to differentiate the ideological position of the fundamentalist woman on the one hand and the one who stands in opposition to the Islamic regime on the other. Acts of adornment, polished nails, the wearing of sheer hose, lipstick, or the few purposeful strands of hair that show from under a headscarf appear in these chronicles as embodied principled positions in a war against a perceived repressive theocratic regime. While such notations appear quotidian and superficial, the distinctions, focusing as they do on the agency of women in transforming the conditions of compulsory veiling and unveiling, "get to the heart of a question that has dominated Iranian politics" in history and memory since the Qajar period—to a question that points up the fault lines of communal belonging, religious identity, class affiliation,

---

imagery of the descent of the *hijab* over all women for the "fifteen centuries that followed" in this paragraph and her subsequent discussions strongly suggests the above reading (1987, 178–79).

21. See Fanon's discussion of the veil in the chapter "Algeria Unveiled" in *A Dying Colonialism* (1967) and Shirazi-Mahajan's discussion of the role of the veil in the Iranian Islamic revolution (1993).

and gender dynamics in the constitution of the nation. It is the question that asks: "Whose country is this?"[22]

Thus, rather than argue that the veil is essentially repressive on the one hand or essentially liberating on other, I want to suggest that the verse of the *hijab* that is said to have been invoked on the Prophet's wedding night, and that has been reappropriated and reinterpreted for various purposes over the course of the thousand-year history of Islam, entered into an apparatus of power and knowledge to configure the limits of communal identity at restless moments in the history of Islam. The female body was subsequently construed as the focal point of this identity. As such it was given the task of protecting communal identity by protecting its own. Islamic identity was thus constituted on a problematic rupture divided on this body's gendered split between nature and culture—and again on its historically constructed hierarchized social divide—a body culturally constituted as vulnerable and perceived as naturally harmful and abject. Having entered into the apparatus of power and knowledge at this level, the verse of the *hijab,* as the historical vacillations of veiling and unveiling have demonstrated in the context of Iranian modernity, marked a problem for closure within Islamic discourses on space, land, and belonging. Its fluctuations within the contending recollections/knowledge that surrounded it, and the political discourses that activated it over the fourteen centuries of its historical persistence, further problematized the constitution of a unified and continuous Islamic identity despite all efforts to construe it as otherwise. My point, put more briefly, is that the veil as a signifier of a fragmented identity has functioned both positively and negatively within the dynamics of power. As a focal point of identity it has become an arena of constant struggle and domination for both Muslim communities and contending colonial and imperial powers. The veil has served as a screen behind which the mysterious, the feared, and the stereotypical and sexually potent female figure could lay dormant, always ready to erupt into the uncertain domain of the public.

Space and its gendered partitioning, as we have already observed, is fundamental in several ways to both the doctrine and the practice of

22. See Asayesh (1999).

Islam. Before we return to the discussion of its disarticulation in the gardens of Badasht, I would like to move our attention to a particularly potent public space that has for centuries fired the imagination of poets and geographers alike. This is the space of the garden.

The Islamic Garden

In the context of the geographical conditions of the area "conquered" by Islamic discourses, the garden is to be seen as a way to ameliorate the often life-denying, arid, and monotonous conditions of the land. People of high and low economic status incorporated a life-sustaining oasis into their own properties, carefully sheltered away with a wall in order to shut out the hustle and bustle as well as the odors of the city. One finds clear evidence of this even if one only casts a passing glance on the various collections of images that have been handed down through Mogul arts and ancient Persian miniatures and carpets. It would also seem, from a consideration of the vegetal imagery introduced into the carpet tradition during the Abbasid period in Iran, that the garden was so greatly valued that it was important to re-create a never-fading image of it onto a transportable medium such as the carpet. The floral carpet would thus introduce the garden's verdant quality to interior spaces.

A brief study of the lifestyle and practices of the Iranian nobility, as depicted especially in the grand narratives of royal history and Iranian (mystical) poetry, may allow us to reach similar conclusions. We learn that gardens were always incorporated into the structures of dynastic residences for the pleasure and traditional rituals of the ruling class. The tales situate the royal garden as a site of romance and hedonistic pleasure, and as spaces where the king would hold court and celebrate his weddings. In allegories of the garden, the space of the garden represents and activates the dynast's dreams, desires, and nightmares. The garden not only enables his daily and ritual activities, it is an integral part of his physical and phantasmagoric realities.[23]

23. See Meisami (1985).

Traditional historiography claims the garden's main function to be the spatial reflection of the paradise of the Qur'an. Its structure in the form of the Persian *chahar bagh,* for example, is said to directly represent the Garden of Paradise described by the Prophet Muhammad himself in this following verse:

> And besides these shall be two gardens,
> green green pastures,
> therein two fountains of gushing water
> therein fruits, and palm-trees and pomegranates
> therein maidens good and comely . . .
> houris, cloistered in cool pavilions . . . (Qur'an 46–75:55)

This description of Paradise is regularly interrupted by the refrain: "O which of your Lord's bounties will you and you deny?" thereby giving room for detailed attempts to figure out a geography of Paradise in the form of two-times-two gardens, a quadrangular layout of many royal Persian gardens called the *chahar bagh,* "four gardens."

Echoing theocratic narratives, historians of the garden return to similar Qur'anic verses about Paradise as a source that unquestionably situates the origin, character, and structure of the Islamic garden for all time. Historians of the Islamic garden place it in the grand narrative of Muslim life and attribute its very structure and continuity to the authority of the Prophet. What is missing from these historical accounts is a sense of discontinuity and change that leaves open to further research the construal of a variety of other influences in the making of the material paradise on earth: considerations for irrigation and traditional horticultural practices are examples of these. Other considerations, like the ease of hunting and concerns about aesthetics and architecture, may also be the reasons behind the garden's formal structure. What is denied in the traditional historical analyses of the Islamic garden, then, is an *analytics* of the social and historical contexts that may signal various sources of authorship and historical influence, not to mention deeply embedded pre-Islamic associations with the garden and its beauties as external conditions for its emergence.

Shaykh Abu Turab's Critique

It is precisely against this kind of historiography that Shaykh Abu Turab's memory of the revolt in Badasht represents a critique. The representation, or rather, the critical practice I attribute to this recollection, presupposes four methodological principles identified by Michel Foucault in his 1970 inaugural lecture at the College de France, "The Order of Discourse": the principle of reversal, wherein the origin, tradition, and authority of the Islamic discourse on space is put to question; the principle of discontinuity, which recognizes the discontinuity of discursive practices regarding space, their crossing, juxtaposition, and exclusion; the principle of specificity, which recognizes the violence of discourse done on things, here Islamic space; and finally the principle of exteriority, which identifies the external conditions of possibility for such a discourse. Let us proceed to a more detailed explanation.

Shaykh Abu Turab's recollections of the proceedings of the Badasht Conference are remarkable in the striking and clear rhetoric that they associate with Qurrat al-'Ayn Tahirih's provocative gesture in a garden, and unequaled, too, as we have witnessed in our perusal of the "Browne chronicles."

Although twelve centuries apart, al-Bukhari's version of Anas's recollections of the events that took place on the threshold of the Prophet's wedding chamber and Shaykh Abu Turab's recollections of Qurrat al-'Ayn's unveiled appearance in Badasht have similar although inverse effects in their appropriation by traditional historical practice. Whereas in the case of the Prophet Muhammad the rhetoric (i.e., the Qur'anic verse) is preserved in historical memory over and above the act of drawing a curtain between two men, in the case of Badasht, Qurrat al-'Ayn's unveiled appearance, rather than her powerful address, is conserved in popular memory. In the case of one, the preservation of the word enabled the opportunity for men to regain control over women, while in the case of the other, the dramatic act of unveiling alone was seized upon by later historians as a figurative construct that would reinforce the national discourse on "Babi" difference (discussed in chapter 1) and the Babi discourse on equality. The preservation of her dramatic action over her more dramatic words constituted the foundation for the appropriation of these early discourses for future feminist purposes. We find evidence of this in numerous essays, texts, and tracts, but it may be useful to cite at least one of the most referenced texts on Iranian feminism, Farzaneh Milani's *Veils and Words: The Emerging Voices of Iranian Women Writers,* in which Qurrat al-'Ayn is placed as the first in the line of liberated/liberating women's voices in Iran. Abbas Amanat's *Crowning Anguish* (1993), which includes the autobiography of Taj al-Saltanih, the Qajar princess and Nasir al-Din Shah's daughter, places Qurrat al-'Ayn Tahirih within a similar trajectory.[24] As we have seen, the order of veiling is solidified in the case of Islamic scholarship hundreds of years after the death of the Prophet and is used as a means to configure the limits of communal identity. The example of Qurrat al-'Ayn Tahirih, on the other hand, framed as "the first example of an Iranian woman's unveiling" and perceived as a singular act of feminist practice, is appropriated in the context of modernity to frame and fashion a conflicted national identity. Both of these historiographic practices, though dealing with events that are separated by at least a hundred years to the time of recording, are examples of the ways in which discourse is a violence done to things. A critical stance against this kind of discursive violence is evident in Qurrat al-'Ayn Tahirih's own rhetorical practices and antidisciplinary gestures as recollected by Shaykh Abu Turab.

If we consider the gestures and rhetoric that are said to have occurred, as reported by Shaykh Abu Turab, as a co-determining whole, we are struck by the recognition in rhetoric and gesture and the awareness Qurrat al-'Ayn Tahirih herself is said to have professed of the place in which she spoke. The conference site is not only a public space that is exclusively reserved for men, but it is also represented as the space of a garden, which for centuries had been associated with the space of the Islamic paradise. In what follows, I will propose that the gesture of unveiling by Qurrat al-'Ayn Tahirih in Shaykh Abu Turab's recollections signals a critical analytics of

24. See Amanat (1993, 59); Amanat also rejects these views in an earlier book (1989, 330). Also, for a delightfully utopian and early account of the coincidence between Qurrat al-'Ayn's "originary" gestures and the concomitant development of the women's movement in the West, see Martha Root (1981).

space on two fronts and an acknowledgment of a violence done to space by discourse on two levels.

On the one hand, we see that in the simple act of appropriating the Qur'anic verse "Amongst gardens and rivers . . . ," Qurrat al-'Ayn Tahirih's speech acknowledges the structural imposition of the discourse of the Qur'an paradise on the space of the garden. On the other, her appearance unveiled in a male domain questions the imposition of Islamic territorial partitioning upon an otherwise undifferentiated public space. In both cases she questions the structural imposition of a so-called Islamic discourse on space. Her use of Qur'anic language at once supports the authority of the Qur'an while simultaneously undoing its *meaning* through a specifically gendered mode of enunciation in the public sphere. She thus appropriates a vocabulary and "turns it against those who had once used it." In this act of appropriation Qurrat al-'Ayn Tahirih effectively re-situates paradise and hell spatially on earth and temporally in the present. Much more than claiming to be a return or a resurrection, which evidently is the manner in which those who were assembled in Badasht recognized her, she is associated by Shaykh Abu Turab with the presence of the present (as the word spoken by the Qa'im or Mahdi). Her reported speech also indicates this association by suggesting that those sitting in the garden, in that very tent, are the pious assembled before the potent King. In her speech and action Qurrat al-'Ayn Tahirih thus reintroduces human agency within the context of history and positions authority and change within the realm of human activity. She questions thereby the contiguous character of historical unfolding as prefigured and predetermined, and therefore unconditioned by mortals.

Qurrat al-'Ayn Tahirih's address at Badasht in Shaykh Abu Turab's recollections questions the homogenous unity established as the source of authorship of the Islamic garden and of the social division of space as well. Her speech and her act of unveiling in the public domain reconfigure the disjunction between the doer and the deed—a disjunction that ironically presupposes a continuity between "the author" of Islam and "his" work/people on earth. Put differently, whereas before it had been a given that it was Allah's will that Islamic space was to be divided by the believers into two territories (male and female), and that the garden should be divided into four, to reflect Qur'anic paradise, Qurrat al-'Ayn Tahirih's action and speech now clearly posit human agency as the external condition of possibility for spatial discourse in Islam. Human activity is the only party responsible for determinations regarding divisions in space. Because of the imbrication of spatiality and veiling in Islam, one can additionally say that if she could unveil despite the so-called injunction to veil (exemplified by the appropriation of the Qur'anic verse), then others could appropriate the veil without that injunction in mind. Human activity alone could therefore be held responsible for the construal of a gendered space and the constitution and the authorship of the garden as the Qur'anic paradise.

Her act and her speech introduce a disjunction between the Islamic discourses on space, "cutting" them off from their assumed Qur'anic injunctions. Shaykh Abu Turab's recollections of Qurrat al-'Ayn Tahirih in Badasht thus situate the deed and the doer within the same discursive matrix. In effect her gesture and speech in Abu Turab's recollections propose the possibility of a reversal in the meaning of that space through the force of rhetorical and practical juxtaposition. The garden previously regarded as the space of paradisical and poetical musings is redressed as a space of activity, change, and resistance. As such, Shaykh Abu Turab's representation of the events at Badasht disentangles them from the disciplining rhetoric of the past and of their direct and coterminous association with Islamic practice.

Qurrat al-'Ayn Tahirih's appearance unveiled in the public and gendered space of the garden also questions the hierarchical structure imposed on the garden as the space reserved for the pious and the noble. In questioning this hierarchical structure, Qurrat al-'Ayn Tahirih is said to claim that her presence in the garden as the word spoken by the Qa'im would put to flight "the chiefs and nobles of the earth." Although physically unveiled, her speech re-veils her (so to speak) as the word spoken by the Qa'im himself, the charismatic leader who abrogates the *shari'ah* (law) and establishes the reign of a new era in religious and political history. Her antidisciplinary gesture, as recollected by Shaykh Abu Turab, thus introduces a "foreign other" into the realm dominated by the rhetorics of authority and power formerly attributed to Qurrat al-'Ayn Tahirih's sexual counterpart. As such, she is made to launch a frontal attack on (Islamic) hierarchical and other-worldly discourse, introducing human activity as the basis for social progress.

According to Amanat, in the days that followed Qurrat al-'Ayn's historical speech, each of the participants at the conference took on a new name, thereby signaling their rebirth into a new era in time. Then, as if to acknowledge Qurrat al-'Ayn Tahirih's gesture, the participants discarded their prayer rugs, which by design orient the pious body toward Mecca, and broke their prayer seals, equating them to idols in a gesture not unlike Muhammad's when he tried to convey the definite break with an era of paganistic devotion by destroying the objects of idol worship. The space of Islam in Shaykh Abu Turab's recollections was confronted by a discourse of antagonism at the Badasht Conference, thereby creating the conditions for a different discourse on space and a new era in (religious) history (1989, 327).

Shaykh Abu Turab's recollections of the events that took place in Badasht reconstruct a consistent, continuous, and antagonistic portrait of a revolutionary movement that through the gestures and words of one of its renowned female representatives introduced discontinuity into the life of the Muslim mind. In appropriating this stance, Shaykh Abu Turab's recollections "cut" our knowledge of Islamic history, disarm its notion of a unified subjectivity, and question its sense of historical continuity. Ironically, this stance is only possible by the appropriation of an undivided subjectivity informed by Shaykh Abu Turab's recollection of Qurrat al-'Ayn Tahirih as a presentable female without equal—a recollection that claims for her the status of the avatar of Fatimih in order to take a somewhat "existentialist" stance.

If we look at other accounts of Qurrat al-'Ayn Tahirih, there is reason to believe that matters are not as straightforward as they seem. Browne's collections of various historical materials suggest that in one of his conversation with Mirza Yahya—known as Azal, the half-brother of Mirza Husayn Ali Nuri Baha'u'llah—it was remarked that Qurrat al-'Ayn never intentionally took off the veil.[25] Browne comments that *if he can remember*

25. This statement may, of course, be understood in terms of the way in which the notion of female unveiling is sometimes conceptualized in Islamic ideology. Unveiling has in

the conversation correctly, Mirza Yahya responded to the question of Qurrat al-'Ayn Tahirih's discarding of the veil with the following words: "It is not true that she laid aside the veil. Sometimes when carried away by her eloquence, she allowed it to slip down off her face, but she would always replace it after a few moments" (Browne 1891, 314).

Nabil's Narrative, Agency, and Effective History

Shaykh Abu Turab's recollections of the Badasht Conference are rather precarious in the context of Babi history because no one seems to elaborate on who Abu Turab is. Browne suggests that Abu Turab was one of the earliest disciples of the Bab and that he was married to one of Qurrat al-'Ayn Tahirih's female students, a woman of "extraordinary virtue and piety" (Browne 1891, 247). Nabil, on the other hand, introduces Abu Turab as a Shaykhi who never really acknowledged the Bab's claims until much later in the Bab's career. According to Nabil he apparently died in the Tehran prison where he was held captive with some well-known Babi leaders, including Mirza Husayn Ali Nuri Baha'u'llah (Zarandi 1996, 30).[26]

To add more complexity to the matter, Abu Turab seemingly plays *the* most insignificant role in the grand and at times grotesque history of the Babi movement as presented in *Nabil's Narrative.* He appears only four

---

different times and places been understood as gesture of female nudity. Its citation therefore is incriminating to the woman and to the pious man in Islam.

26. In personal correspondence with me, Moojan Momen helped me assemble some facts on Shaykh Abu Turab, known as Shyakh Abu Turab Ishtihardi in Babi and Baha'i historiography. He was a student of Sayyid Kazim Rashti in Karbala and studied with many of the Bab's early followers including Mulla Husayn Bushru'i. Shaykh Abu Turab was married to Varaqat al-Firdaws, the sister of Mulla Husayn and he became a Babi as soon as the message of the Babi reached Karbala, in all likelihood by way of Mulla 'Ali Bastami. When Qurrat al-'Ayn Tahirih moved to Karbala he was part of her circle there and then later returned to Iran where he was closely associated with Mirza Husayn 'Ali Baha'u'ullah. It is clear from his description of the events that Abu Turab was present at Badasht, but then he returned to Karbala sometime later. Ishtihard is a town about a hundred kilometers due west of Tehran where Abu Turab established the Baha'i community after Baha'u'llah's declaration of his mission (E-mail Jan. 5, 2003).

times in the more than seventy years of history narrated by Nabil: once as the chronicler of the Badasht Conference (Zarandi 1996, 211); a second time as Qurrat al-'Ayn's bodyguard after the conference (216); a third time as the harbinger of glad tidings at Shaykh Tabarsi;[27] and finally as a character witness against Haji Mirza Karim Khan Kirmani in his recollections of Sayyid Kazim (29–31).

It is the latter moment that I would like to pause and reflect on because here, once again, Abu Turab's recollections are drawn upon to elucidate a critical situation. In Nabil's historiography, Abu Turab's recollection of Haji Mirza Karim Khan Kirmani is brought into the picture only paragraphs before Sayyid Kazim Rashti's death is characterized. It is obviously a moment that if not negotiated carefully would create a potential crisis for Babism's legitimacy as a religious movement.

Sayyid Kazim was known as the religious leader of the Shaykhi school, a heterodoxy of Shi'ite Islam situated in Karbala (Iraq). According to most sources, he had taught the Return of the Twelfth Imam (the Qa'im or Mahdi) for years and prepared his students to investigate this Return were it to occur in their lifetime. The Bab's initial claims regarding his gatehood to the Mahdi in 1844 were directed at Sayyid Kazim's students at the Shaykhi school, many of whom accepted it after the teacher's death.[28] In effect the Bab took on "the successorship" of the Shaykhi school. Shaykh Abu Turab is said to be one of Sayyid Kazim's prominent students who accepted the Bab's subsequent claims to Mahdihood.

The positioning of Abu Turab's recollection in the context of Nabil's historiography becomes clear if we consider the role played by the third party to this recollection: Haji Mirza Karim Khan Kirmani, another prominent student of Sayyid Kazim, who left the Shaykhi school some years before the death of Sayyid Kazim and established himself in Kirman, where he started his own branch of the school (called the Kirmani school). Although familiar with the Bab's claims, Kirmani rejected the Bab and was for years involved in the agitation of the remainder of Sayyid Kazim's students against the Bab and his followers.

27. For a discussion of the battle at Shaykh Tabarsi, also known as the "Mazandaran upheavals," see Momen (1983).

28. For a more detailed account of the Shaykhi school and its history, see Bayat (1982).

Abu Turab's recollections, situated (in textual terms) only moments before Sayyid Kazim's death in *Nabil's Narrative,* give Abu Turab's words a highly charged task: to recall a moment in which Sayyid Kazim rejects his own student, Karim Khan Kirmani. In Abu Turab's recollection of this conversation, Sayyid Kazim is said to have referred to Karim Khan Kirmani as one "accursed," whose doctrines are "heretical" and "atheistic" and "who has grievously erred in his judgment" (Zarandi 1996, 29). Abu Turab's recollection of this conversation with his own teacher can be read as a self-serving character assassination. But its strategic positioning at a crisis point in Nabil's historiography clearly situates its content in a historiographic place that rids the reader of any doubt as to the successorship of Sayyid Kazim before the historical crisis is even recounted. For *Nabil's Narrative,* Abu Turab's recollections situate the necessary continuity of his narrative of the Babi movement's revolutionary history and its legitimacy.

But why is this important? What relevance does this textual positioning have for a revolutionary history that relentlessly posits itself as the driving force for social change, and that uses strategy in the face of chance to disrupt the foundations of Islamic thought by revealing discontinuities in its history?

Abu Turab's role, although infinitesimal in Nabil's narration of Babism's history, is played on a measured field of continuity and discontinuity. Abu Turab's recollections of Badasht in the *Narrative* launch an account of the movement's discontinuity with Islamic traditions and values, forcing a break between Islam and Babism through a detailed representation of the conference. Abu Turab's recollections of Qurrat al-'Ayn Tahirih's actions and words in Badasht, much like his portrayed role as her bodyguard after the conclave, suture the necessary subjectivity that would then posit human agency up against an identity in crisis. His recollections thus situate a continuous subjectivity against a decrepit identity. (The conference participants' collective appropriation of new names, we should note, is important in the configuration of this identity.) For Nabil, this still leaves the question of the movement's legitimacy unanswered. Here, as we have already observed, the "Browne narratives" resort to messianic redemption.

In drawing on Abu Turab's recollections, Nabil, by contrast, situates the Babi movement's legitimacy in Sayyid Kazim's rejection of his pupil,

Karim Khan. More important, he does this before the teacher's death. Indeed, through this rejection, and almost fortuitously, he posits the Bab as the legitimate claimant to Sayyid Kazim's successorship, creating through Abu Turab's recollections a continuity between the two schools of thought: Shaykhism and Babism. Legitimacy is established in the face of every claim directed at the movement from it opponents.

The figure of Abu Turab must be seen as problematical. Divided on the juncture between insignificance and infinite signification, split on the critical line dividing continuity and change, and called upon to bear witness to the movement's legitimacy and Qurrat al-'Ayn Tahirih's illegitimate gesture, Abu Turab is made to exemplify the Babi movement as such. For as Fischer and Abedi remark, the Babi movement as a revolutionary movement can be seen as a "mixture of progressive ideas and initiatives and reactionary theocratic ones" (1990, 231).

It is precisely within this ambivalence that we must locate the significance of Qurrat al-'Ayn Tahirih's unveiled appearance in *Nabil.* While it is clear that female unveiling *did* occur in Shrine protests to demonstrate that the proper "order" of things was out of kilter and should be restored, this citation of unveiling epitomizes a force that is not restorative, as much as it is transformative. It configures a drastic break from an old order and points toward the need to establish a new reign.

A *ta'ziyeh* from this period uses the gesture of unveiling as a restorative of order. In the *Ta'ziyeh of Imam Husayn,* Zaynab (Imam Husayn's sister) threatens to tear off her veil when Husayn asks her to "bring his old, dirty ragged garment to put on" (Pelly 1879, 90–91). By this gesture of unveiling she expresses her confusion and suggests that she perceives Husayn's request as a disruption of order in the world: "What has an old garment to do with being a king?" (91). Husayn proceeds to put on the tattered garments underneath the new, saying, "neither the old nor the new of this world can be depended on" (91). To Zaynab's protests he then answers, "Rend not thy dress, modest sister, nor pull off thy head-covering. There is a mystery involved in my action. Know that what Husain [Husayn] has done has a good meaning in it. His putting on an old garment is not without signification" (91–92).

While the rending of the veil in this *ta'ziyeh* further reinforces gestures of distress and emphasizes a call for order, in *Nabil* the unveiling motif calls for the transformation, rather than the restoration of a preestablished and fixed order. As such, Abu Turab's recollections of Qurrat al-'Ayn's unveiling neither draw on the dramatic representation of Islam in the *ta'ziyeh* nor mimic its demands. They evoke instead what Benjamin regards as "the archaic." In his *Arcades Project* on the modernity of Paris, Benjamin attempts to show the ways that the new, by constituting a break with the old, resurrects not the immediate past but a distant one—"the archaic." In the *Arcades Project* he demonstrates this by "rescuing" and assembling scraps of cultural products from nineteenth-century Paris to illuminate the conditions of his own present.

Writing about the theory behind his project, Benjamin notes that history decomposes into images, not narratives. This move involves an immanent critique of the concept of progress. In nineteenth-century Paris, Benjamin finds a restorative impulse evident in its new technologies. There photography mimics traditions in painting, and the first railroad car follows the design of stagecoaches. Iron ornaments are shaped like leaves and are made to resemble wood; electric light bulbs are shaped like gas flames; the first department stores, with immense glass roofs, are made to resemble Oriental bazaars (Buck Morss 1989, 111). Technology, Benjamin argues, expresses the "not-yet" of its new nature in archaic symbols rather than in new forms commensurate with it. In nineteenth-century Paris, these technological innovations were not "emancipated" and were still in a mythic stage, however. In Benjamin's conception, modern technological innovations were not emancipated because they supported a conventional imagination that saw the new as a continuation of the old. In the collective imagination the innovations therefore signaled "progress." Of course, Benjamin would reject any temptation to argue that these "archaic reproductions" were a return to past myths. On the contrary, he saw in the traces of the ur-images (in the archaic) within the new technologies a motivation for future emancipation, that is, not figuratively a restoration of the past, but in fact, the return of the archaic with a new twist. These "ur–temporal elements" within the new innovations were indexes that, like unseen and unconscious details in a photograph, were marked for future redemption. This is a future that, from Benjamin's standpoint, the era could only "begin to surmise" (Buck Morss 1989, 114–20).

In my view, it is the ur–temporal element within Shaykh Abu Turab's recollections of Badasht that situates Babism's fundamental break with the immediate old, that is, from its continuity with the traditions of Shi'ite Islam in *Nabil.* Briefly, that ur–temporal element lies hidden in the heart-wrenching image of Isfahani's self-mutilation at the sight of an unveiled Tahirih. In Shaykh Abu Turab's recollections of Badasht, it is this image that is indexed for redemption. The image of Isfahani's self-mutilation at the sight of an unveiled Tahirih recalls an archaic kernel, a Qur'an story that constitutes a *gushe* or prologue to the *ta'ziyeh.* This *gushe* is based on the Qur'an's "Best of Stories" or the story of Joseph. The retelling of that story's highlights deserves a brief digression, after which we will once again return to the archaic index hidden within Shaykh Abu Turab's recollections of Badasht.

The Best of Stories

In the much-loved story of Joseph in the Qur'an, Joseph is represented as a delicate and comely man. In the tale, he is repeatedly tested for his ability to endure hardship without losing his faith. His jealous brothers throw him into a pit from which he is saved by a caravan and then sold to an Egyptian named al-'Aziz. This first portion of the tale commonly precedes *ta'ziyeh*s as a *gushe* and thus gives weight to the representation of Imam Husayn's hardships as equal to, even surpassing that of the prophets of old.

In al-'Aziz's household, sura 12 of the Qur'an continues to record, Joseph was seduced by al-'Aziz's wife. For untold reasons he was imprisoned, and his endurance was tested again. In the end, and upon his release, Joseph was vindicated. Al-'Aziz's wife confessed her guilt over the adultery, and Joseph became the ruler of Egypt and a prophet.

Joseph's seduction, as Gayane Karen Merguerian and Afsaneh Najmabadi point out, is "narrated as part of a series of tests of prophethood" (1997, 488). Joseph is tempted and tries to flee the scene of temptation. Al-'Aziz's wife tries to grab him and tears his shirt from behind. "Confronted by her husband, she accuses Yusuf [Joseph] of attempted transgression. The torn shirt is suggested, by 'one of her people,' as a test of truth: had Yusuf attacked her, the shirt should have been torn from the front" (88; my addition). The verses 30–32 of sura 12 tell us that al-'Aziz's wife was not the only one to have been seduced by Joseph's beauty. She invites the town's women to her home for a banquet and calls Joseph to the banquet so that they, too, can see him. The town's women were equally seduced. Enamored, one and all, they cut themselves with knives. The self-mutilation that takes place at the sight of Joseph's beauty by the town's women is the key archaic index buried in the ur-image that is recalled by Abu Turab in his recollection of Qurrat al-'Ayn in Badasht. Key here is the Qur'an verse that reads:

> In the city, women were saying: "Al-'Aziz's wife has sought to seduce her servant. She has conceived a passion for him. It is clear that she has gone astray." When she [al-'Aziz's wife] heard of their intrigues, she invited them to a banquet prepared at her house. To each she gave a knife. She then ordered Yusuf [Joseph] to present himself before them. So struck were they by his beauty that they cut their hands with the knives,[29] exclaiming "God preserve us! This is no mortal, but a gracious angel." "This is he," she said, "on whose account you blamed me. I attempted to seduce him, but he was unyielding." (Merguerian and Najmabadi 1997, 488; my additions)

This passage, unlike much of sura 12 of the Qur'an, has no parallel in Genesis, though Merguerian and Najmabadi argue that it may have its source in a Hebrew midrash that could have been transmitted to the Arabs through the Jews of Yemen (Merguerian and Najmabadi 1997, 489). But it is noteworthy that although it is not generally included as part of the *ta'ziyeh* prologue, the townswomen's mutilation sequence is represented in pictorial form on tile paintings of the nineteenth-century *takiyeh*s, indeed adjacent to the representation of Joseph's trials and informing them in literalized form.

29. One translator renders this as "they pressed their fingers between their teeth" and "they gnawed their fingers" (see Merguerian and Najmabadi 1997, 504; Khan 1991, 221 and 223).

As with the tile images of women's mutilation connoting Joseph's beauty, Shaykh Abu Turab's recollection of Qurrat al-'Ayn Tahirih's unveiling at Badasht situates the poet as the object of a gaze that disturbs the Isfahani zealot so much that he cuts his own throat. The disruptive beauty, restraint, and purity are not, in Shaykh Abu Turab's recollections of Badasht, those of the comely prophet Joseph, but that of the poet, the avatar of Fatimih herself. In a patient reading of the recollection in *Nabil,* it becomes evident that while Abu Turab connects the self-mutilation of the Isfahani with the ur-image of Joseph and of his stunning appearance in the assemblage of townswomen in the Qur'an, he gives this image a gendered twist. A female beloved emerges out of that cliché that bears witness to the beauty and purity of the male beloved, Joseph. Joseph, who was called into the assemblage of women, takes image form. This image is intimately linked to Tahirih's image, which, in a different time and place and in contrast to the banquet sequence in the Qur'an, shows her bringing herself to the assemblage of men. She proceeds adorned and unveiled into the assemblage of men, seeing that her demands to speak to Quddus have fallen on deaf ears. The image of Joseph, whose striking appearance causes the women "to gnaw" at their own fingers, an image of exquisite desire and relentless pleasure, is developed in Shaykh Abu Turab's graphic recollection to take on a new form in the portrait of a beautiful poet, Tahirih, within whose figurative presence the frightful force of change and, indeed, the horrors of the Bab's uncompromising vision of revolutionary transformation are crystallized. The horror and pleasure of this Babi's unveiled presence is signaled by the disruptive bloodshed that follows.

On Qurrat al-'Ayn Tahirih's Unpresentability

The contrast between the representation of Qurrat al-'Ayn Tahirih in the "Browne chronicles" and Shaykh Abu Turab's recollections is unsettling. That is perhaps only so if one expects an over-abundance of tabloid commentary on an unexpected or unseemly gesture such as the one reported by Shaykh Abu Turab in *Nabil's Narrative.* However, it seems precisely for this reason that the unveiling and the literal assumption of power are left unpresented in the chronicles assembled by Browne. Historians, whose work is involved in a process of documentation, cannot tell us why the author of Browne's *Nuqtat al-Kaf* ignores Qurrat al-'Ayn Tahirih's unveiling, but I would submit that a comparative cultural and literary analysis such as the one I have attempted creates a significant frame for the analysis of such questions. I have argued that much of early Babi historiography, and the *Nuqtat al-Kaf,* in particular, rely on the tropes of the Karbala passions to achieve political ends. *Nuqtat al-Kaf* uses those tropes that are familiar to the audiences of the Karbala eulogies and *ta'ziyehs* to engage the emotions and actions of its national constituents. In each instance the actions and persons of the Babi leaders and the spaces in which they move, like those of the actors on the *ta'ziyeh* stage, are uniquely tied to that of the early Muslims heroes and the Shi'ite vision of their resurrection on *al-yaum,* the Day of Judgment. Mulla Husayn is Imam Husayn. Shaykh Tabarsi is Karbala. And the Bab is the Mahdi returned. The day—*al-yaum*—of the present is indexically redeemed and mimetically connected to both the vision of a reenacted past and to the return of that moment on the day made special for its significance as Judgment Day. In this context, the unveiling of Qurrat al-'Ayn Tahirih must be seen as a severance of all unique ties with the Shi'ite past, in that it in no way replicates it or is answerable to its traditions. Indeed even her appropriation of Fatimih's legacy, as Amanat notes, involves a revaluation of her place in the traditions of old. The contrast is revealing: "Qurrat al-'Ayn's Fatima was one of independent will and action. The leadership she assumed . . . in Badasht was the realization of this paradigm" (1989, 331). Forced to account for Qurrat al-'Ayn's actions outside the confines of the known, *Nuqtat al-Kaf* renders her physical unveiling only in a metaphorical remark, where it regards the days in Badasht as a time in which the fruits of the Bab's revelation reached their height of ripeness—a ripeness that tore open the fruit's own skin *(az shiddat-i rasidigi pust ra parih nimudand)* to reveal an exquisite kernel *(maghz-i dilkash)* (Browne 1910, 145). But even that remark, we must admit, is a meager attempt at representation. For in its graphic depiction of the torn skin and of the ripeness of the time, it recalls the exchange between Imam Husayn's daughter, Fatimih, with her bridegroom, Qasim, in the *ta'ziyeh* of their wedding during the Karbala battle. Here Fatimih, addressing her vanquished groom, asks: "How may I know you on the Day of Resurrection? Tell me by what sign may I recognize you? Give me a sign now, O lord, so I may be able to find you by that sign." Qasim, her groom, replies: "With ripped sleeve, with sorrowful eyes, with a body torn in a hundred places, among the group of martyrs, along with Akbar and Abbas, in the service of your father, king of the thirsty-lipped [Imam Husayn], you will recognize me on Doomsday" (Petty 1982, 226; my addition). For the Babi author(s) of *Nuqtat al-Kaf*—a text that is at once a history, a drama, and a document of national regeneration—the present of the chronicle returns in the guise of the recognized and desired utopian time—the "now time" of Judgment. The "now" of Babi action appears in the garment of the known but unredeemed, not in the robe of the unknown.

So what of the momentous unveiling of the poet in these chronicles?

While the other significant Babi events that are represented in *Nuqtat al-Kaf* are uniquely linked to a messianic time and are characterized by the eschatological meanings assumed by *al-yaum* ("present" but also Judgment Day), the moment of the poet's unveiling issues an unpresentable "now-time." Her unveiling, in other words, is severed from both early Muslim history and the Shi'ite vision of Judgment Day. It is a "now" that ruptures both the perception of continuity in history and its mimetic reenactment in the Karbala passion on that everyday that is considered to be Judgment Day. As such, the act of unveiling represents an act and a present that can only be the subject of the reports of the most recent day, that is, the proper object of a newspaper. The account of everyday life in Iran as the proper topic of the newspaper did not appear until 1851. (The first of these, according to Browne, was "ruznama-i Waqayi-i Ittifaqiyya"; see Browne 1983). But the shock of this un-present-able rupture in the continuity of history emerged systematically and emphatically in the accounts of everyday acts in the personal journals and poetics of Qajar subjects from the 1850s to as late as the 1930s. This shock makes its presence known in images of the stereotypical and fetishized "Babi" in passing remarks that suggest the subject's abjection. These images, often marked by a reference to objects of clothing, cast "the Babi" as the ambivalent emblem of modernity, the carrier of the vices and virtues of European cultures and the innovators of sartorial fashions. The modern Iranian self, here, appears in image form, as the image of the abject "Babi," as an other within.

In contrast to the topical nature of newspapers, photographs, and journals, *Nuqtat al-Kaf*'s view of history, as most Babi accounts of that era, must be characterized as redemptive. (Redemptive, yet unable to recognize the technologies necessary for the representation of the topical present.) Redemption assumes that the chronicler of history represents the occurrences of his time *only* insofar as he can cast them in the mold of a time known, envied, or desired. Characteristic of the practices of nineteenth-century *ta'ziyeh*s, redemption demands a firm grasp of the past, which connects singular moments in the present with that of an archaic, messianic one. *Nuqtat al-Kaf*'s history as an analogous activity of redemption remains in the fluctuating space, unable to speak of a present (such as Badasht) that is detached from a unique, mimetic connection with messianic time.

A similar stance can be argued for *Tarikh-i-Jadid.* Any attempt to assemble the Babis under the banner of the Return would be negated precisely because an unveiled Qurrat al-'Ayn Tahirih could not be understood in terms of Fatimih's return. Hence, as a project that represents the Babi period as a fold in Islamic time, the act of unveiling is a literal laceration. It punctures the very call to reform that is the obvious next step (continuity) for a nation fluctuating between the standards of Shi'ite Islam and those signaling European progress. The success of *Tarikh-i-Jadid*'s project depends on the reader's perception of continuity between the traditions of Shi'ite Islam and the actions of the Babis. The visual technology for the representation of the Babi present—as a present without equal—is as yet "unemancipated" in this text.

Nabil's Narrative is essentially a historical project that, while redemptive, articulates the Babi movement as sustained by a revolutionary and thus a progressive potential. In its portrayal of the Badasht conclave, the historical narrative clearly points up the fact that the movement raised the clarion call for a new moment in time, a moment severed from Islam. *Nabil's Narrative* uses Shaykh Abu Turab's recollections for the archaic kernel that it holds. It draws on an archaic image, crystallized in the Qur'an's "Best of Stories" and then transformed in Abu Turab's recollections to take on a new meaning. Indeed, rather than relying on *ta'ziyeh* tropes, the *Narrative* draws on the literarized images surrounding the *ta'ziyeh* stage, those details of the "Best of Stories" adorning the *takiyeh* walls. Although dramatic in form, the story of Badasht comes together by an appeal to the archaic image preserved in the present in these mural paintings—in paintings representing the townswomen's banquet sequence. Using the Qur'an tale of Joseph as if it were a photographic cliché, a photographic negative, Abu Turab's recollection develops the detail of the banquet sequence buried within it, and in the process transforms the story to an infinitely reproducible and mutable image. "Details of structure," Benjamin writes, "with which technology and medicine are normally concerned—all this is, in its origins, more native to the camera than the atmospheric landscape or soulful portrait. Yet at the same time, photography reveals in this material physiognomic aspects, image worlds, which dwell in the smallest things—meaningful yet covert enough to find a hiding place in waking dreams, but which, enlarged and capable of formulation, make the difference between technology and magic visible as a thoroughly historical variable" (Benjamin 1999b, 512). A transformation such as the one developed from the Qu'ranic detail and rendered into movement like "pictures which flitted by the onlooker under pressure of the thumb" (Benjamin 2003c, 280n 39), once thought a product of magic, reveals itself as a technological possibility in the camera's re-rendition of the historical. In Shaykh Abu Turab's rendering of the detail, Qurrat al-'Ayn is Joseph, except for her gender. He is ordered into an assembly of women. She, on the other hand, brings herself to an assembly of men. Joseph's beauty is so striking that it rivets the women assembled in the women's banquet, exhibiting a spontaneous physical response that accounts unimaginable pleasures. Qurrat al-'Ayn's appearance, by contrast, leads to a scene of crimson horror and is followed by a century of associations that represent the modern Iranian self in corresponding images of abjection. The transformed archaic image of the prophet Joseph's matchless beauty works as a kernel within *Nabil's Narrative* to constitute the decisive break with the past in the prophecy of a future that has in fact arrived, unperturbed, unveiled, and uninhibited but in the embodied figure of a woman without equal.

In Shaykh Abu Turab's memory, Joseph appears as a cliché—a photographic negative that is progressively developed. In negative form, a pure and comely male prophet appears transformed into a photographic positive—a portrait—of Tahirih, "the pure one." Her very presence in the assemblage of men calls for the severance of the present from all time. While securing the Babi moment's continuity and legitimacy within religious history, Abu Turab's recollection of Qurrat al-'Ayn, in its development of a known cliché, signals the potential of new visual technologies capable of capturing Iran's shocking modernity. His recollection of Badasht recognizes in the image a potential that that era could only "begin to surmise." "For it is an irretrievable image of the past which threatens to disappear in any present that does not recognize itself as intended in that image" Benjamin 2003a, 391). As the new technology of the camera displaced the old media for historical representation (such as the *ta'ziyeh* and the sacred wall paintings of the *takiyeh*), the photographic image began to assume its full potential in representing Iran's unpresentable modernity. Each flitting imprint that was transformed into the next like a photo-booklet under the pressure of the thumb was "a predecessor of the celluloid photogram in a privately regulated motion picture device not yet readied for mass public consumption" (Stewart 1999, 4).

5

Purifying the Nation Through Representation

> For Benjamin, nothing can take place before the photograph, before the event of the photograph. Effecting a certain spacing in time, the photograph gives way to an occurrence. What the photograph inaugurates is history itself, and what takes place in this history is the emergence of the image.
>
> —Eduardo Cadava, *Words of Light*

In photographs dating to the late nineteenth and the early twentieth centuries, court eunuchs look into the camera lens, leaning on tables that are loaded down with leather-bound books. Ever present, the background matte, which is a made-for-the-studio European-garden landscape with marble pillars and gargoyles, suggests to us looking back, the haunting presence of old Europe in the Persian court. In European photographs such pillars represented the emblem of a "well-rounded education" (Benjamin 1999a, 677). Framing the photographs of the servants of the interior, the foreign setting produced by the studio matte attests to a universal perception: photography was seen as an opportunity of becoming other. Photography was not necessarily a means by which we could capture the spirit or the ghost of the subject of portraiture, as some obviously had thought, but was rather a means by which we could create other histories, reveal other selves. In gestures that consign to photography the opportunity to live "spectrally," servants and eunuchs put on costumes and strange straw hats in the Qajar court (Benjamin 1999a, 688). In these photographs, courtiers made themselves look like women, hedgehogs, and flowerpots. In the transformations they effected through the new technology, they articulated what the old forms retrieved by Shaykh Abu Turab's Badasht recollections could only begin to surmise.

A caption for one photograph rendered in *Ganj-e Peyda* reads as follows: "Moshir ol-Hokama (later titled Hakim ol-Molk) examining a patient." In the photograph, the "patient" is prostrate on an ornate Persian rug. He is surrounded by nine men, one of who is blocked by the "assistant's" hat (Tahimi 1998). Another haunts the frame with a booted presence along the right edge of the image. If this is the site of a medical examination, it is a strange one. The tubes balancing on the patient's stomach are made of plastic and resemble coiling intestines. The "doctor's" helpers casually hold wrenches and screwdrivers in their hands and in the background, a frame within a frame, is a pillared British garden landscape, now mounted on an interior wall in the Persian court. A curious smile and a trickster gesture—one finger of a hand to the edge of his mouth and another open and pointing at "the patient." Here a character within the photograph interprets the image for us. He speaks where the contemporary caption falters. His gesture orients our vision toward the ontogeny and phylogeny of a technological ambivalence that embedded itself in the dreams of invention associated with early inscriptive technologies. The play on the magical and the real, on seeing oneself as other and seeing oneself becoming other than oneself in this and many of the photographs belonging to Muzzafar al-Din Shah's court, configures the historical unconscious of the camera as it comes into its own as constitutive of Iranian modernity.

This chapter traces the introduction of visual and aural representational technologies to Iran. It sets the genealogy of these technologies within a history of confluence—a history of exchange, in other words—between the East and the West. This historical exchange is itself nested, I will suggest, in the practices of inscriptive technologies, and as such continues to affect both their representations and their modes of enunciation over time. This history charges an ambiguity in the language of representation and determines it. I will argue that this hidden ambiguity, animating representational technologies from their beginnings, ominously affects, indeed haunts, postrevolutionary Iranian cinema's isolationist strategies today. Focusing on *Delshodegan,* a highly popular postrevolutionary Iranian fiction film by director Ali Hatami that highlights the history of representational technologies, I will attempt to draw out the confluence of these contradictions and chart the ambiguities that surface in close readings of the film's thematic contents and in the organization of its discourse. In longer forays into the history of the technologies of sound and vision—that is, of cinematic technologies—and their role in the representation of the nation, I will consider the repercussions of the cultural confluence that informs processes of representation in the national cinema of the Islamic Republic of Iran. At a time when social historians are asking if a continuous Iranian identity can be established on the basis of a national history, I will submit that contemporary Iranian cinema, as the much celebrated space of the national imaginary and of the projection of its postrevolutionary identity, shows the premise of "continuity" and "purity" in relation to national identity, a premise deeply fraught.[1] As we have observed in readings of nineteenth-century chronicles such as *Tarikh-i-Jadid,* and noted in the cultural transvestism of the *ta'ziyeh,* nineteenth-century imaginary on the modern nation articulated an unsettled ambivalence in relation to such notions of purity. This, I argue, haunts Iran's self-representation in its cinema today.

Postrevolutionary Iranian Cinema

"There is no better example of a nation that is both a discursive construct and an image regime than the Islamic Republic of Iran," writes Roxanne Varzi. And "Khomeini was not only the interpreter and guide of this symbolic world, but he helped to create that world" (2006, 34). Khomeini's role in the constitution of the Islamic Republic of Iran under the direction of the Shi'ite jurists has had a significant impact on the political system, but the transformations that took place in the culture and in the social life of the nation have been tremendous. It is perhaps the regime's insistence on the role of film in the production of a postrevolutionary national identity that has been most noteworthy. Iranian cinema has not only been important to the Islamic government's will to regenerate culture, it has

1. See Chehabi (1997).

also been the means by which the postrevolutionary government's values have gained notoriety in the world at large (Pena 2006, 40–41). Iranian films have participated in film festivals all over the world since the late 1980s, winning awards at numerous festivals, including Cannes, Locarno, Toronto, and New York. As director Abbas Kiarostami once suggested, Iran's greatest export after the Iranian Revolution of 1978–79, besides pistachios, has been its cinema.

After the establishment of the Islamic Republic, the government intervened significantly in the cultural sphere to make access to the means of film production more democratic. Institutions affiliated with the government supported filmmakers and launched massive national campaigns to bring film as a means of public education to villages all over the country. As part of a campaign initiated in the early 1980s, the Ministry of Islamic Guidance provided funds for a mobile cultural and cinematic unit with the ability to project 35 mm films. This unit would travel to remote villages in Iran and provide rural dwellers with the opportunity to borrow books and videos and watch films that would otherwise be inaccessible to them.

The most significant transformation affecting the film industry was aesthetic, however. This change in aesthetics was to be significantly shaped by the film industry's relation to the female body. The enforced veiling of women aimed to purify an artform and an industry that was previously associated with vice and Western values. The industry, now purified from vice, was suddenly being shaped by women who wanted to be behind the camera. More women entered the industry after 1982 than in the century of cinema in Iran prior to the Revolution (Naficy 1994). The enforcement of modesty laws and the rule of veiling constricted women's representational presence in cinema considerably, however. Following the announcement of new government regulations for the industry in the early 1980s, postrevolutionary Iranian cinema dictated that both women and men abide by the rule of modesty. Women were strictly veiled, and in the early 1980s men and women were forbidden to exchange glances in close-up shots or to look at each other directly on screen. The arrested exchange made one of the tools conventionally used in cinema to convey conversation next to impossible. The ban on heterosexual exchange on screen, a ban that, as we shall see, confronted the defining roots of the medium in Iran, constricted the use of the shot/reverse shot, a conventional pattern inextricably linked to Hollywood classicism and promoted throughout the world by the standardizing measure of the American film industry.

During the years that immediately followed the Iranian Revolution and the Iran-Iraq war (1980–88), close-ups of women were strictly forbidden as well. A close-up of a woman's face on screen would put a nonfamilial or unrelated male in the audience in close and intimate proximity to her in representational form. Government censors saw this representational frame in cinema as a violation of the doctrine of modesty. A sustained insistence on modesty forced filmmakers to think of new representational strategies and plotlines. While this constriction on cinematic language was altered over the years, the veil and modest garb for women on screen would continue to be strictly enforced. Restrictions of this sort were aimed at the purification of the industry and, through it, a cleansing of the culture itself from all perceived foreign influence. To an Iranian audience, Muslim or not, however, the veiling of women's bodies in both public and private narrative spaces on screen would appear unrealistic. For while women must wear the *hijab* in public space according to the laws of the Republic, the veil is not considered obligatory in the privacy of the home. Yet these laws, as they are addressed to the film industry, insist on the veiling of women in all narrative spaces, public or private. Like the use of veiling during the Medinese civil war in the early years of Islam, the Islamic Republic saw the veiling of screen women as a way to protect the national community from all impurities associated with outside influence. Thus under the new laws of the Islamic Republic, veiling was key to the representation of Iran's national identity and independence in cinema.

To create a national cinema attached to the veiled and modest body of the female was commensurate with the creation of a national culture that was protected from and independent of both East and West. But as the vibrant life of the Islamic Revolution was being knit to the history of cinema, Iranian film journals engaged in debates around cinema's function in relation to lived reality and Iranian cinema's national character. What is a cinema of resistance? they asked. What is a cinema with a message?

How does a film industry show its national characteristics? In disregarding the imperialist and commercial impulses of Western films, how does Iranian film communicate and to whom? What constitutes a cinema's national difference? (Sadr 2002, 236, 241, 245). And how can a national cinema make its presence known when it makes its own subjects and its spaces unpresentable?

For director Ali Hatami, the fundamental first step in creating a national cinema after the 1979 revolution was to construct a new *optique,* a different style and an altered national form for Iranian cinema. In his view, the fundamental assertion of difference in Iranian film, that is, the constitution of a so-called national cinema, could not occur on the level of the narrative and mise-en-scène. The "Iranian difference" in national cinema had to go beyond showing characters that speak in Persian, cook Persian food, and sit on Persian rugs. Clearly the quotidian does determine elements of Iranian cultural life. This is true. And these elements are incorporated to lend national character to his films. But for Hatami, the specificity of cultural difference was to be inscribed within the processes of production itself and, more precisely, on the level of cinematic enunciation, where narrative meaning is produced, patterned, and organized. For Iranian cinema to be national, this process of ordering and patterning would have to signal the national difference. "I cannot tell an Iranian story on the patterns and production processes of the West. What I mean is, I have seen musicals or films about music in European and global cinemas and I have seen many of them and with a great deal of attention. But what I am attempting to do, and this is where my efforts have converged in the last years, is to realize a language, a style, a production process that arrives through the clarity of Persian speech and Persian storytelling" (Rawhani 1378 [1999], 545). What Hatami means in referring to speech and narration is not dialogue precisely. National difference in his film must be conditioned by the specificity of "technique" and "style." Thus national difference for Hatami is the difference that emerges not out of a difference in content and dialogue so much as in the determined ordering of undetermined elements—enunciation, more specifically (Elsaesser 1995 ,12). Homi Bhabha maintains that in cultural analysis as with cultural production itself, this shift of focus away from epistemology (on function and intention, which is essentially locked into "the hermeneutical circle") and toward enunciation, relocates cultural production to "alternative, hybrid sites of cultural negotiation" (1994, 177–78). The shift from the epistemological, totalizing view of culture, to culture as an enactive, discursive, and enunciatory site, as we shall see, also, and perhaps unconsciously and unwittingly, "opens up possibilities for other 'times' of cultural meaning (retroactive and prefigurative) and other narrative spaces (fantasmatic, metaphorical)," too (178). From a Benjaminian perspective the resistant kernel, the historical index, hides precisely in this unconscious cultural arrangement. It is here, in the organizing "source" of postrevolutionary Iranian film that "the Babi" image, the image of the self as abject other, nests. But this already anticipates too much. A brief discussion of Ali Hatami's cinematic production after the Revolution will be more suited to the task of delineating the national coordinates of his postrevolutionary films and suggest the means by which we can access contemporary Iran's attempt to represent its identity through them.

Delshodegan: Neither East nor West

Ali Hatami was one of Iran's most prolific contemporary filmmakers until his untimely death in 1998 and was lauded as the master poet of Iranian cinema. The overwhelming popularity of his work for the screen in Iran has been noted for its heavy emphasis on dialogue and rich poetic language and composition. Although involved in the film industry before the Islamic Revolution, his work after the Revolution is primarily known for introducing new innovations in genre. Hatami's engagement with the cinema in the postrevolutionary period involved the elaboration of what he has referred to as "the historical genre." In 1982 Hatami made *Haji Washington,* a film about the tribulations of the Persian ambassador to the United States during the reign of the monarch Nasir al-Din Shah Qajar (1848–96). Two years later, in 1984, Hatami made *Kamal ul-Mulk,* a fiction film about the famous nineteenth-century Iranian painter in the court of Nasir al-Din Shah. Made in 1990, *Madar,* (Mother), is one of Hatami's best-known films in the West. It excavates buried histories of forced Westernization under Reza Shah Pahlavi (1925–41).

Hatami's *Delshodegan* (1992; sometimes rendered in English as Love Stricken, The Enamored, or Haunted by Love), produced two years after *Madar,* follows a group of Iranian musicians who travel to Europe to record traditional music on the early gramophone. The film is set during the rule of Sultan Ahmad Shah Qajar in Iran (r. 1909–25). Hatami emphasizes in an interview with Omid Rawhani about the making of *Delshodegan* that his aim, however, was not to represent a specific historical persona or an actual historical period. Indeed, he suggests that the events that are directly portrayed in *Delshodegan* may have occurred either before or immediately after the reign of Ahmad Shah. Like the *ta'ziyeh*'s atomistic conception of time, the fictive era that is represented in the film does not necessarily coincide with Ahmad Shah's rule. According to Hatami, although the film is about the processes involved in the recording of music, "the specific historical figures" associated with the recording of traditional music are unimportant to the film itself. Every person, he says, has a unique "ideological stance and world view and is conditioned by the political and cultural atmosphere of his/her time, but my subject matter and my objective was to attend to music itself" (Rawhani 1999 [1378], 541–45). In the course of his career and in making historical films, Hatami says, he realized that it was possible to give birth to characters in film that were in essence allegorical or metonymical representations of certain personalities who lived or who may have lived in a given era. In *Delshodegan,* therefore, his aim was to create characters that had no other identity except the musical one: "I created personalities and wrote ones that were derived from historical figures, not only from the Qajar era, but also figures who live in this present era. For example the character of the drummer in the film has more of Hassan Tehrani [the actor who plays the character], than of a historical figure, but I brought him [Tehrani] back to the Qajar era" (541). Hatami's reflections on the characters created for the film point up the fact that *Delshodegan* is not quite a chronicle of national history, nor is it entirely a cinematic reflection on the present. Although the film deals with the question of modernity, Hatami sees *Delshodegan* as a fictionalized history in film. More than a documentary about the nation's past, the film is a reflection on the inscription and standardization of traditional music. As such, the film deals with the *longue durée* of contingencies that have surrounded and continue to inform the historical inscription of "the national" in representational technologies. As with *ta'ziyeh* representations of antiquity that create correspondences with the present of happening, the nation's past and present are coeval in *Delshodegan* and, as such, are cast as part and parcel of the cinematic mediation and woven into the genealogy of the film's technologies. The temporal index operating here belongs to the *ta'ziyeh,* then. Here, all time determines the now-time of representation. It is this confluence of times that provides the setting for the reception of the historical drama.

Characters drawn from the present become embodiments of the past in the film and give shape to its "historical" perceptions. Their insights are historical, though they remain their own and in turn become ours as well. True to *ta'ziyeh* form, national spaces, whether fictional or indexical, historical or contemporary, are transformed through the intervention of the film's technologies into sites with uncertain historical and spatial boundaries. They become orientations more than fixed locations and sites (more like allegories of the *takiyeh*) where the past and the present of national culture can interact in representational form. This insight is borne out in Hatami's discussion of the choices he made in directing the film: "I thought it would be interesting to show that early sound recording devices are curiosities not only for the contemporary audience of the film, but for my characters as well" (Rawhani 1999 [1378], 544). Fictional characters on the screen and audience members present before the screen are seen as inhabiting synchronous positions vis-à-vis mediating technologies—technologies that simultaneously plot the course of the narrative and that constitute and represent the nation's identity, past and present. The film's narrative becomes the landscape of music, a landscape in which the fullness of the past is redeemed in the present of production and reception. The film's temporal index heralds, in the manner of the "Browne chronicles," the site of Judgment Day, the day that for every believing Iranian Shi'ite is the everyday.

Positing the coevalness of the past and present in the film, Hatami speaks of the film not only as a project that is preoccupied with the status of sound, music, and its recording, but also as an enterprise that reflects on the status of the cinematic object as such, its technologies, and the work involved in producing its narrative. Indeed, in his rejection of models for his films, whether formal or stylistic, he seems to suggest his project as involved in the "struggle over the cultural politics of standardization"—a struggle that, although not solely embedded in the hierarchies of cultural distinction historically rooted in the technologies of film, played a historical role in configuring the medium's uses with the coming of sound to cinema (Mowitt 2004, 397). The temporal confluence that the film's diectics inherited from the *ta'ziyeh,* is used as a means to revolt and to resist the determining marks of standardization, which, put forthrightly, is the stamp of the imperial domination of Hollywood in cinemas all over the world. The "all-time" of musical history in *Delshodegan* is in this way brought into a messianic and revolutionary confrontation with the dominant forces that standardize vision and hearing in cinema, at a moment in time—a now-time—that configures the present as the redemptive moment of national purification in cinema.

Historically speaking, recorded sound was precisely what came to be seen as that which distinguished "national cinemas" from Hollywood. As John Mowitt's genealogical analysis of the regulatory discourse that has linked film, language, and foreignness in the United States demonstrates, sound served as a decisive locus for the coordination of domestic and "foreign" industrial strategies. "This coordination," he writes, "vital in certain respects to the capitalist aim of vertical integration, did not simply standardize a certain technological system; it also displaced the infancy of the pre-linguistic era of the cinema. In other words, with the exportation of standardized sound practices, the cinema entered language, or, as Fitzhugh Green famously put it, film found 'its tongue'" (2004, 396). In the international history of film we know that sound gave the European film industries a "new weapon against American domination" (Sklar 1994, 222). Foreign films could talk. Indeed they could talk back. With wagging tongues they could compete with American films for a market share. Yet, according to Mowitt, the Academy of Motion Pictures, Arts, and Sciences (AMPAS), like many other national institutions in the 1930s through the 1950s, explicitly intervened in the "domain of indigenous cultural practices not only to impose the capitalist logic of standardization, but also, in effect, to eliminate foreignness from the cinema" (Mowitt 2004, 398). This intervention in cultural practices identifies precisely the site of struggle for Hatami, a struggle that he also sees as any national cinema's struggle against the homogenization of the medium of film itself. In order to confront the history of Hollywood domination, he configures a temporal now-time that embraces the messianic all-time of musical recording, musical representation, and reception. Grounded in the confluence of a redemptive and messianic "all-time," Iranian national cinema is able to confront the imperial effects of standardization in the international film industry on the national front.

The standardization of cinema sets limits. These limits not only mold the formal and material components of film, they also come to determine, in large part, the habits of film reception and viewing. Standardization is responsible for the disciplining of film and film audiences both. In referring to his Iranian viewers who have been habituated to the codes and conventions, or "patterns," of Hollywood cinema primarily, Hatami identifies his own struggles in his attempt to produce a national feature film against the disciplining force-field of standardization. This gesture casts his project as antidisciplinary in nature:

> I have always said that the difficulties that my more privileged viewers, cinéphiles and film critics, have had in watching my films has been [based on] their desire to think through my films by using previously established patterns and formulas, but my work . . . has no such models. It is important to emphasize that this is a new phenomenon in Iranian cinema. Perhaps there have been documentaries that exist somewhere and that I have not seen, but in feature fiction films, there is no extant pattern. There is no film, that is, about the conditions of Iranian traditional and classical music in the late Qajar and early Pahlavi era and about the recording of music and voice. Perhaps in American cinema, . . . *Singing in the Rain*, for example, which is essentially different in style and production, so it could not be a model for my film. (Rawhani 1378 [1999], 544)

The process involved in the material transfiguration of silent to sound film, which is one of the main narrative threads of Donen and Kelly's *Singing in the Rain* (1952), had, as Mowitt demonstrates, immediate consequences for the chain that links language, film, and foreignness—a configuration that reaches "as does the structure of the commodity [of sound film] itself, into the cultural practices of filmmakers world wide" (2004, 397).[2] In this context, Mowitt continues, "Resistance is not exactly 'futile,' but it is constrained to a degree that projects glaring light on 'modernity at large,' that is, on the social, economic and cultural constellation that re-frames 'indigenous' practices even as quite unevenly developed realities adjust this constellation's focus" (397).

Hatami's elaborate references to making films without models, films that are genuinely national, echo his emphasis on making an emphatically ahistorical film in order to represent the nation's confrontation with the consequences of modernity, exemplified by "the first" recordings of Iranian traditional music abroad. To confront the disciplining imperial practices that have deprived cinema of its national characteristics, to make a cinema that is neither of the East nor of the West, means that a national cinema must stage a revolutionary confrontation with the cultural practices of standardization. In doing so, it must address both the past and the present of the processes and technologies that mediate a national culture to itself and situate the transformation of modernity's constellations over a *longue durée* of historical change. Once again the *ta'ziyeh*'s emplotment of historical time serves as a model for this revolutionary confrontation on the part of the nation.

Hatami's insights into the lack of prefabricated techniques in his films seem to suggest this line of reasoning and to emphasize a resistance to conventional classification systems of foreign language films, which merely "situate foreignness on the sound track and in the speech of those 'foreigners' recorded there" (Mowitt 2004, 398). For Hatami, making an Iranian film means more than just producing a film with a Persian soundtrack. In making Iranian films, Hatami continues: "I do not consider whether or not my mise-en-scène can be compared to this or that foreign film—that I have also seen—or not. I am fully aware that there are things that one can convey with the movement of a tilt or a pan or can capture with a traveling

2. For an overview of the processes involved in the coming into being of sound film and the talkies, see Crafton (1997).

shot. But I sometimes desist and pursue my own path. I am looking for a unique style and a special technique to tell a unique story in a singular form. . . . I want to reach that elegance of style, that elegance of production, of weave and form that appears in the Persian carpet. I am a carpet weaver" (Rawhani 1378 [1999], 545).

Hatami's insistence on the nonstandardized, or rather, antidisciplinary and artisanal character of his films, his resolute insistence on representing the singularity of Persian life and cultural history without imitating given models and techniques, foregrounds the need to search out criteria for the analysis of his *Delshodegan.* In my reading, Hatami's emphasis on the processes of production underscores the significance of cinema's productive technologies and the most obvious technological fork in film, namely that which separates the production of the visual from the aural component of film. Hatami's focus on the international history of cinema and on the processes of national production, by contrast, underscores the importance of that history to his project, emphasizing the international alongside the unique—and he insists, national—engagement with the mediating technologies that make films.

In light of this, the focus of my analysis of *Delshodegan,* a work that attempts to build a national film language in form and style, will be a close reading of the meanings, messages, and contradictions forwarded on two tracks, namely those of sound and of image. In this chapter I will argue for the need to attend to and uphold the contradictions that arise within a secondary forking, namely those produced through the alternative positioning of the film narrative on the one hand and of enunciation on the other in order to read the workings of both the narrative and filmic enunciation (or address) as they evoke "the national." True, this approach abandons the hermeneutics of reading film as narrative, but it allows for a reflection on the enactive sites of culture in which the utopian image of the nation is produced. It is this utopian image of the modern nation that reveals postrevolutionary cinema's uncanny response to the figure of "the Babi," the specter of the other within. Although much attention has been given over to narrative analyses in the study of national cinemas, giving emphasis to film narratives as allegories of "the nation," my aim in this chapter will be to show the importance of attending to filmic enunciation in order to pursue the specificity of national address. To my mind, understanding the coordinates of a national cinema, its address—who speaks, to whom, from where, and at what moment in time—involves the pursuit of this, the cinema's narratological landscape, the much-neglected base term in film studies, *enunciation.* A brief digression on the history of the entry of this term to film studies and its use will set the terms of the analysis of *Delshodegan,* to follow.

Enunciation in Film

As briefly noted in the introduction, enunciation or discourse in linguistics is an instance of communication between a sending and a receiving subject or a speech act, the meaning of which depends on the circumstances configuring an utterance (i.e., the who, to whom, the place, and the time of an utterance). As such, a text inscribes its own situatedness with deictic markers. In film studies, enunciation is much more readily a "correlation of subjectivity," a correlation in which, according to Christian Metz, the "'source' (or origin) of the enunciation and the 'enunciative target' (or destination)" rely to a lesser extent on pronouns and on embodied subjects—representative bodies at the source and at the sites of reception—than on machines (1995, 141). We recall from the distinction that Emile Benveniste makes between (hi)story and discourse, that for Benveniste, deixis (time, place, pronoun suggesting the speaking or receiving subject) in a statement is evidence of the moment of enunciation inscribed in it. Pronouns, for example, foreground the time, place, and identity of the subject making a statement. In film this subject is not necessarily the director or the film's auteur. Metz argues that, applied to film, deixis is less a marker of the pronoun (which stands in for the filmmaker, for example) and more fundamentally the marker of the film's reflexivity—the film's way of identifying the location of its own address. "Not being an I, the source of enunciation does not produce a YOU answering the I," Metz observes, "the film, far from being an absent instance stuck between two present ones, would resemble rather a present instance stuck between two absent ones, the author who disappears after the fabrication, and the spectator, who is present but does not manifest his presence in any respect"

(150–51). Metz maintains that while film is traditionally presented as a narrative or story, it is the film's discourse and the very principle of that discourse's effectiveness that obliterates the traces of filmic enunciation and hence presents film with the coherence and continuity that we call "the story" (91). The sense of continuity and coherence in the film narrative depends on the ability of film to hide the traces of its production—that is, its enunciation and address—from the audience before the screen. The seamlessness of the narrative and the concealment of the operation of the film's productive technologies is effected by embedding the latter's workings—that is, the film's discourse—in the narrative, in the story's settings, in the mise-en-scène, and in the body of the characters shown on screen. What this suggests, of course is that unlike shifters in discourse, deictic markers in film ("I," "you," "here," "there," "now," etc.) are hidden and are instead evidenced in the narrative as moments where the film reflects on the process of its own coming into being as a film, marking in this way the sites and locations of the film's own address. When in his 1987 reflections in "The Impersonal Enunciation or the Site of Film: In the Margin of Recent Works on Enunciation and Cinema" Metz takes up the notion of discourse or enunciation in film, he does so to evoke enunciation in terms of this filmic reflexivity. In "The Impersonal Enunciation," reflexivity marks moments of metafilmic splitting within the narrative:

> All figures of enunciation consist in metadiscursive folds of cinematic instances piled on top of each other. . . . It is as if the film could manifest the production instance that carries it only by talking to us about the camera, the spectator, or by pointing at its own filmitude, that is, in any case, by pointing at itself. Thus, in places, a slightly sliding-off layer of film is constituted. It detaches itself from the rest and settles at once through this very folding that puts it, as it were on a double lane on the register of enunciation. (159)

Thus for Metz, the story we watch on screen is understood to chart the trajectory of its own enunciation, but reflexively. These moments of reflexivity fold the film up onto itself, producing metafilmic splittings. Such moments enable the film, and with it the audience, to reflect on the film's own production processes or to envision the ideal setting and circumstance for its future reception. According to Metz, these moments are typically inscribed in the story by the presence of door frames, windows, mirrors, cameras, sound equipment, fictional audiences, and so forth. Such inscriptions alert the viewer to his or her positioning within, or in relation to the media producing and projecting the film narrative on screen. These moments mirror the fact that the spectator's vision is mediated by technology. A window in the film frames a landscape in ways that are similar to the way the film itself frames; an audience in a fictional theater on screen reminds the viewer of his/her positioning in the film theater in front of the screen. The reflexive hem marks the characteristics and trajectories of the film's address and manifests the inscription of enunciation in the film narrative. In this light, to read the film narratives in terms of national cinema means to understand them not as allegories, but as stories that operate in such a way as to repress the enunciative processes of cultural and national production. The hem of enunciation, of national production and address, like the hem of the veil, folds inward and hides behind the seamless narrative that is the film's most obvious statement. This process, which is in fact the process of national production in representation, suggests that if the nation is posited as the subject of the filmic statement, namely its narrative, it must also be said to be at a remove (in both time and space) from the film's own enunciation. The story folds over and seamlessly covers over the film's processes of production. The production process is constitutive, however. It configures the ground and meaning of the film's national address and representation. Enunciation is the term that stands for that which joins the film narrative to the sources and sites of film production. "The national" in national cinema is nested here.

Reading national cinema's address by attending to the space of enunciation as well as its narrative must therefore involve attending to the entire topography of filmic space, not the narrative alone. Reading for the national address implies that we see a whole geography of differences configuring the film's meanings and messages. Because of the contradictory forces that mark the source of the national address in cinema, this address often emerges as ambiguous. The enunciative address of film is an address that is both temporally and spatially distant from the film's narrative representation. That is to say that at moments of narrative rupture in film, where the film is most self-reflexive, the "spoken statement" represents a site that is at a temporal and spatial remove from other parts of the film's address. The meanings that are forwarded by the film are both embedded within and deferred from the film's narrative constructions. As a commodity used in the context of the Islamic Republic of Iran to shape and represent the nation, film can therefore be said to produce and proliferate an extraordinary configuration of splittings and forkings—configurations of contradiction and difference, of delay and distance, that necessarily unsettle any notion of fixity in cultural statements. In the context of a national cinema, such as the one envisioned by the Islamic Republic after the revolution of 1979, one could even say that the source/subject of the filmic enunciation—at a temporal and spatial remove from the product/statement of a film—speaks from other places, from an elsewhere and in a different tongue.[3]

Representational Technologies in *Delshodegan*

As a film preoccupied with the processes involved in the production and inscription of sound and of national representation, *Delshodegan* forwards a reflection on its own processes of production, that is, on what Metz refers to as filmic enunciation. In reading *Delshodegan* as a film made by one of the most deeply religious and committed popular filmmakers of the postrevolutionary period, a film that problematizes the evocation of "the national" in representational technologies through their history, and in focusing on the inscription of the national in their histories, I will attempt to show the ways in which enunciation, as the landscape that inscribes the topography of film production and the unconscious site of the national address, self-reflexively reveals what contests messages and meanings produced by the film's narrative statements. In reading *Delshodegan,* I will discuss the ways in which narrative statements regarding the identity of

3. John Mowitt's important intervention on the role of enunciation, as that which joins text to industry in cinema, fleshes out this very cursory discussion of the unconscious site of national address in the present work. See Mowitt (2005).

the nation, the nation's history, and its representation, are contradicted by the histories and identities embedded within the film's representational technologies and enunciative sources. Against the statement of national purity on the narrative track, the nation emerges in the enunciation—from the site of filmic production—as a product of cultural confluence, a product that the nation has historically deemed other than itself in the figure of the nineteenth-century "Babi."

Based in turn-of-the-century Iran, *Delshodegan* (1992) traces the peregrinations of a group of early-twentieth-century musicians to Paris to record traditional music on a newly invented gramophone. Historical in its leanings, the film narrative itself is preoccupied with the processes involved in the production of musical instruments and of sound recordings. This preoccupation with processes of production and inscription consistently reflects on the film's own processes. Thus the issue of production, national and aural, is clearly one of the concepts the film offers up for analysis.

Delshodegan's narrative spans the period under the reign of Ahmad Shah, who ruled Iran during the revolutionary riots of 1909, riots that ultimately established a constitutional monarchy in Iran. While the film itself is emphatically ahistorical in its choice of characters and in its representation of historical events, it may be important to remark that the period in which the narrative is set is a period of enormous turmoil in which Iran suffered a sad fate in the hands of an incompetent young monarch, a monarch unable to resist the political and economic imperialism of the European powers. The latter is a point left unacknowledged in the film narrative, which anachronistically overturns the conventional cultural hierarchies buried in the history of the film's own technologies and instead constructs Iran's contemporary post-1979 moral economy in parity with the Western technological, economic, and political superiority at the turn of the twentieth century.

In the film, the young monarch, Ahmad Shah, is approached by one of his foreign advisors to assemble a traditional group of musicians to go to *"farang." Farang* is a word used indiscriminately in Persian to denote "the West" or "Europe," but literally translates to "France." The traditional musicians are assembled to record music on the new foreign equipment. In effect they are to do what many did in this period, which is to traverse the space separating Tehran and Paris to bring back to Iran the product of a national modernity. This, the film's thematic preoccupation with the history of sound recording in the Iranian Constitutional era, self-reflexively recalls the historical role played by the gramophone as studio sound displaced live musicians with sound that was prerecorded on a wax plate abroad.

The Phonograph

Although Edison's phonograph was invented in 1878, the mass distribution of records and gramophones occurred first in Iran under the reign of Muzzafar al-Din Shah Qajar in 1323/1906 (Sipanta 1998, 133). At the time of its invention, Edison promoted the phonograph "as an invention that would revolutionize print" (Gitelman 2003, 157). Thus, even before the Iranian Constitutional Revolution of 1906–11, the phonograph entered a bureaucratic network and facilitated a public sphere in which the record, like print, became important to formulating the fundamental characteristics of the emerging civil society in Iran.

In his travelogues Muzzafar al-Din Shah's father, Nasir al-Din Shah, attests to the use of the phonograph among the upper classes *(khavas)*. On Monday, January 8, 1889, Nasir al-Din Shah wrote that the phonograph was put in the middle of a gathering. Although many felt that "the early, imperfect phonograph produced only faint sounds obscured by scratchy surface noise," Nasir al-Din Shah observes that this type of phonograph was different from other talking machines found in Tehran (Gitelman 2003, 157). This one produced much clearer sound. As Gitelman notes, "The first scratchy phonograph records . . . reportedly sounded 'just like' the sounds they recorded," but this "perceptual condition of sounding 'just like' has continued to change over time and according to expectation" (1999, 18). First, Nasir al-Din Shah notes, the phonograph "played back the music that had been recorded in it. It was very good and clear. Then, they spoke and it played analogously" (Rijai'i 1994, 29). The phonograph belonged to Dust Mohammad-khan Muayer al-Mammalik. On it, he recorded the voice of his wife, Ismat al-Dawlih, the daughter of Nasir al-Din Shah. Muayer al-Mammalik's phonograph was also instrumental in recording the work of the most accomplished musicians in Iran at the time, including Aqa Hussaingholi (Sipanta 1998, 146).

A recording on the night of January 28, 1899, inscribes the voice of the daughter of Nasir al-Din Shah on a cylinder: "If I were to describe the inventions of this period, it will take too long . . . so let me be brief. One of these fascinating inventions is this phonograph which records my words and will reproduce them anytime I wish," (quoted in Sipanta 1998, 379). Like many of her male contemporaries, including the author of *A Traveller's Narrative,* she reflects on the loss of national power, though less as it concerns the loss of territory than in terms of Europe's comparative greatness in light of its technological advances: "Consider that once we were more powerful than all of our neighboring governments and our authority surprised and astonished all foreigners. But now it has come to pass that we are astonished by their inventions and industry. We have been around since the ancient times, but they are new; we must discover the reasons and the causes of this" (quoted in Sipanta 1998, 379). In a culture that was structured almost exclusively by two homosocial spheres separated by walls and veils, the phonograph functioned to penetrate divisions and level distinctions. Mohamad Tavakoli-Targhi suggests that the historical conjoining of male and female voices in representational technologies such as that of the printing press "made possible the formation of an imagined national sphere that sanctioned the mixing of 'national sisters and brothers'" in Iran (2001, 113–14). The invention of the phonograph emerged from Edison's laboratory "into and amid a cluster of mutually defining literary practices, texts, and technologies, among them shorthand reporting, typescripts, printing telegraphs, and silent motion pictures" (Gitelman 1999, 1). Such "metal embodiments," as the phonograph records were first called, made "written texts seem inadequate for capturing history" (Gitelman 1999, 21, 22–23). The new representational technologies took the place of the court chronicler and the fictive role of the objective foreign observer in the twentieth century. Even as they inscribed the passing of time, the phonograph needle and reproducer became catalysts for the reinscription of spaces, destabilizing at the same time the traditional boundaries that were demarcated by sexual difference, demarcated, that is, by veils and walls.

In 1906 Maxime Pick, a salesman for gramophones and typewriters, received permission from Muzzafar al-Din Shah to distribute the gramophone in Iran. Following the lead of Edison agents who rushed to prominent statesmen and artists to demonstrate the superior sound of the new machine by recording and then mass-distributing their voices, Pick hurried a letter to the court of Muzzafar al-Din Shah. Requesting that the shah issue an order *(farman)* to the Iranian community of musicians and singers, Pick argued that a recording of their voices would in return "be a source of joy for Shah" (Rijai'i 1994, 30). Relentless and thorough in his eagerness to reach the Iranian populace, which he regarded as lacking a significant middle class able to purchase the Edison product, Pick asked that the shah's *farman* also grant "The Gramophone Company" permission to distribute and sell the machine in Iran. The *farman* was not granted easily. Pick himself was to go to the shah's court to record the voice of the royal personage and thereby show the potential of the new machine to the shah himself.

Five records were made in the course of this visit. Two of them bear the seal and signature of the shah, dated January 16, 1906 (Rijai'i 1994, 32). A third one, that according to Pick imprinted the shah's praises of the gramophone, ironically lacks his penned signet. Pick comments, as he registers this regrettable failure in a letter to the home office in England, that the "Shah is old . . . kneeling on the floor is difficult for him" (quoted in Rijai'i 1994, 67). Writing about Edison technologies, Lisa Gitleman observes that the "moment when an inscription bears evidence of itself, is the hallmark of inventing representational technologies" (1999, 161). It could be claimed, then, that despite that absent seal, Muzzafar al-din Shah himself was instrumental in an innovation in sound technology. Lest we forget, his celebratory presence in the first Iranian motion picture carries a comparable territorial claim.

The Cinematograph

Muzaffar al-Din Shah, who, like his father, was an early dynastic enthusiast of the modern camera, notes in his travelogue that he took part in a festival of flowers in Osted, Belgium, in August 1900. Continuing the tradition of *voyages photographique* (photographic voyages) that made their appearance in the *Salon de Photographie* in 1859, his entry on this festival arrests moments of visual exchange between parading European women and himself.[4] The scene, which is captured by his cameraman, Mirza Ibrahim Khan Akkasbashi Sani-al Saltanih, combines a mixture of decorum and titillating circumstance, a pleasing sensuality that also conditioned the production of the early phonograph clocks to which both Edison and Bellamy refer (Gitelman 1999, 85). The shah notes that Akkasbashi's motion-picture camera, most likely a Gaumont purchased during this trip, captured an exchange between the shah of Iran and the Belgian women. He writes in his diary of that momentous event:

> It was a very interesting festival. They had decorated the coaches with flowers, inside and out, and the wheels were covered with flowers so that one could hardly see the coaches through them. The ladies were riding the coaches with bouquets of flowers in their hands and they passed in front of us. Akkasbashi was busy photographing with the cinematograph. There were more than fifty coaches passing by, one after another, with the rhythm of music. There was quite a crowd there. When the coaches reached us they threw bouquets of flowers to us continuously and we also threw back flowers to them. (Qajar 1982, 160)[5]

According to Gitelman, "Phonographic and cinematic inscriptions fit the logic of ethnography exactly. The recording phonograph and the camera interceded between the ethnographer and his subject, offering a rhetorically valuable sense of technological impartiality and receptivity" (1999, 123). In both media, phonograph and camera, the subject of the inscription was frozen in time and place. Transformed into matter, and "concretized" as a "live" specimen, the subject could be studied at an objective distance again and again. The medium itself thus positioned the seer and the seen, the hearer and heard, in opposition to one another and in doing so enabled "questions and conflict over matters of identity and cultural

4. On photographic voyages, see Benjamin (1999b, 684).

5. Translation in Issari (1989, 59).

hierarchy." The phonograph and camera became party to habitual and manifold hierarchical distinctions between "us" and "them" and enabled modes of distancing that would root themselves, as Gitelman suggests, at "different depths" in the culture of recorded sound and image (123, 160).

The hierarchies historically and ideologically embedded in the technology of film were somewhat upset in Belgium. During the parade in 1900, the specimen frozen for "further study at home" was not a person pure and simple, but an exchange, in effect a movement—a movement of desire between the shah and European women, who, unlike women on the streets of Tehran, were moving about unveiled. As Tavakoli-Targhi observes, "Seeing oneself being seen, that is, the consciousness of oneself as at once spectator and spectacle, grounded all eighteenth- and nineteenth-century Oriental and Occidental *voy(age)eurs'* narrative emplotment of alterity" (2001, 36). Both European and Asian travelers took note of such exchanges in their travelogues, "providing multiple scenarios of self-fashioning. Whereas Europeans reconstituted the modern self in relation to their non-Western Others, Asians and Africans began to redefine the self in relation to Europe, their new significant Other" (4). This consciousness informed the thrilling exchange between the shah and the women in the flower parade and became material as that narrative trace that would condition the evolution of the new technology at home. The camera, as a technology of inscription, continued a textual history of cultural exchange that was formative in fashioning Iranian national identity. "Asians gazed and returned the gaze and, in the process of 'cultural looking,' they, like their European counterparts, exoticized and eroticized the Other" (36). The exchange between the shah and the unveiled European women at the Belgian flower festival historically overdetermined Iranian cinema's enunciative site by a visual exchange of the Eastern gaze westward, a conscious gaze that returned the gaze of the West on the Eastern subject. The inscription of this loaded exchange by Akkasbashi's camera implied a gesture of internal labeling, an inscription, as we have noted, necessary for the invention of inscriptive technologies marshaled to provide what Gitelman calls "the evidence of the technology's own existence" (1999, 161–62; Tavakoli-Targhi 2001, 138). Like a stamp marking the birth of the film camera in the context of Iranian history, the exchange provided for the camera's "creative relocation within a different textual and political universe" (Tavakoli-Targhi 2001, 138). The camera provided for the continuity of the East-West exchange and the self-reflexivity we witnessed in earlier chapters in the turn-of-the-century chronicles and in the *ta'ziyeh*'s discursive quest to situate the self from the perspective of a valued outsider in a modern world. Thus the camera became party to measures that were to shape the nation's modern identity as well (Tavakoli-Targhi 2001, 138). This haunting history of film technology's preoccupation with the mutual exchange (of glances) on the anticipatory eve of modernity was overwritten years later by the veiling of all women from the voyeurism of the gaze and the Islamization of desire for the contemporary Iranian screen.

Be that as it may, as Hatami's film attempts to articulate, there is no doubt about the transformation of the gramophone's function after its introduction to Iran, in ways similar to the cinematograph. Like the film camera, the gramophone was to become a chronicler of passing days, a representative of national culture, and the engraving site for the will of the nation's leader almost immediately.

Key to the conceptualization of the gramophone as a site for the enunciation of national history, national desire, and national identity are the sealed and signed records that document two exchanges between Muzzafar al-Din Shah and his courtiers. On the first record, the shah thanks his grand vizier and his foreign minister for the services they have granted his court and the nation. In his response to the shah on this record, the vizier observes that he has been in the service of the court for forty years and adds that if he were to live a hundred more, he would want to continue his service at the court. Joining in, the foreign minister, too, adds a few rather tepid words about his hope to continue his service to the court, to which the shah responds that he is pleased with the minister's services as well (Rijai'i 1994, 34). The second record proceeds similarly, though here the shah comments on the good weather and on how much he has enjoyed the day. "This winter was much fun and I hope," the shah says to his vizier, "that your services are rendered in such a way that We shall always enjoy Ourselves." The shah also advises his vizier to serve the people of Iran *(ahaliy-i Iran)* so that they, too, enjoy themselves. The gramophone takes on the role of a witness in these conversations, oddly understood in terms of earlier textual chronicles such as *A Traveler's Narrative* and optical innovations such as the camera.[6]

Two weeks later, on January 31, the American vice consul general, John Taylor, certifies to having been at the royal palace on January 18 and to having witnessed the interest and the amusement of the shah and his ministers. Taylor observes that the shah "hoped the Gramophone Company would have a successful career in the future in Persia," and that though "he had seen many Talking Machines . . . none of them could be compared to the Gramophone." Finally, in a closing remark Taylor writes, "Although I have known His Majesty for many years I have never seen him so bright, cheerful, and happy before" (Rijai'i 1994, 36).

What punctuates the introduction of the gramophone to Iran, and its transformation with the voice and the signet of the Qajar monarch, is the inscription of a fleeting tactile temporality: of the seasons, of contentment, of pleasure, of desire, and of government, not on paper but on wax. The gramophone becomes a diary of a sort, a record of the newest day, making the pleasures of the present palpable for the future. The phonograph could "stereotype any object introduced into its funnel. A cat in the funnel produced kittens; strawberries berried out of season; money reproduced itself" (Gitelman 1999, 64). Sound, like the visual exchange captured by the motion picture six years earlier, became "an object." Having been made material through technology, it provided the historical impulses informing film technology's future in Iran.

Muzaffar al-Din Shah's stately gestures lay the groundwork for the recording of Iranian music and its future mass distribution on the gramophone. Rijai'i observes that the three early ventures to London, Paris, and Tiflis by leading Iranian musicians were to pursue the foreign "Gramophone Company's" objective to record Iranian sound on a new invention. And although it may appear as a slight groove in the otherwise extensive chronicle of sound recording, it could be established, as Hatami does in *Delshodegan*, that a group of well-known musicians traveled abroad to record traditional Iranian music on the newly invented sound-recording

6. For more on the role of inscriptive technologies as witnesses, see Gitelman (1999, 87).

device.[7] This traversal in space came toward the end of a civil war in Iran in which the nation's past, its history, became the primary loci of struggles over the constitution of the nation's modern identity (Tavakoli-Targhi 2001, 142). The constitutionalists would in this struggle eventually take over Tehran, depose the shah, and execute some of the anticonstitutionalists. The messianic temporal configuration that conditions Hatami's historical film suggests that these events both precede and follow the film's narrative setting. In the film, the present is a time out of time, associated with the resurrection scheduled for the Day of Judgment. On this day, a day configured from the historical perspective of the *ta'ziyeh,* the nation arises with Imam Husayn to confront the injustices of all time for the last time. As we shall see, the temporal configuration informing this national film, *Delshodegan,* positions its frame in opposition to one unjust ruler in particular. This ruler rules the world of film, issuing standardized processes for the production of films, processes that have by all accounts blemished the representational strategies of the nation with Hollywood's imperial seal. The film replaces American cinema's inauspicious mark with a uniquely national seal from the start.

A Genealogy of National Music

Delshodegan opens with a close-up shot of the interior of a mechanical music box, decorated on the exterior with a clock. Sultan Ahmad Shah stands next to the music box, enjoying the *"voix celeste."* Seated outside the royal palace, after an abrupt transition to the subsequent scene, Ahmad Shah expresses his desire for the world to be a music box "in which every voice is the sound of music and every conversation a song." His minister informs him that a Monsieur Joli, a foreigner with a plan for recording music, has asked permission to gain audience with the shah. As the modern monarch

7. Born in 1853, Aqa Hussaingholi (d. 1915) went to Paris to record music on the new gramophone with Baghir Khan Ramishgar; Assadullah Khan, who played the *tar* and the *santoor;* Muhammad Baghir, who played the *zarb;* and the singer Siyyid Ahmad Khan. Baghir Khan made two subsequent trips to record his music in Western cities. The second was to London and the third to Tiflis (Sipanta 1998, 50, 71; Rahgani 1998, 397).

rides his bicycle in the park surrounding the royal palace conversing with the foreigner, in scene 3, he agrees to Monsieur Joli's plan to gather up and record the sound of the traditional Iranian musicians abroad.

Together, these three scenes locate the historical, technological, and emotive contexts for the national inscription of traditional music on the phonograph record. What is important to note here is that "the idea" of the phonograph is introduced in the film narrative, after the shah has expressed his musical vision of the world. In the film, the national monarch's (Ahmad Shah) enjoyment of the music box is given as the motivating force behind the introduction of recorded music to Iran. Against the historical claims made about the forced commercialization of sound recording by the foreign "Gramophone Company," the film formulates a historically motivated local (or rather national) rationale for the importation of recorded sound. In this way, the film's opening sequence adjusts the sight lines of its audience to provide an altered perspective on modern national history and a different look at the formation of Iranian identity in relation to it. In the film, the music box—a measure of temporality associated with its adorning clock—provides the genealogical ground, as well as the technological motivation, for the production of mechanized sound in Iran. It is the young monarch's desire that is set up by the film to sustain the technology that will etch the groove of Iranian sound on a foreign wax plate. The shah's imaginary world, like the world of the film, situates the nation as a modern world envisioned, mediated, and produced by mechanized music and song. Framed by the *ta'ziyeh*'s atomistic temporal sense, in which now-time is the all-time of universal history, this world, the world of the film, is born of national desire.

The Overture: Film Production

Scene 7, the scene that bears the overtures of the film, doubly emphasizes the issue of production, this time national, artisanal, and technological. The scene depicts an old craftsman working on various parts of a new type of *tar,* a traditional Iranian string instrument made out of wood. In close-ups and medium shots of the craftsman and the parts of the instrument that he is working on, the camera focuses on the steps involved in giving shape to the wood as the craftsman sands it, glues the parts of the instrument together, and finally polishes and strings the *tar.* Nondiegetic string music plays over this scene and rhythmically ushers the coming-into-being of a new instrument that advances innovations in Iranian traditional music.

The overture, customarily a self-reflexive sequence in which films reflect on the means of their own coming into being, introduces *Delshodegan*'s actors, its film crew, and its director by name. As these credits roll, *Delshodegan* simultaneously catalogues the investment that the film has in interrogating the genealogy of an aural medium—a medium that comes to function as a mediator of national tradition. The credits roll as the old craftsman works on the *tar.* Those producing the world of the film (the crew) and the craftsman producing what will come to represent the nation to the world are introduced together in text and image form. Together these productive forces come to fulfill the young monarch's vision of a world imbued with song and music. In accenting the processes of manufacturing, both visually and textually, the overture doubly signals the film's interest in the processes of production. This emphasis not only posits Iran's musical history as a subject of cinematic reflection, but in the film's reflection on itself as a produced object, that is, as a film about "a moment" in the history of national representation, it also shows itself interested in interrogating the mediating processes by which any representation of nationhood comes to be.

What can be said about the genesis of the modern nation? What grounds this history and what motivates its evolution? Can traditions be said to be the foundations of the national? Are dreams such foundations? Are hopes? Are the wishes and the dictates of a monarch? What mediates the nation's constitution? What role do foreign influences have in a nation's evolution? What fashions a nation's identity and its national character? What goes into making the mediating technologies that will later represent it as a modern nation? What histories, what ideological impulses, what sounds and images inscribe themselves in these technologies? What are the processes by which a modern nation comes into being in and through these representational media? What marks and tempers national identity in this process of mediation? The emphasis on the processes of production in the opening sequences of the film pressures the historical context for the inscription of national representations and the influences of such representational technologies in the making of modern Iran and in crafting its identity. The questions that are implicitly raised in the opening sequence of *Delshodegan* thus weigh the Islamic Republic's demands on the Iranian film industry—demands to represent a pure and uncontaminated national culture and to build a model for Islamic citizenship through cinema's representational technologies. Can a national culture be produced through cinema, the film asks? Can cinema constitute Iran's postrevolutionary Islamic identity even as we focus our attention on the history shaping its representational technologies?

The juxtaposition of innovations in traditional and modern musical technologies in the image track and the nondiegetic sound of studio-recorded string music on the sound track of the overture sets the foundation for the questions that become fundamental for the film itself. The simultaneity of the two representations produces an analogic relationship between transformations in traditional representational media *(tar* music) in Iran and the technological innovations in (studio) sound recording associated with *farang* (Europe) in the film. Although the two innovations are posited as equally new, modern, and progressive in the film's overture, the juxtaposition of studio sound and the visual attention to the process involved in the production of the traditional string instrument, split between the sound and the image track, reflexively recalls the historical role played by the gramophone as it displaced live musicians (who, we should remember, were artisans not unlike the craftsman) with recorded film sound in the early years of film production everywhere. Thus the film seems to mourn an auratic national loss, while celebrating the gramophone's reproducible sound—a celebration of a medium that was responsible for so many cultural and technological innovations, including sound films, which, far from being "talkies," were more like primitive musicals, not unlike *Delshodegan* itself. As Michael Chanan argues, "the technique of reproduction detaches the musical work from the domain of the tradition that gave birth to it, and destroys what Benjamin calls the aura which signals its authenticity; except that it also creates new types of musical objects which do not belong to a particular domain, but rather, anywhere a loudspeaker (or earphones) may be found . . . this process redefines the audience, which comes to be constituted quite differently from before" (1995, 9). The mechanization of sound reshapes the temporal and spatial components of a musical score. Displacing its own origins, the film also displaces its audience, for whom it is destined. A film's audience, not unlike the audience for mechanized sound, can be anywhere, unbounded by borders and by temporal limits, indeed at a distance, elsewhere.

The film's historically motivated meditation on the production of representational technologies and the displacement of traditional live music by mechanically reproduced sound in the overture thus reflects on the constitution of the audience now before a screen—a screen that employs mediating technologies to produce national identity through national sound on foreign equipment. The film spatializes its address, disrupting the groundedness of both the object and the receiver in space, time, and tradition. One could say, then, that the film sees itself and its audience as mediated, formed, represented, and addressed through technology in much the same ways as the *ta'ziyeh* articulates the nation in its adoption of a messianic temporal confluence. There on the *ta'ziyeh* stage, as much as in the process of technological mediation, every day is Ashura and every place is Karbala. In *Delshodegan,* film technology itself becomes the site for the figuration of the national.

The scene in which the musicians are introduced opens to a group of four musicians testing the *tar* assembled in the course of the overture. The music is diegetic in this scene, emphasizing by contrast the use of nondiegetic studio music we hear in the scene setup in the overture. The mise-en-scène is structured as if on the set of a photo studio. In the scene, the musicians are framed by two landscape paintings and white pillars. Left over from the days of the daguerreotype, when it was necessary for the photographic subject to lean and stand still during a twenty- to thirty-minute exposure time of "inorganic immobility," such painted British garden backdrops consistently frame photographs taken during the reigns of Nasir al-Din Shah and Muzzafar al-Din Shah Qajar. In these photographs of court eunuchs, servants, and the shah himself, taken on what are seemingly outdoor terraces, the combination of painted landscape and typical white pillars provide the setting for the seated subject of the portraiture (Tahimi 1998, 27, 43, 104).

Delshodegan's gesture of framing within the film frame suggests the film's self-reflexivity. As such, the scene provides an overdetermined enunciative site that simultaneously ties the film to the early history of photography and the camera's historical relation to the introduction of film technology to Iran. This scene, in which traditional live musicians play a newly invented national instrument against a photo-studio landscape, reflects on the genealogy of representational arts and their relation to the history of national modernity. In this genealogy, photography provides the earliest images of the encounter between machine and man (Benjamin 1999a, 678). This scene, representing the musicians testing the new *tar* in *Delshodegan,* suggests that advancement in aural representative forms follows innovations in the visual arts in the Tehran palace. Historically speaking, in other words, the national subject has already traversed his/her groundedness in a specific geographic environment and interior landscape with the invention of the camera (referenced here by the presence of the studio landscape), at the very moment when national sound loses its auratic context.

The Harem Master

Nasir al-Din Shah, the first monarchical enthusiast of the camera, himself a photographer, was instrumental in displacing images of interior, private spaces into the public realm of visibility. The shah's role as a photo-collector of everyday life, a role that Jean Baudrillard rightly designates as the role of the harem master, situates the superficial mechanical click of the shah's camera as the sound that unsettles rigid traditional boundaries formed by walls and veils. Whether his images were brought to the public eye in his own time is of little consequence. This gesture of spatial transgression by the visual apparatus and the accumulation of images of interior life, staged by the master of the harem himself, made the quotidian, that is, everyday, acts, everyday gestures, and everyday concerns, the very subject of public opinion and politics. His camera transported the *haram,* the forbidden, the unpresentable, from the veiled realm of the *baten* to the realm of the public visibility, the realm of the *zaher.* Inscribing the life of women in his harem on the surface of a photograph affected the constitution of the public sphere, not only by marking a new period in the representational arts, but also by bringing previously inaccessible, indeed, unpresentable subjects "in conversation" and "contact" with other, public ones.

After the establishment of the Tehran Polytechnic, Dar al-Funun, in 1852, the shah sent one of his favorite valets, Aqa Reza, to study photography. He appointed him "Akkasbashi," and some years later took up photography himself, amassing a collection that may comprise over twenty thousand photographs of all kinds. Among these are a series of images of Europe's reigning families and an assortment of photographs of women in the imperial harem in what Angelo Piemontese calls "impudent and lascivious poses" (Piemontese 1972). One of the earliest photographs taken by Nasir al-Din Shah is a self-portrait dated 1865. In a profile shot in front of a port, he stands in the idealized studio style of the French photographer Nadar, wearing a combination of European and Persian clothes: top hat, elaborate necktie, European overcoat, and checkered trousers. Another of Nasir al-Din's early portraits is of his mother, the Mahd-i ulya; it shows the powerful harem manager seated on an ornate chair with her hands clasped: "She is modestly dressed in all her finery, with emphasis on the lavish material textures and precise disposition of draperies" (Stein 1983). Immortalizing the private sphere of the harem, Nasir al-Din Shah fashions through many such portraits an image of Iran's national modernity that is transported to an exterior space and reinternalized to inform a rearticulation of national identity.

Spectral Images

The Iranian minister Itimad al-Saltanih writes in his *Diaries* that "Nusrat al-Dawla had sent gifts on behalf of his father Nasir al-Dawla. He had also sent a photo of Nasir al-Dawla holding a tome [*sic*] in which there was some money. It made me laugh a lot, for nothing could be more vulgar than this photograph. It implied that the money which he was holding was for royal offering" (Afshar 1983, 266). The photograph communicates a set of core values to the minister. Representing what is not spoken, the photograph speaks volumes about the interior character *(baten)* of the boastful photographed subject. The minister records another illustrative example of this recovered otherness in early photography in Iran. In his *Diaries,* Itimad al-Saltanih writes: "The Court Photographer . . . by order of [Nasir al-Din Shah] took a picture of His Excellency the Hajji Mulla Hadi and because until then His Excellency the Hajji had not witnessed the action of photography and considered it against the laws and scientific proofs of sages, he was infinitely surprised." We could speculate that this sense of surprise arose from the ancient belief that shadows (which have no materiality) could only gain permanence and be transported through bodies. Just as there is no material thing without a shadow, the shadow cannot exist without the presence of the body that it shadows. Thus it was thought that it was only the mind and spirit of the human being that was capable of imprinting and recording fleeting images, not paper or glass. The faculties of inscription and memory were beyond the scope of "man-made" machines (Afshar 1983, 264). Apparently, upon seeing his own image, the Haji was shocked and agreed that scientific knowledge had conquered the rhapsodies of the ancients.

Thus, immersed in the realm of the unpresentable, photography revealed an exceptionally complicated and hybrid realm of interiority beyond the veil of Islam. In the early Qajar photographs of culture and private and social life taken by the shah himself, there is already a presence of otherness or difference marking the national body. This "other" discloses itself in the realm of the visual, through the clothing, the objects, and the poses adopted from classical styles of Western portraiture. It reveals itself not only as content, but also in the form of the photographically visual and in the process of recording and imprinting.

Representing the Unpresentable

Early Western photographers in Iran, like Ernst Hoeltzer and Antoin Sevruguin, used the camera as a means to document the life, culture, folklore, crafts, and architecture of the nation. With the growing influence of modern technologies and the influx of European values, the last remnants of what Hoeltzer calls "a primitive Persian lifestyle" began to disappear under Qajar culture (Stein 1983, 268). The camera was thought to capture an old world for what was considered the more progressive world and the modern Western gaze.

Sevruguin, who was a prolific commercial photographer in Iran from 1880 to 1930, produced a wide variety of photographs that were used to illustrate travel books and narratives. His photographs, like Hoeltzer's, provide a journalistic record of aspects of Iranian life, including some exoticized images intended for Western collectors who juxtaposed these with the much-circulated photographs of European cityscapes. Such images of Iranian traditional culture, that is, of a quaint Orient with its costumes and strange rituals, taken largely by foreign photographers, stood in stark contrast to the images of an emerging *Paris moderne,* images that captured throngs of people moving about the new city in the icons of modernization: trams, buses, and personal cars. Paris in these photo-postcards was by no means an auratic city, but a city devoid of excess value, that is, of anything but use value. Such functionalism informed the new buildings of glass and steel, but in doing so, it also defined the type of subjects represented in the postcards. The photo-postcards represented the new Paris through the coming of age of female urban mobility. Modern Paris was allegorized by the secular goddesses of *nouveau Paris:* the female coach drivers at work.

Contrasted with such widely circulated images of urbanity, Nasir al-Din Shah's photographs of his harem captured the space of private life. In his photographs, harem women are framed as women of leisure. Leaning on couches, coyly resting on steps, or leaning out of doorways to take a look at the world outside, these images construct the modern Iranian subject as an equal to the occidentalist imagery of the unveiled European woman in dress. What is striking, by contrast, is the way that the photographs, by the very poses they occupy, defy the emerging conventions of what European photography conceived as "the modern." Certainly, the modern Iranian women are unveiled, much like their European counterparts in these photographs, but unlike the secular goddesses of the Paris postcards, the women of the harem are not at work. They are dressed in their finery and outfitted in an excess that defies functionalism. Dressed in long white stockings, awkward, fanning garments, jewelry, and fashionable shoes, they lean on extravagant imported sofas and coyly gaze back at us.[8]

Nasir al-Din Shah's photographs capture not the flurry of urban public life but the leisured life of the interior—private spaces that are inextricably tangled in the confluence of cultures. Each photograph fixes this state of interiority as an indexical present in which the archaic past and the as-yet-unimagined future of Iranian modernity is nested.

Confronting Western Heterosexuality in Film

The European garden landscape that is represented in the photo-studio screen in *Delshodegan*'s early scene provides the backdrop for the reproducibility of the national subject in effigy. The film foregrounds in this way the logic of transformation and the reconstitution of selves in and through the representational technologies of film. The subjects of the camera, in this scene, are transformed and transported into other settings through the process of mediation. Iranian men, playing traditional instruments, sit against the backdrop of a European landscape. Like any societal shift, such cultural encounters with technology demand significant transformations of the technologies that mediate, as well. Not unlike its component parts—the aural and visual technologies signaled as the film's own predecessors in the mise-en-scène—film, too, must go through significant metamorphoses in Iranian hands in order to become national. This claim, postulated by the development and setting of the plot in the opening scenes of *Delshodegan,* is evidenced in later scenes where a third medium is affected in the process of transference between two parties, serving like the gramophone to communicate messages and mediate other meanings in the context of the curtailed domain of contemporary Iranian cinema.

The scenes representing the musicians' farewells with their families are instructive in this regard. As the traditional musicians prepare to travel and traverse the space separating Tehran and Paris to bring back to

8. For a discussion of clothing practices in the harem interior, see Armstrong-Ingram (2004).

Iran the transformed product of an indigenous modernity, the film camera insists on its own groundedness in the time and space of the present under the watchful eye of the Islamic Republic. Scene 21 is particularly provocative in illustrating what this groundedness comes to mean for cinematic representation. So it is here, where Vahabi, the *santoor* player, and his wife discuss the musician's imminent journey to *farang,* that we drop the needle once more.

The scene opens with a long shot of the wife packing Vahabi's clothes. She is wearing a headscarf and is outfitted in the clothes worn in the photographs of the harem interior in the late Qajar period. Vahabi and his wife sit down by a round table on which a set of books, a *santoor,* and a cat rest. The two discuss the things that join them in their affection for one another and review the promises and sacrifices they have made in their devotion to Vahabi's music. The wife speaks to Vahabi with an averted gaze while she strokes the *santoor*—the signifier of their common love—with the palm of her hand.

This scene's opening long shots are followed by nine shot/reverse shots at medium length signifying "a conversation." In these shots, the wife is framed with the *santoor,* looking obliquely to the right of the frame, and Vahabi is shot with the cat resting by his arm, alternately looking away from left frame, looking down, and finally gazing directly to the left of the frame (see fig. 4). In this last sequence of shots, Vahabi tells his wife that his mission to Europe differs from that of his companions. He not only intends to record what he knows, but he also seeks to learn from the Europeans what he does not. Supportive, his wife agrees that no matter how long the journey may take, the gift of knowledge is the best gift of all. The scene alternates between long shots and medium shots. The closing shot is the only close-up to appear. Ironically distancing itself from the representation of husband or wife, the close-up shot frames the cat, Babri, whom we first see being stroked by Vahabi's hand, and then by his wife's hand, as they exchange their vows to stay bound by the music that unites them.

Under the guidelines for modesty in postrevolutionary Iranian cinema, this scene, depicting a heterosexual relationship, gives shape to a new convention—a convention that inscribes the film in the contemporaneity of the Islamic Republic. As modesty laws concerned with the unpresentability of women force the film crew to forgo close-ups of the faces

4. *Scene 21, from* Delshodegan, *Ali Hatami, 1992.*

of the lovers, a medium-long shot frames Vahabi's wife stroking Vahabi's *santoor.* Far removed from the Hollywood convention of the affectionate gaze, the palm of the wife's hand on her husband's *santoor* and their gesture of mutual affection for the cat in close-up stand as mediators of filmic affection under the watchful eye of the Islamic Republic. Rather than conjuring a moment of historical happening—a moment belonging to the late Qajars—these allegorical tropes mark the enunciative present and the modest address of the contemporary nation to the world. As tropes they take a forceful stand against standardized conventions. Although the "conversation" is connoted through the classical Hollywood convention of the shot/reverse shot, love itself finds its expression elsewhere. Though not central to the mise-en-scène or the frame, the couple's hands become the site of love, and gestural meaning combines with the shot convention of the close-up on Babri to communicate where the standardized Hollywood convention of the heterosexual embrace is prohibited. The cat becomes an allegory of the cinema's resistance, guided by the Islamic Republic's rule of modesty.

This resistance to the dominant Western values as embedded in standardized representational strategies features prominently in another such farewell scene. This is the scene in which the drummer converses with his wife and his mother about going to *farang*. The drummer's wife asks if *farang* is the same place she has seen in the *Shahr-i farang* (literally, "Europe City," a popular peepshow in Iran that projected fantastic images of Europe), where the mosques have towers, she says, instead of domes? Inquiring about the distance of *farang* from Tehran, she says that she's seen the *farangi* women in the *Shahr-i farang*. She describes their perfumes and clothes and remarks that they look just like dolls. She warns her husband not to let them "get into his frame" (*narand tu jeldet*! Or, "don't fall for them"). Predictably, it is precisely these women that enter and disrupt the seams of the filmic frame as the musicians start recording their nationalist music on wax abroad.

Traversing Heterosociality

As if to emphasize post-1979 restrictions on heterosexual exchange, imposed anachronistically on the turn-of-the century farewell scenes set in Tehran, and to underscore reflexively the young wife's plea not to let the *farangi* women into her husband's frame, the next scene opens with a long shot of a European cityscape in which European men in tophats and suits walk arm in arm with European women in Victorian garments, bonnets, umbrellas, and white gloves. This scene, which represents the arrival of the musicians in Europe, also marks, by contrast, the freedom of heterosexual exchange in the West at the turn of the century. Repeated, such scenes reveal a stark contrast between Iranian women who walk around the capital city, Tehran, covered by the veil and the unveiled women who the musicians encounter on the streets as they traverse the Parisian city, instruments in hand. This scene from the musicians' traversal of the Paris streets recalls eighteenth- and nineteenth-century travelogue entries by Iranian voyagers to the West who describe Europe in terms of the status of European women and the public display of heterosexuality.

Studio Sound

In *Delshodegan,* the scene signifying the musicians' arrival in Europe by staging a heterosocial mise-en-scène is taken in long shot. As such it comments on the film's preceding scenes. In its juxtaposition of cultural differences (between the travelers and the Europeans they pass on the Paris streets), the film articulates its own struggle to find a representational grammar in keeping with contemporary national modesty laws. On the level of the film narrative, these juxtapositions compare the moral superiority of an imagined "uncontaminated" and chaste Islamic culture of the present to a generalized sense of European moral laxity. This representation of the European in the film contrasts strongly with the nineteenth-century representation of the European ally in *ta'ziyeh* performances and the deference given to the European traveler in reform tracts of the period. A popular presence in the nineteen-century passion play, the European "elci farangi" corroborated the superiority of the Shi'ite Iranian over his Sunni Arab oppressor, articulating the Shi'ite and the European as one under drag. Maintaining a short lens, the scene in *Delshodegan* anachronistically shows itself critical of European heterosociality and thus eludes censorship in contemporary Shi'ite Iran. But this self-consciously anachronistic overture to contemporary isolationist sensibility is merely a precursor to the actual site of recording, where the film's argument regarding the production of modern national identity and the function of representation in this context is forged. The gramophone, identified by the film as the historical site for the construction and inscription of a modern Iranian identity, becomes the focal point of this articulation.

The musicians' arrival at the Parisian studio foregrounds the film's emphatic preoccupation with the enunciative site of this national identity: as if obsessed with its displacement of the book as sole chronicle of national history and identity, the film repeatedly returns to the question and the role of representational culture and technology in relation to it. In this scene, the presence of recording equipment in the mise-en-scène reflexively and deliberately underscores the status of the film's narrative as mediated by film technologies. The indisputable association between the place of the silent viewer and his or her equivalent in the role of the engineer behind the posted "silence" sign in the recording studio also reflexively points up and reaffirms (on the level of enunciation and address) the preoccupation of the film with its status as a constructed narrative for a viewing audience. As audience, we cannot fail to note, in other words, that we are situated by the film as silent witnesses, witnessing a production process similar to the one the film passes through, but which the film by necessity erases in order to uphold narrative coherence. Thus the film reflexively shows its seams, marking the scene as an important site for the reading of filmic enunciation. Marking the process of technological inscription, the film marks the site of national production alongside it.

In the lead-up to this scene, the musicians walk out of the Pension de Paris to traverse the city in their stroll toward the recording studio (fig. 5). At the entrance, the English sign "Recording Studios" signals the Persian tongue's indifference to the specificity of *farang,* as if to say "The other speaks in a foreign tongue, and we do not care if it is English or French." Indoors, the next scene is set in the recording studio and emphasizes the status of recorded diegetic and nondiegetic sound as fundamental to the modern constitution of national identity through cinematic technologies. In this scene, as musicians set up and as the recording begins, what we hear on the sound track is diegetic sound. In other words, the music that we, as audience, hear on the sound track is coming from the instruments the musicians are actually playing within the visual frame. There is a sound synchronicity with the instruments being played on screen.

5. *Scene at the Pension de Paris, from* Delshodegan, *Ali Hatami, 1992.*

As the singing begins, however, there is a cutaway to outside scenes, and the musicians start their stroll along the Parisian city streets once again (fig. 6). The sound we hear over the outdoor scene is studio recorded sound and it is nondiegetic (in shots 2 and 3), that is, no instrument is

6. Scene at the recording studio, from Delshodegan, *Ali Hatami, 1992.*

shown to be playing the musical score that plays over the visual frame. Studio-recorded music continues to play the score we heard the musicians play in the studio but the musicians now walk and look about the Parisian city streets.

What we hear as the scene returns to the recording studio (shots 4 and 5 of fig. 6) is a continuation of this nondiegetic studio recorded musical score. The soundtrack no longer synchronizes with the instruments we see the musicians playing. The music that played outside (in shots 2 and 3) wanders into the studio and plays independently of the musicians' movements. Indeed what seems to have taken place in the musicians' traversal of the city on the visual track is so disruptive to the process of the recording that the drummer stops playing the score (shot 4) and starts wandering about the recording studio to satisfy his curiosity about the recording process itself (shot 7).

This is strange. What is marring the otherwise seamless montage in this scene? Why are the image and sound tracks so off-kilter? Oddly enough, the process of narrative construction—that process involved in the construction of a national identity through the film's mediating technologies—seems to be unsettling the synchronous harmony between sound and image. It is as if what takes place on the street—the heterosocial visual exchange in the foreign sites and the nondiegetic Iranian sound that accompanies the musicians' traversal of the foreign city—is now being brought into the studio and recorded along with the national music. That is the message that is scopically mediated through the recording tube as the audience duplicates the drummer's gaze as he peers into the tube to see the needle inscribing the sights of Paris and the sound of Iran on wax (shot 8 of fig. 6). This slippage on wax is the enunciative backdrop to an ironically patriotic lyric poem that is sung into the gramophone. The repeated refrain in this poem identifies the singers as "the enamored" worshippers of neither East nor West and the lovers of the beloved nation, rendered symbolically by the iconography of the lion and the crowning sun—the century-old symbol of Iran. The poem reads as follows:

> We the enamored ones take refuge in the majesty of the lion,
> We are in love with the moon-faced beauty of that crowning sun,
> Of two worlds, except you, our love, we want nothing,
> Of two worlds, except you, our love, we want nothing

The love-struck musicians are rendered as the ones who will bring joy to the heart of the nation and those who will remove her pain and sorrow.

7. After-images, from Delshodegan, *Ali Hatami, 1992.*

In a subsequent scene in which the musicians regroup to play the same piece of music in a park, the question of enunciation is underscored anew (fig. 7). Here the scopic and the aural become incommensurable and nonsynchronous, once again.

Set outdoors, the scene opens to a shot of a photographer and his female model. The model poses before the camera in the manner typical of late nineteenth-century *carte de visite* studio poses set against the backdrop of a European garden landscape. In this session, however, the conventional painted studio backdrop is absent (fig. 7, shot 1). Contrasting with the early scene in which the musicians test the new *tar* against the painted European landscape, the natural Parisian garden landscape takes the place of a studio screen. The oddity of playing out the scene of portrait photography outdoors is here underscored by the conversation that follows between photographer and model, where at the end of the session the model asks in French if they are going to do it again and he answers, "yes, tomorrow, if the weather is good." The exchange between the photographer and his model emphasizes the history of early phototechnology, which depended on the predictability of light available only indoors—in other words, only in studio spaces.

The presence of the camera in this first shot situates the scene as a site of enunciative self-reflexivity for the film. In this scene, once again, the audience is alerted to the status of its own vision as mediated by foregrounding the technology that enables the images the audience sees on screen. With this emphasis on the mediating role of the camera, the musicians, in effect, become the after-images of the unveiled European model, the model who, earlier in the sequence, is captured by a camera that stands within the narrative for that other camera that gives the audience access to the screened narrative. As after-image, the figure of the musicians, representative of Iran abroad, forcefully wedges the questions of national identity and cultural difference into an open ambivalence. While in the earlier scenes of the musicians' arrival the camera kept its distance from the staging of heterosexuality on the Paris streets, thus asserting the superiority of Iran's contemporary values, this scene situates both Europe and Iran within the same frame, simultaneously framed by the same lens. This comparative lens, more ambivalent than that used to stage the musicians' arrival, asks where contemporary Iran stands in relation to Europe past and present. Given Iran's dependence on mediating technologies that share an international history, how is the nation able to claim national purity in representation?

The status of sound becomes as important as the status of the visual in this scene. As the musicians start their practice, it becomes quite clear that the music that we are hearing is a studio recording (fig. 7, shot 2). The soundtrack adopts studio recorded sound here to play over the outdoor landscape. What has happened to the national music is precisely what should have, but did not happen to the photographer's session. Studio sound plays outdoors, and the outdoors becomes the site of *carte de visite* poses.

In this way, the film reiterates the nonsynchronicity of the scopic and aural. This enunciative incommensurability pressures the issue of national identity by mapping the production of national identity onto traversals in space, where what is being inscribed as modern Iran in its representational technologies is constantly externalized and then reconstructed and internalized on the backdrop of an intimate visual exchange between the European gaze eastward and the westward gaze of Iranian travelers. These gazes, we recall, grafted the exchange of desire onto the history of the nation's visual technologies at the moment of the technology's birth in the hands of Akkasbashi in Belgium. That exchange clearly continues to haunt Iranian cinema even as it attempts to construct the nation as independent of all external influence. The significance of this chronicled exchange is emphatically underscored as the European model reenters the shot and hauntingly stares at the seated musicians at the site of her own photo session (fig. 7, shot 4).[9]

Delshodegan foregrounds what Iranian films from the 1980s and 1990s have demonstrated repeatedly in the form of a quiet political protest on the level of enunciation: appearing on the narrative level to comply with the demands put on the industry to construct a national culture that shows Iran as isolated from Western influence, they accept the imposition of veiling and modesty laws to avoid censure and represent the national lifestyle as "Islamic," "traditionally Shi'ite," and "pure," even if anachronistically so by implication. Like *Delshodegan,* many films made after the establishment

9. The review here of the history of photography and film in Iran should be sufficient in suggesting that the unveiled female body is the productive site of Iranian cinema. The Iranian film camera is shaped not only by the history of Nasir al-Din Shah's photographic ventures into the harem, but also by the Iranian film camera's first encounters at the Belgian festival. Christian Metz (1982) suggests that although our primary identification with film is with its productive mechanism—its discourse, associated with the camera—it is this element of the film that must be repressed in order for the film to narrate its story effectively. Discourse, the site of production, in other words, must be repressed for the film to have narrative continuity and conventional meaning. What I am calling up here by the term "repression," then, is not patriarchal silencing per se, but the repression of the enunciative or the constitutive and meaning generating principle of film. Iranian cinema is marked at birth by its association with the unveiled female body. It is this productive site that has been and still is repressed in Iranian national cinema. Although one can argue that the "repression" of the enunciative is necessary for film in general, its association with the female body has significant political and cultural consequences for postrevolutionary Iranian cinema in particular. For more on this dynamic in postrevolutionary Iranian cinema see Mottahedeh (1999).

of the Islamic Republic of Iran configure a temporal index adopted from the *ta'ziyeh* tradition to form an atomistic confluence that shifts the terms of the real and the magical. In their adoption of a messianic temporality, the films articulate a now-time which confronts the standardization of cinematic strategies that have persistently bent all narrative tropes to conform to disciplinary Hollywood procedures of causality, continuity, and closure. In drawing on messianic *ta'ziyeh* tropes to pattern and organize a revolutionary and contestatory enunciation for postrevolutionary Iranian films, government demands for national purity in representation are contested and rearticulated as well, repeatedly showing how the modern nation and its cinema is produced on the grounds of cultural confluences, wedged in the contradictions of a forked tongue.

Conclusion

> The historian's work . . . is a work of representation in many senses, but it is representation with respect to something that is not representable, and that is history itself. History is unpresentable, not in the sense that it would be some presence hidden behind the representations, but because it is the coming into presence, as event.
>
> —Jean-Luc Nancy 1990, 166

That I begin this work with the stereotypic image of the Babi in scraps of chronicles, travelogues, and memoirs and end with that productive yet unpresentable enunciative site that is the confluence of cultures informing Iran's modern identity in its contemporary cinema, may seem somewhat idiosyncratic. But it is precisely this flitting image that must be seized as it suddenly appears, as Benjamin would put it, "in a moment of danger" forming in this way a constellation with the present (Benjamin 2003a, 391).

In our present, when the cinematic image is recruited by the Islamic Republic to purge Iranian identity and culture of all foreign influence, the urgent task that the filmmaker Ali Hatami sets himself is to ask how it might be possible for this pure identity to be represented through the mediating technologies of the cinema. Although clearly committed to creating a national cinema, Hatami's preoccupation with the history of representational technologies uncovers forces capable of halting the overdetermined processes that are currently intent on constructing Iran's history as one detached and pure from both the East and the West. The historical constellation of past and present informed by the *ta'ziyeh*'s messianic model of time and space is used to confront the overpowering disciplinary forces of standardization derived from Hollywood cinema and to create instead a film that is representative of a national cinema. As the nineteenth-century Babi chronicles recognized over a century ago, the *ta'ziyeh*'s spatial and temporal tropes are the very means by which the national is signaled and defended against aggression. Yet this very constellation unearths the constitutive sites that alone, as Herbert Marcuse notes, hold the revolutionary corrective for the present.

Benjamin, whose historical concepts inform mine, attempts to unite dialectical images with dialectical arguments. The force of his work thus lies in the multiple ways in which past experience forms a constellation with as yet unfulfilled traces of the present. Thus, his work situates historiography not as a labor that produces "continuities," but that traces within history's discontinuous images that redemptive index that could inform the future.

Structured in this late antique way of understanding being in time and space, resonant with the *ta'ziyeh*'s own, Benjamin's concepts of history are not only relevant to Iranian nineteenth-century conceptions of historical representation, but his "dialectical images" signal the very tools necessary to recover the repressed potentialities inherent in them—potentialities for understanding modernity and the after-images of that modernity as they develop in the present—from negative clichés to moving images on the screen of contemporary Iranian cinema. Marcuse glosses this approach as a "negative dialectics" and defines it as "an approach to the world which is negative in its very structure, because that which is real opposes and denies potentialities inherent in itself—potentialities which themselves strive for realization" (1987, 447). Dialectics is the "[i]nterpretation of that-which-is in terms of that-which-is-not." Dialectical thought strives therefore to recover the repressed content of historical thinking.

What I have attempted to recover in my readings of differential representations of Iranian modernity is the other face of the proverbial moon—the repressed content of contemporary thought on its modern history and its disciplinary representation. Alternative discourses of the modern, as Keya Ganguly notes, "have often proceeded simply by assuming that all accounts follow or simulate patterns of the paradigm case of Europe" (1996, 157). But it is clear from my readings of Browne's own disciplinary work on the Babis, and the contrasting thinking that operates within the texts that he introduced to the West, that the two views are incommensurable. Contemporary disciplinary models, on the one hand, fail to recover the historical conditions for Iranian perceptions of modernity precisely because of their imbrications in disciplinary systems. Persian modernist attempts, on the other hand, constantly fall short in their representation of Iran as mimetic of European models of progress. In close reading, these representations articulate their failure by revealing the constitutive cultural confluence that informs the nation in the tropes, the images, and the captions represented by them to their readers.

The haunting questions of *Representing the Unpresentable* have been the following: Why are modern acts, often articulated in terms of dress or veiling, associated with the dissent of the Babis? And why does this image of "the Babi" appear as a dialectic of modernity, fluctuating between images of Western secularism and unveiling on the one hand, and as unpresentable images of Shi'ite antiquity, on the other? At least two chroniclers cryptically answer these questions and do so in their articulations of Qurrat al-'Ayn Tahirih's unveiling in Badasht—one (Sipihr) in the appropriation of the phantasmagoric image of paradise associated with *farang* (Europe), and the other (Shaykh Abu Turab) in the appropriation of *takiyeh* tile images from the "Best of Stories" as the *literarization* of the *ta'ziyeh* representations of Joseph.

In Benjamin's work, thought is actualized through this force field of past and present. "Where thinking comes to a standstill in a constellation saturated with tensions, there the dialectical image appears. It is the caesura in the movement of thought" (1999a, 475). The dialectical image, for Benjamin, is thus the pause— in the movement of history, past and present, and is "identical with the historical object" (475). In the present of my reckoning with Iran's modern history, I have located Qurrat al-'Ayn Tahirih's unveiling in Badasht as that corresponding space in the past where thinking stops. In contrast to the locomotive of reform and progress in the "Browne chronicles," I see the cryptic recollections by Shaykh Abu Turab and Sipihr as the reach for the emergency brake. The emergent images reveal what the narratives of Babism erase in their narratization. An unveiled Babi emerges in the archaic—now as Fatimih, now in the beauty of Joseph. She appears, too, in the utopic—now as the proto-type of Europe and now as the *houri* of the Qur'anic paradise. The representation of this modern act of unveiling is made possible only by an appeal to the image, which, in the recollections of Shaykh Abu Turab, appears ultimately reversed by gender and in Sipihr's crafty scene is situated not in the here and now of modernity but in the utopian image of the West constructed by Iranian travelers in terms of a Qur'anic paradise. Modernity is articulated by the recovery of ur-images, images rescued from their context and given new form. As such, the ur-images inform modernity's *Jetztzeit*.

The shocking act of unveiling by the Babi as the condition of Iran's dialectical modernity thus comes to us in image form. The formal quality of the image is identified as the technology commensurate with Iran's modernity. The hybrid image—marked as it is, in both form and content, by its historical vacillation between interiority and infinite exposure, between the shocking, the phantasmagoric, the archaic, and the utopian, in the interstices between East and West—must be recognized as the dialectical site (past and present) where the battle over Iran's contemporary identity is now waged. The unveiled Tahirih is not the first unveiled woman to appear in public, as some historians have claimed, but she is Iranian modernist historiography's first simulacrum, its first stuttering ghost. It is her ghostly figure that comes to haunt Iranian cultural representations as the national government attempts to claim an unsullied Iranian identity in a globalized world. The contemporary attempt to purify the image in cinema can be understood once its dialectical "other" is situated—in the presentable image of Iran's modern scapegoat, "the Babi."

Works Cited

Index

Works Cited

Abdu'l-Baha. 1981. *The Secret of Divine Civilization.* 2d ed. Translated by Marzieh Gail. Wilmette, Ill.: Baha'i Publishing Trust.

Afaqi, Sabir, ed. 2004. *Tahirih in History: Perspective on Qurrat al-'Ayn from East and West.* Studies in the Babi and Baha'i Religions, vol. 16. Los Angeles: Kalimat Press, 2004.

Afary, Janet. 1996. *The Iranian Constitutional Revolution, 1906–1911:Grassroots Democracy, Social Democracy, and the Origins of Feminism.* New York:Columbia Univ. Press.

Afary, Janet, and Kevin B. Anderson. 2005. *Foucault and the Iranian Revolution: Gender and the Seductions of Islamism.* Chicago: Univ. of Chicago Press.

Afnan, Muhammad, and Hatcher, William. 1985. "Western Islamic Scholarship and Baha'i Origins." *Religion* 15:29–49.

———. 1986. "Notes on MacEoin's 'Baha'i Fundamentalism.'" *Religion* 16:187–92.

Afshar, Iraj. 1983. "Some Remarks on the Early History of Photography in Iran." In *Qajar Iran: Political, Social and Cultural Change, 1800–1925,* edited by Edmond Bosworth and Carole Hillenbrand, 261–90. Costa Mesa, Calif.: Mazda.

Aghaie, Kamran Scot. 2005a. "Gendered Aspects of the Emergence and Historical Development of Shi'i Symbos and Rituals." In *The Women of Karbala: Ritual Performance and Symbolic Discourses in Modern Shi'i Islam,* edited by Kamran Scot Aghaie, 1–21. Austin: Univ. of Texas Press.

———. 2005b. "The Gender Dynamics of Moharram Symbols and Rituals in the Latter Lears of Qajar Rule." In *The Women of Karbala: Ritual Performance and Symbolic Discourses in Modern Shi'i Islam,* edited by Kamran Scot Aghaie, 45–63. Austin: Univ. of Texas Press.

Ahmed, Leila. 1992. *Women and Gender in Islam: Historical Roots of a Modern Debate.* New Haven: Yale Univ. Press.

Akhundzadih, Mirza Fath Ali. 1985. *Kamal al-Dawla,* published as *Maktubat.* Edited by M. Subhdam. N.p. [Germany]: Mard Imruz. (Orig. pub. 1863–64.)

Amanat, Abbas. 1989. *Resurrection and Renewal: The Making of the Babi Movement in Iran, 1844–1850.* Ithaca: Cornell Univ. Press.

———, ed. 1993. *Crowning Anguish: Memoirs of a Persian Princess from the Harem to Modernity,* by Taj al-Saltana. Washington D.C: Mage Publishers.

Anon. 1892. "Review of *A Traveller's Narrative* trans. Edward Granville Browne." *Oxford Magazine,* May 25, 394.

Arjomand, Said Amir. 1984. *The Shadow of God and the Hidden Imam: Religion, Political Order, and Societal Change in Shi'ite Iran from the Beginning to 1890.* Chicago: Univ. of Chicago Press.

Armstrong-Ingram, Jackson. 2004. "The Shah, the Skirt and the Ballet: A Menage a Trois, or Just Ill-Founded Gossip?" *Qajar Studies: Journal of the International Qajar Studies Association* 4:91–107.

Arnold, Matthew. 1871. "A Persian Passion Play." *Cornhill Magazine,* Dec., 668–87.

Asayesh, Gelareh. 1999. *Saffron Sky: A Life Between Iran and America.* Boston: Beacon.

Atkins, John B., ed. 1927. *A Persian Anthology: Being a Translation from the Persian.* London: Methuen.

Bab, Sayyid Ali Muhammad Shirazi. 1987. *The Persian Bayan.* In *Selections from the Writings of E. G. Browne on the Babi and Baha'i Religions,* edited by Moojan Momen. Oxford: George Ronald.

———. 2006. "Excerpts from the *The Persian Bayan." Selections from the Writings of the Báb,* 99–146. Wilmette, Ill.: Bahá'í Publishing Trust.

———. n.d. *Risala furu al-adliyya.* Tehran Baha'i Archives 5010C. In Arabic with Persian translation.

Baghdadi, Aqa Muhammad Mustafi. 1991. "Sharh hal-i Hazrat-i Tahirih." In *Chahar Resalih-i-Tarikhi Dar Bariyih-i-Tahirih-Qurratu'l-'Ayn,* edited by Abu'l Qasim Afnan, 18–45. Wienacht, Switzerland: Landegg Academy.

Baktash, Mayel. 1979. "Ta'ziyeh and Its Philosophy." In *Ta'ziyeh: Ritual and Drama in Iran,* edited by Peter J. Chelkowski, 95–120. New York: New York Univ. Press; Tehran: Soroush Press.

Balfour, Ian. 1991. "Reversal, Quotation (Benjamin's History)." *MLN* 106:622–45.

Balyuzi, H. M. 1970. *Edward Granville Browne and the Baha'i Faith.* London: George Ronald.

Bayat, Mangol. 1982. *Mysticism and Dissent: Socioreligious Thought in Qajar Iran.* Syracuse: Syracuse Univ. Press.

Beeman, William O. 1979. "Cultural Dimensions of Performance Conventions in Iranian Ta'ziyeh." In *Ta'ziyeh: Ritual and Drama in Iran,* edited by Peter J. Chelkowski, 24–31. New York: New York Univ. Press; Tehran: Soroush Press.

———. 1982. "A Full Arena: The Development and Meaning of Popular Performance Traditions in Iran." In *Modern Iran: The Dialectics of Continuity and Change,* edited by Michael E. Bonine and Nikki R. Keddie, 361–81. Albany: State Univ. of New York Press.

———. 1986. *Language, Status, and Power in Iran.* Bloomington: Indiana Univ. Press.

Beiza'i, Bahram. 1996. "At the End of a Hundred Years." *Iran Nameh* 14, no. 3 (Summer): 363–82.

———. 2000. *A Study of Iranian Theatre.* Tehran: Roshangaran and Women's Studies Publishing.

Benjamin, Walter. 1983. *Charles Baudelaire: A Lyric Poet in the Era of High Capitalism.* London: Verso.

———. 1992. "What Is Epic Theatre?" 1st and 2d versions. In *Understanding Brecht,* translated by Anna Bostock, 1–23. London: Verso.

———. 1999a. *The Arcades Project.* Konvolute J. Edited by Rolf Tiedemann, translated by Howard Eiland and Kevin McLaughlin. Cambridge, Mass.: Harvard Univ. Press, Belknap Press.

———. 1999b. "The Little History of Photography." In *Selected Writings, Volume 2: 1927–1934,* edited by Michael W. Jennings, Howard Eiland, and Gary Smith, translated by Rodney Livingstone, 507–30. Cambridge and London: Harvard Univ. Press, Belknap Press. (Orig. pub. 1931.)

———. 2002. "The Storyteller: Observations on the Works of Nikolai Leskov." *Selected Writings, Volume 3: 1935–1938,* edited by Michael W. Jennings and Howard Eiland, translated by Edmund Jephcott, Howard Eiland, and others, 143–66. Cambridge and London: Harvard Univ. Press, Belknap Press. (Orig. pub. 1936.)

———. 2003a."On the Concept of History." *Selected Writings, Volume 4: 1938–1940,* edited by Michael W. Jennings and Howard Eiland. Translated by Edmund Jephcott and others, 389–400. Cambridge and London: Harvard Univ. Press, Belknap Press. (Orig. pub. 1940.)

———. 2003b. "Paralipomena to 'On the Concept of History.'" *Selected Writings, Volume 4: 1938–1940,* edited by Michael W. Jennings and Howard Eiland, translated by Edmund Jephcott and others, 401–11. Cambridge and London: Harvard Univ. Press, Belknap Press. (Orig. pub. 1940.)

———. 2003c."The Work of Art in the Age of Reproducibility [Third Version]." *Selected Writings: Volume 4, 1938–1940,* edited by Michael W. Jennings and Howard Eiland, translated by Edmund Jephcott and others, 251–83. Cambridge and London: Harvard Univ. Press, Belknap Press. (Orig. pub. 1939.)

Benveniste, Emile. 1971. "Correlations of the Tense in the French Verb." In *Problems in General Linguistics Series No. 8,* translated by Elizabeth Meek, 205–15. Coral Gables: Univ. of Miami Press.

Bhabha, Homi K. 1994. *The Location of Culture.* London: Routledge.

Biddiss, Michael D. 1970a. *Father of Racist Ideology: The Social and Political Thought of Count Gobineau.* New York: Weybright and Talley.

———. 1970b. "Introduction: Human Inequality and Racial Crisis." In *Gobineau: Selected Political Writings,* edited by Michael Biddiss, 13–35. London: Jonathan Cape.

———. 1977. *The Age of the Masses: Ideas and Society in Europe Since 1870.* Hassocks, U.K.: Harvester Press.

Brook, Peter. 1979. "Leaning on the Moment: A Conversation with Peter Brook." *Parabola* 4, no. 2:47–59.

Browne, Edward G., trans. 1891. *A Traveller's Narrative Written to Illustrate the Episode of the Bab,* by Abdu'l Baha. Cambridge: Cambridge Univ. Press.

———, ed. and trans. 1892. "Catalogue and Description of Babi MSS." *Journal of the Royal Asiatic Society* 24:433–99, 637–710.

———, ed. and trans. 1893. *Tarikh-i-Jadid or New History of Mirza Ali Muhammad—the Bab.* Cambridge: Cambridge Univ. Press.

———, ed. 1910. *Kitab-i Nuqtatu'l Kaf (Nuqtat al-Kaf)* Reprint, 1998, H-Bahai publications Web site, Lansing, Mich. http://www.h-net.msu.edu/~bahai/.

———. [1918] 1961. *Materials for the Study of the Bábí Religion.* Cambridge: Cambridge Univ. Press. (Orig. pub. 1918.)

———. 1924. *A Literary History of Persia.* Vol. 4, *Modern Times: 1500–1924.* Cambridge: Cambridge Univ. Press.

———. 1926. *A Year Amongst the Persians: 1887–1888.* 2d ed. Cambridge: Cambridge Univ. Press.

———, ed. and trans. 1983. *The Press and Poetry of Modern Persia.* Los Angeles: Kalimat Press.

Browne, Edward G., and Nicholson, Reynold Alleyne. 1932. "Shaykhi and Babi Mss." In *A Descriptive Catalogue of the Oriental Mss Belonging to the Late E. G. Browne.* Cambridge: Cambridge Univ. Press.

Buck-Morss, Susan. 1989. *Dialectics of Seeing: Walter Benjamin and the Arcades Project.* Cambridge, Mass.: MIT Press.

Butler, Judith. 1993. *Bodies That Matter: On the Discursive Limits of "Sex."* New York: Routledge.

Cadava, Eduoardo. 1997. *Words of Light: Theses on the Photography of History.* Princeton: Princeton Univ. Press.

Calmard, Jean. 1983. "Muharram Ceremonies and Diplomacy (a Preliminary Study)." *In Qajar Iran: Political, Social, and Cultural Change, 1800–1925,* edited by Edmond Bosworth and Carole Hillenbrand, 213–28. Costa Mesa, Calif.: Mazda.

Certeau, Michel de. 1988. *The Practice of Everyday Life.* Translated by Steven Rendall. Berkeley: Univ. of California Press, 1988.

Chanan, Michael. 1995. *Repeated Takes: A Short History of Recording and Its Effects on Music.* New York: Verso.

Chehabi, Houchang. 1993. "Staging the Emperor's New Clothes: Dress Codes and Nation Building under Reza Shah." *Iranian Studies* 26 (Fall): 209–33.

———. 1997. "Ardabil Becomes a Province: Center-Periphery Relations in Iran." *International Journal of Middle East Studies* 29, 2:235–53.

Chelkowski, Peter J. 1971. "Dramatic and Literary Aspects of Ta'zieh-Khani—Iranian Passion Play." *Review of National Literatures: Iran* 2, no. 1 (Spring): 121–38.

———. 1979. "Ta'ziyeh: Indigenous Avant-Garde Theatre of Iran." In *Ta'ziyeh: Ritual and Drama in Iran,* edited by Peter J. Chelkowski, 1–11. New York: New York Univ. Press; Tehran: Soroush Press.

———. 1988. "When Time Is No Time, And Space Is No Space: The Passion Plays of Husayn." In *Ta'ziyeh: Ritual and Popular Beliefs in Iran,* edited by Milla Riggio, 13–23. Trinity College: Hartford Seminary.

———. 2005. "Time Out of Memory: Ta'ziyeh the Total Drama." *Drama Review* 49, no. 4 (Winter): 15–27.

Cixous, Hélène. 1981. "Castration or Decapitation?" Translated by Annette Kuhn. *Signs* 7, no. 11, 41–55.

Cole, Juan R. I. 1993a. "'I Am All the Prophets': The Poetics of Pluralism in Baha'i Texts." *Poetics Today* 14, no. 3 (Fall): 447–76.

———. 1993b. "Shaykh Ahmad al-Ahsa'i on the Sources of Religious Authority" Paper given at the Center for Iranian Studies, Columbia Univ. Oct. http://www-personal.umich.edu/~jrcole/papers.htm.

———. 1994. "The World as Text: Cosmologies of Shaykh Ahmad al-Ahsa'i." *Studia Islamica* 80: 145–63.

———. 1996. "Marking Boundaries, Marking Time: The Iranian Past and the Construction of the Self by Qajar Thinkers." *Iranian Studies* 29, nos. 1–2 (Winter–Spring): 35–56.

———. 1997. "Individualism and the Spiritual Path in Shaykh Ahmad al-Ahsa'i." Occasional Papers in Shaykhi, Babi, and Baha'i Studies 1, no. 4 (Sept.). H-Bahai publications Web site. http://www.h-net.msu.edu/~bahai/.

———. 1998a. *Modernity and the Millennium: The Genesis of the Baha'i Faith in the Nineteenth-Century Middle East.* New York: Columbia Univ. Press.

———. 1998b. "Nuqtat al-Kaf and the Babi Chronicle Traditions." Research Notes in Shaykhi, Babi, and Baha'i Studies 2, no. 6 (Aug.). H-Bahai publications Web site. http://www.h-net.msu.edu/~bahai/

Copjec, Joan. 1995. *Read My Desire: Lacan Against the Historicists.* Cambridge: MIT Press, October Books.

Corbin, Henry. 1971–72. *En Islam Iranien,* vol. 3. Paris: Gallimard.

Crafton, Donald. 1997. *History of the American Cinema.* Vol. 4, *The Talkies: American Cinema's Transition to Sound, 1926–1931.* New York: Macmillian Library Reference.

Easterman, Daniel [Denis MacEoin]. 1992. *New Jerusalems: Reflections on Islam, Fundamentalism, and the Rushdie Affair.* London: Grafton.

Elsaesser, Thomas. 1995. "From Sign to Mind: A General Introduction." In *The Film Spectator: From Sign to Mind,* edited by Warren Buckland, 9–17. Amsterdam: Amsterdam Univ. Press.

Fanon, Frantz. 1967. *A Dying Colonialism.* Translated by Haakon Chevalier. New York: Grove.

Fath-Ali Beygi, Davoud. 1990. "Majlis Ta'ziyeh Dokhtar-i Hindu." *Fasl-Namah-i Teatre* 11–12 (Summer): 221–46.

———. 1992. "Gushe dar ta'ziyeh." *Fasl-Namah-i Teatre* 14 (Summer): 229–73.

Fischer, Michael, and Mehdi Abedi, eds. 1990. *Debating Muslims: Cultural Dialogues in Postmodernity and Tradition.* Madison: Univ. of Wisconsin Press.

Flynn, Thomas R. 1997. *Sartre, Foucault and Historical Reason.* Vol. 1. Chicago: Univ. of Chicago Press.

Forrester, John. 1990. *The Seductions of Psychoanalysis: Freud, Lacan, and Derrida.* New York: Univ. of Cambridge Press.

Foucault, Michel. 1979. *Discipline and Punish: The Birth of the Prison.* Translated by Alain Sheridan. New York: Vintage.

———. 1980. *Power/Knowledge: Selected Interviews and Other Writings, 1972–1977.* Edited and translated by Colin Gordon. Brighton: Harvester Press.

———. 1981. "The Order of Discourse." In *Untying the Text: A Post-Structuralist Reader,* edited by Robert Young, 48–78. New York: Routledge.

———. 1991. "Politics and The Study of Discourse." In *The Foucault Effect,* edited by Graham Burchell, Colin Gordon, and Peter Miller, 53–72. Chicago: Univ. of Chicago Press.

Freud, Sigmund. 1962. "Neuropsychosis of Defense." *Standard Edition of the Complete Psychological Works of Sigmund Freud.* Vol. 3. Translated by James Strachey, 45–61. London: Hogarth Press.

———. 1971a. "Negation." *Standard Edition of the Complete Psychological Works of Sigmund Freud.* Vol. 19. Translated by James Strachey, 235–39. London: Hogarth Press.

———. 1971b. "On Fetishism." *Standard Edition of the Complete Psychological Works of Sigmund Freud.* Vol. 21. Translated by James Strachey, 149–58. London: Hogarth Press.

———. 1971c."Recapitulation and Problems." *Standard Edition of the Complete Psychological Works of Sigmund Freud.* Vol. 17. Translated by James Strachey, 29–47. London: Hogarth Press.

———. 1971d. "Three Essays." *Standard Edition of the Complete Psychological Works of Sigmund Freud.* Vol. 17. Translated by James Strachey, 125–245. London: Hogarth Press.

———. 1971e. "The Uncanny." *Standard Edition of the Complete Psychological Works of Sigmund Freud.* Vol. 17. Translated by James Strachey, 219–56. London: Hogarth Press.

Ganguly, Keya. 1996. "Carnal Knowledge: Visuality and the Modern in *Charulata.*" *Camera Obscura: Feminism, Culture and Media Studies* 37 (Jan.): 157–87.

Garber, Marjorie. 1998. "Dress Codes, or the Theatricality of Difference." In *Routledge Reader in Gender and Performance,* edited by Lizbeth Goodman with Jane de Gay, 176–81. New York: Routledge.

Girard, René. 1986. *The Scapegoat.* Translated by Yvonne Freccero Baltimore: Johns Hopkins Univ. Press.

Gitelman, Lisa. 1999. *Scripts, Grooves, and Writing Machines: Representing Technology in the Edison Era.* Stanford: Univ. of Stanford Press.

———. 2003. "Souvenir Foils: On the Status of Print at the Origin of Recorded Sound." In *New Media, 1740–1915,* edited by Lisa Gitelman and Geoffrey B. Pingree, 157–73. Cambridge, Mass.: MIT Press.

Gobineau, M. le Comte de. 1900. *Les Religions et les Philosophies dans l'Asie Centrale.* Paris: Ernest Leroux.

———. 1933. *Correspondance entre le comte de Gobineau et le comte de Prokesch-osten (1854–1876).* Paris: Plon.

———. 1970. *Gobineau: Selected Political Writings.* Edited by Michael Biddiss. London: Jonathan Cape.

Godzich, Wlad. 1994. "The Tiger and the Papermat." In *The Culture of Literacy,* 159–70. Cambridge, Mass.: Harvard Univ. Press.

Gordon, Colin. 1991. "Governmental Rationality: An Introduction" In *The Foucault Effect,* edited by Graham Burchell, Colin Gordon, and Peter Miller, 1–51. Chicago: Univ. of Chicago Press.

Gulpaygani, Mirza Abu'l Fadl, and Sayyid Mihdi Gulpaygani. 1991. *Kashf al Ghita.* Tashkent, 1991.

Haeri, Shahla. 1989. *Law of Desire: Temporary Marriage in Shi'i Iran.* Syracuse: Syracuse Univ. Press.

Hamid, Idris. 1998. "The Metaphysics and Cosmology of Process According to Shaykh 'Ahmad Al-'Ahsa'i Critical Edition, Translation, And Analysis of 'Observations in Wisdom'" Ph.D. diss., State Univ. of New York at Buffalo.

Hone, J. M. 1914. *The German Doctrine of Conquest; A French View, by E. Seilliere's Philosophy of Imperialism.* Dublin: Maunsel and Co.

Howard, Jean E. 1998. "Cross-Dressing: The Theatre and Gender Struggle in Early Modern England." In *Routledge Reader in Gender and Performance,* edited by Lizbeth Goodman with Jane de Gay, 47–51. New York: Routledge.

Issari, M. Ali. 1989. *Cinema in Iran, 1900–1979.* London: Scarecrow Press.

Itzutsu, Toshihiko. 1964. *God and Man in the Koran* Tokyo: Keio Institute of Cultural and Linguistic Studies.

Kashani-Sabet, Firoozeh. 1999. *Frontier Fictions: Shaping the Iranian Nation, 1804–1946.* Princeton, N.J.: Princeton Univ. Press.

———. 2000. "Hallmark of Humanism: Hygiene and Love of Homeland in Qajar Iran." *The American Historical Review* 105, no. 4, 70 pars. Accessed Jul. 5, 2006. http://www.historycooperative.org/journals/ahr/105.4/ah001171.html.

Khan, Muhammad Zafrulla. 1991. *The Quran: The Eternal Revelation Vouchsafed to Muhammad, the Seal of the Prophets.* New York: Olive Branch Press.

Kristeva, Julia. 1982.*Powers of Horror:An Essay on Abjection.* Translated by Leon S. Roudiez. New York:Columbia Univ. Press.

Kurzman, Charles. 2005. "Weaving Iran into the Tree of Nations." *International Journal of Middle East Studies* 37, no. 2 (May): 137–66.

Lacan, Jacques. 1982. *Feminine Sexuality.* Edited by Jacqueline Rose and Juliet Mitchell. New York: Pantheon Books.

Lawson, B. Todd 1987. *The Qur'an Commentary of Sayyid Ali Muhammad, the Bab.* Ph.D. diss., McGill Univ.

MacEoin, Denis. 1979. "From Shaykhism to Babism: A Study in Charismatic Renewal in Shi'i Islam." Ph.D. diss., Faculty of Oriental Studies, Univ. of Cambridge.

———. 1982. "The Babi Concept of Holy War." *Religion* 12:93–129.

———. 1983. "From Babism to Baha'ism: Problems of Militancy, Quietism and Conflation in the Construction of a Religion." *Religion* 13:219–55.

———. 1986a. "Afnan, Hatcher and an Old Bone." *Religion* 16, no. 2:193–95.

———. 1986b. "Baha'i Fundamentalism and the Academic Study of the Babi Movement." *Religion* 16, no. 1:57–84.

———. 1992. *Sources For Early Babi Doctrine and History: A Survey.* Leiden, Netherlands: E. J. Brill.

———. 1997a. "Deconstructing and Reconstructing the Shari'a: The Babi and Baha'i Solutions to the Problem of Immutability" Paper presented for the British Society for Middle East and Islamic Studies in Oxford, July 9.

———. 1997b. "The Trial of the Bab: Shi'ite Orthodoxy Confronts Its Mirror Image." Occasional Papers in Shaykhi, Babi and Baha'i Studies 1, no. 1 (May). http://www.h-net.msu.edu/~bahai/.

Marcuse, Herbert. 1987. "A Note on the Dialectic." In *The Essential Frankfurt School Reader.* Edited by Andrew Arato and Eike Gebhardt, 444–51. New York: Continuum.

Mazandarani, Asadu'llah Fadil. n.d. "Tarikh-i Zuhur al-Haqq." Vol. 2. Manuscript in private collection. East Lansing, Mich.: H-Bahai, 2000.

McCants, William, and Milani, Kavian. 2004. "The History and Provenance of an Early Manuscript of the *Nuqtat al-Kaf* Dated 1268 (1851–52)." *Iranian Studies* 37, no. 3 (Sept.): 431–49.

Meisami, Julie Scott. 1985. "Alegorical Gardens in Persian Poetic Tradition: Nezami, Rumi, Hafez." *International Journal of Middle Eastern Studies* 17:229–60.

Merguerian, Gayane Karen, and Najmabadi, Afsaneh. 1997. "Zulaykha and Yusuf: Whose 'Best Story'?" *International Journal of Middle Eastern Studies* 29, no. 4 (Nov.): 485–508.

Mernissi, Fatima. 1975. *Beyond the Veil: Male Female Dynamics in Modern Muslim Society.* New York: Wiley and Sons.

———. 1991. *The Veil and the Male Elite: A Feminist Interpretation of Women's Rights in Islam.* Translated by Mary Jo Lakeland. Reading, Mass.: Addison-Wesley.

Metz, Christian. 1995. "The Impersonal Enunciation, or the Site of Film: In the Margin of Recent Works on Enunciation and Cinema." In *The Film Spectator: From Sign to Mind,* edited by Warren Buckland, 140–63. Amsterdam: Amsterdam Univ. Press.

Milani, Farzaneh. 1992. *Veils and Words: The Emerging Voices of Iranian Women Writers.* New York: Syracuse Univ. Press.

Miller, William McElwee. 1969. *Ten Muslims Meet Christ.* Grand Rapids: W. B. Eerdmans Pub. Co.

Momen, Moojan, ed. 1981. *The Babi and Baha'i Religions, 1844–1944: Some Contemporary Western Accounts.* Oxford: George Ronald.

——— 1983. "The Social Basis of the Babi Upheavals in Iran: A Preliminary Analysis." *International Journal of Middle Eastern Studies* 15:157–83.

———. 1985. *An Introduction to Shi'i Islam.* New Haven: Yale Univ. Press.

———, ed. 1987. *Selections from the Writings of E. G. Browne on the Babi and Baha'i Religions.* Oxford: George Ronald.

Mottahedeh, Negar. 1999. "Bahram Bayza'i's Maybe Some Other Time: The un-Present-able Iran." *Camera Obscura: Feminism, Culture and Media Studies* 43:163–91.

Mowitt, John. 1992a. "Algerian Nation: Fanon's Fetish" *Cultural Critique* 22 (Fall): 165–86.

———. 1992b. *Text: The Genealogy of an Antidisciplinary Object* Durham, N.C.: Duke Univ. Press.

———. 2004. "The Hollywood Sound Tract." In *Subtitles: On the Foreignness of Film,* edited by Atom Egoyan and Ian Balfour, 381–401. Cambridge, Mass.: MIT Press.

———. 2005. *Re-Takes: Postcoloniality and Foreign Film Languages.* Minneapolis: Univ. of Minnesota Press.

Munis al-Dawleh. 2001 [1380 A.H.]. *Khatirat.* Edited by Sirus Sa'd-u Nadiyan. Tehran: Zarrin Publications.

Naficy, Hamid. 1994. "Veiled Vision/Powerful Presences: Women in Post-Revolutionary Iranian Cinema." In *In the Eye of the Storm: Women in Post-revolutionary Iran,* edited by Mahnaz Afkhami and Erika Friedl, 131–50. Syracuse: Syracuse Univ. Press.

Nafisi, Azar. 2003. *Reading Lolita in Tehran.* New York: Random House.

Naghibi, Nima. 1999. "Bad Feminist or *Bad Hejabi?:* Moving Outside the Hejab Debate." *Interventions* 1, no. 4:555–71.

Najmabadi, Afsaneh. 2001. "Gendered Transformations: Beauty, Love, Sexuality in Qajar Iran." *Iranian Studies* 34, nos. 1–4:89–102.

—m——. 2005. *Women with Mustaches, Men Without Beards: Gender and Sexual Anxieties of Iranian Modernity.* Berkeley: Univ. of California Press.

Nancy, Jean-Luc. 1990. "Finite History." In *The States of Theory,* ed. David Carroll, 149–72. New York: Columbia Univ. Press.

Nietzsche, Friedrich W. 1974. *The Dawn of Day.* New York: Gordon Press.

———. 1989. *Genealogy of Morals and Ecce Homo.* Translated by Walter Kaufmann and R. J. Hollingdale. New York: Vintage.

Pelly, Lewis. 1879. *The Miracle Play of Hasan and Husain.* 2 vols. London: W. H. Allen.

Pena, Richard. 2006. "Iranian Cinema at the Festivals." *Cineaste* 31, no. 3 (Summer): 40–41.

Peterson, Samuel R. 1979. "The Ta'ziyeh and Related Arts." In *Ta'ziyeh: Ritual and Drama in Iran,* edited by Peter J. Chelkowski, 64–87. New York: New York Univ. Press; Tehran: Soroush Press.

Petty, Rebecca Ansari. 1982. "The Ta'zieh: Ritual of Renewal in Iran." 2 vols. Ph.D. diss., Indiana Univ.

Piemontese, Angelo. 1972. "The Photograph Album of the Italian Diplomatic Mission to Persia (Summer 1862)." *From East to West* 22, nos. 3–4 (Sept.–Dec.): 249–311.

Qajar, Muzzafar al-Din Shah. 1982 [1361 A.H.]. *Safarnameh-ye Mobarakeh-ye Muzzafared-Din Shah Beh Farang.* Transcribed by Mirza Mehdi Khan Kashani. 2d ed. Tehran: Ketab-e Foruzan.

Qajar, Nasir Din Shah. 1874. *Diary of the Shah of Persia During His Tour Through Europe in 1873.* Edited by J. W. Redhouse. London: John Murray.

Rabbani, Ahang. 2007. *The Babis of Nayriz.* Vol. 2 of *Witnesses to Babi and Baha'i History.* http://ahang.rabbani.googlepages.com/nayriz.

Rabbani, Shoghi Effendi. 1970. *God Passes By.* Wilmette, Ill.: Baha'i Publishing Trust.

Rafati, Vahid. 1979. "The Development of Shaykh'i Thought in Shi'i Islam." Ph.D. diss., Univ. of California, Los Angeles, University Microfilms.

Rahgani, Ruh'angiz. 1998. *Tarikh-i musiqi-i Iran.* Tehran: Pishraw.

Rawhani, Omid. 1999 [1378 A.H.]. "Ali Hatami: Kargardan-e Delshodegan, 'Man Ghali Mibafam.'" *Film: Mah Nameh-ye Sinema* 2: 541–45.

Rijai'i, Farhang. 1994. *Ganji Sukhtih: Pajuheshi dar Musighiye Ahdi Qajar.* Tehran: Shirkatih Ahya-yi Kitab.

Ronell, Avital. 1989. *The Telephone Book: Technology, Schizophrenia, Electric Speech.* Lincoln: Univ. of Nebraska Press.

Root, Martha. 1981. *Tahirih: The Pure One.* Los Angeles: Kalimat Press. (Orig. pub. 1938.)

Sadr, Hamid Reza. 2002. *An Introduction to the Political History of Iranian Cinema (1900–2001).* Persian ed. Tehran: Ney Publishing House.

Samandar, Shaykh Kazim. 1991. "Sharh hal-i hazrat-i Tahirih." In *Chahar Resalih-i-Tarikhi Dar Bariyih-i- Tahirih-Qurratu'l-'Ayn,* edited by Abu'l Qasim Afnan, 45–64. Wienacht, Switzerland: Landegg Academy.

Sanjabi, Maryam. 1995. "Rereading the Enlightenment: Akhundzada and His Voltaire." *Iranian Studies* 28, nos. 1–2 (Winter–Spring): 39–60.

Sante, Luc. 2004. "Introduction." In *Camera Obscura,* edited by Abelardo Morell, 7–9. New York: Bulfinch Press.

Satrapi, Marjane. 2003. *Persepolis.* New York: Pantheon.

Scarce, Jennifer. 1976. *Isfahan in Camera: 19th Century Persia Through the Photographs of Ernst Hoeltzer.* London: AARP.

Shirazi-Mahajan, Faegheh. 1993. "The Politics of Clothing in the Middle East: The Case of Hijab in Post-Revolutionary Iran." *Critique* (Spring): 54–63.

Sipanta, Sasan. 1998. *Tarikh-i tahavvul-i zabt-i musiqi dar Iran.* Tehran: Mahur.

Sipihr, Muhammad Taqi Lisan al-Mulk. 1958 [1353 A.H.]. *Nasikh at-Tavarikh.* 4 vols. in 2 eds. Tehran: Talib Sirahih and Muhammad Baqir Bihbudi.

Sklar, Robert. 1994. *Movie-Made America: A Cultural History of American Movies.* New York: Random House. (Orig. pub. 1975.)

Spellberg, D. A. 1994. *Politics, Gender and the Islamic Past: The Legacy of 'Aisha Bind Abi Bakr.* New York: Columbia Univ. Press.

Stein, Donna. 1983. "Early Photography in Iran." *History of Photography* 7, no. 4:253–91.

Stewart, Garrett. 1999. *Between Film and Screen: Modernism's Photo Synthesis.* Chicago: Univ. of Chicago Press.

Tahimi, Gholam Reza, ed. 1998. *Visible Treasure/Ganjeh Peyda.* Tehran: Cultural Research Bureau.

Tancoigne, M. 1820. *A Narrative of a Journey into Persia and Residence at Teheran.* London: William Wright.

Tavakoli-Targhi, Mohamad. 1990a. "Imagining Western Women: Occidentalism and Euro-Eroticism." *Radical America* 24, no. 3 (July–Sept.): 73–87.

———. 1990b. "Refashioning Iran: Language and Culture During the Constitutional Revolution," *Iranian Studies* 23:77–101.

———. 2001. *Refashioning Iran: Orientalism, Occidentalism, and Historiography.* Hampshire and New York: Palgrave Macmillan.

ter Haar, Johan G. J. 1993. "Ta'ziyeh: Ritual Theatre from Shi'ite Iran." In *Theatre Intercontinental: Forms, Functions, Correspondences,* edited by C. C. Barfoot and Cobi Bordewijk, 155–74. Amsterdam: Rodopi.

Thaiss, Gustav. 1972. "Religious Symbolism and Social Change: The Drama of Husain." In *Scholars, Saints, and Sufis,* edited by Nikki Keddie, 349–66. Berkeley and Los Angeles: Univ. of California Press.

Varzi, Roxanne. 2006. *Warring Souls: Youth, Media, and Martyrdom in Post-Revolution Iran.* Durham: Duke Univ. Press.

Walbridge, John. 1996. "The Babi Uprising in Zanjan: Causes and Issues." *Iranian Studies,* nos. 3–4 (Summer–Fall): 339–62.

———. 1998. "Document and Narrative Sources for the History of the Battle of Zanjan." Occasional Papers in Shaykhi, Babi and Baha'i Studies 2, no. 4 (May). H-Bahai publications website. http://www.h-net.msu.edu/~bahai/.

White, Hayden. 1976. "The Fictions of Factual Representation." In *The Literature of Fact,* edited by Angus Fletcher, 21–44. New York: Columbia Univ. Press.

Wirth, Andrzej. 1979. "Semiological Aspects of the Ta'ziyeh." In *Ta'ziyeh: Ritual and Drama in Iran,* edited by Peter J. Chelkowski, 32–39. New York: New York Univ. Press and Tehran: Soroush Press.

Wishard, John G. 1908. *Twenty Years in Persia: A Narrative of Life under the Last Three Shahs.* New York: Fleming H. Revell Company.

Zarandi, Muhammad. 1996. *The Dawn-Breakers: Nabil's Narrative of the Early Days of the Baha'i Revelation.* Edited and translated by Shoghi Effendi Rabbani. Wilmette, Ill.: Baha'i Publishing Trust.

Zizek, Slavoj. 1991. *Looking Awry: An Introduction to Jacques Lacan Through Popular Culture* Cambridge, Mass.: MIT Press.

———. 1993. *Tarrying with the Negative: Kant, Hegel, and the Critique of Ideology.* Durham, N.C.: Duke Univ. Press.

Index

www.ingramcontent.com/pod-product-compliance
Lightning Source LLC
Chambersburg PA
CBHW030505100426
42813CB00002B/347